Critical Crosscurrents in Education

Critical Crosscurrents in Education

Michael Collins

KRIEGER PUBLISHING COMPANY
MALABAR, FLORIDA
1998

Original Edition   1998

Printed and Published by
**KRIEGER PUBLISHING COMPANY
KRIEGER DRIVE
MALABAR, FLORIDA 32950**

Copyright © 1998 by Krieger Publishing Company

All rights reserved. No part of this book may be reproduced in any form or by any means, electronic or mechanical, including information storage and retrieval systems without permission in writing from the publisher.
No liability is assumed with respect to the use of the information contained herein.
Printed in the United States of America.

FROM A DECLARATION OF PRINCIPLES JOINTLY ADOPTED BY A COMMITTEE OF THE THE AMERICAN BAR ASSOCIATION AND A COMMITTEE OF PUBLISHERS:
This publication is designed to provide accurate and authoritative information in regard to the subject matter covered. It is sold with the understanding that the publisher is not engaged in rendering legal, accounting, or other professional service. If legal advice or other expert assistance is required, the services of a competent professional person should be sought.

Library of Congress Cataloging-In-Publication Data

Collins, Michael, 1939–
  Critical crosscurrents in education / Michael Collins. — Original ed.
    p.   cm.
  Includes bibliographical references (p.) and index.
  ISBN 0-89464-755-5 (hardcover : alk. papaer)
  1. Critical pedagogy. 2. Critical theory. 3. Continuing education. I. Title.
LC196.C65   1998   97-52360
370.11′5—dc21   CIP

10 9 8 7 6 5 4 3 2

CONTENTS

Introduction	vii
1. Schooling and Society: Reappraising Ivan Illich	1
2. The Deskilling of Educators	31
3. The Prison as Metaphor	55
4. Dimensions of Critical Pedagogy	63
5. Education and Work	79
6. Reflections on Lifelong Learning and Lifelong Education	109
7. Participatory Strategies	139
8. Internationalist Pedagogy	171
References	187
Index	193

INTRODUCTION

The graduate student was giving her views about books and articles on critical education: "The trouble with all this academic critical analysis is that teachers just don't understand it." Her concern carried weight with the rest of the class. She was a part-time graduate student with many years of teaching children and adults. Like most of the people she was addressing, she read and understood critical writings on education. And she subscribed to the notion, implicit in such writings, of education as a means for democratic social change toward a more *just society*.

Responses from fellow students, most of whom had the same kind of practical experience and intellectual commitment as this critic of critical education, echoed her concern. Someone suggested that many ideas from academic writing on critical education have been passed on in distorted form, raising false hopes and ill-advised enthusiasms. "Yet still," came another response, "it's preferable to the methodological pap and mindless 'how-to-do-it' junk that many schoolteachers and adult educators now seem to depend on." Someone interrupted impatiently: "Let's face it, teachers don't want to reflect critically on the meaning of their work. Most of them don't have the intellectual capacity to understand critical theory." This unflattering assessment was met with a barrage of protests.

The conversation ended on a less strident note. Critical writing about education is worthwhile, it was agreed. The relevant task now is to make it accessible to more educators and members of the public who are concerned about education.

It cannot be denied. Few educators read what academics write about the need for teaching practices based on a critical rather than a merely taken-for-granted view of today's society. Yet so much has been written for a largely academic readership in recent years about critical practice in education. Scholarly journals on education and educational conferences where academics attract the limelight abound with discussions on critical pedagogy. But how has this academic enthusiasm for educational discourse which takes a critical view of our advanced industrial society and its priorities influenced practitioners? (The notion of *discourse* used in this book refers us to actual, normative practices as well as the way of talking about them.) What have teachers been able to make of academically formulated ideas about education as a primary means to effect democratic changes toward a more just society? So far, precious little. Writing by academics on critical issues in education is even less accessible to noneducators who, in a society which invokes democratic principles, have a responsibility in the shaping of public education.

So far the practice and theory of critical pedagogy are matters of concern mostly for small groups of university-based educators and their students. And, allowing for the old adage about there being nothing as practical as a good theory, the emphasis is more on theorizing than practicing. No doubt any tendency to enthrone unreflective (thoughtless) practice at the expense of theory needs to be resisted. Yet there is a juncture at which a preoccupation with critical theory leads to "theoryglut" even in the academy. This juncture is reached when practical commitment and understanding are left behind by a theoretical discourse intended to be not merely a guide to practice, but integral to practice. Although there are notable exceptions (among the intellectuals of some activist groups, for example), a concern for critical pedagogy scarcely features in the staff room conversations of schoolteachers and other educational practitioners. Their immediate work agenda tends to focus on how to manage learning situations under increasingly difficult circumstances. Education for a change from this perspective has to do with learning how to cope in a world of multiple learning deficiencies where, allegedly, knowledge changes at an ever accelerating pace. Much of what is known now will be obsolete by Christmas next year. The tempo and the contradictions are almost too overwhelming to contemplate.

Educators have little time or inclination to reflect critically on pedagogical practice. Increasingly, the classroom situation is being shaped by forces beyond the control of the teacher. Relentless cutbacks in publicly funded education are sapping the will of educators to make a convincing case for the necessity of their vocation in these times.

Although the theoretical insights of academic critical pedagogy have scarcely trickled down to the level of educational practice, bureaucratic interventions in education have become more forceful. Academic critics on education are able to understand which interests are being served by these bureaucratic forays into public education, but do not seem to appreciate the power vested in authorities which shape modern educational policy and practice. Recommendations from these critics that educators as intellectuals should resist educational practices that favor status quo interests are often naively unrealistic. The majority of educators, unfortunately, are reluctant to acknowledge their roles as intellectuals (the same can be said of many academics), many favor status quo arrangements and, in any case, they sense that there is a price to pay for resistance even when it is backed by a critical understanding of what is at stake. Nevertheless, this book is beholden to many of the theoretical perspectives which have been sustained within academic critical thought about education during the neoconservative ascendancy.

This book takes a different view of the educational enterprise, and of the educator's role, from one which calls for coping skills and pre-packaged curriculum as a response to changes which can seem to be almost beyond our control in these times of relatively fast-paced change. The position taken here is that educators could still choose to play a critical role in helping determine the nature, pace, and direction of change toward knowledgeable participation in a genuinely participatory democratic process. It is crucial at this time for educators in many contexts to recognize that there is a vital part for them to play in today's society so that they can muster the collective will to argue against cutbacks and defend against the prevailing ideological assault on publicly funded education. This is not a call for careless activist protests that represent infantile challenges to the status quo. Angry, useless gestures against authority are dysfunctional where they merely serve to reinforce feelings of frustration and powerlessness. A primary purpose of a critical perspective in these times is to identify "sensible" strategies and relevant occasions for making progressive, emancipatory, educational practices more widely accessible.

The emphasis placed here on the "sensible" is deliberate. This book does not subscribe to that kind of sanguine rhetoric around critical pedagogy which pays insufficient attention to the power of status quo arrangements. Teaching against the grain and planning alternative educational initiatives for progressive change do not occur in favorable circumstances of our own choosing. By the same token, this text also parts company with any overly pessimistic critical perspective that views the self-perpetuating (reproductive) potential of prevailing institutional arrangements and relationships of power as being too well entrenched to overcome. In these regards, neither the naive activism of the radical idealist nor the seemingly critically informed detachment of the cynical pragmatist can be productive for a critical pedagogy in these times. Given a well-reasoned appraisal of educational institutions and pedagogical practices in today's society, practitioners are right in believing that they can do something to transform the status quo.

Along with writings on critical pedagogy in general, the chapters in this text explain that education is inherently political. In this view, the notion still advanced in some quarters that educational discourse (curriculum and policy development, philosophy and research, and so on) can be apolitical is tenable only to the extent that its own political bias and ideological assumptions are naively, or willfully, ignored.

Critical Crosscurrents in Education is written for busy schoolteachers, adult educators, teachers in training, community-based educators, public service workers who see their work as educational, and others who believe that education should be a means for the realization of a more just and peaceful world than presently exists. In seeking to identify prospects for democratic social change through nonmanipulative educational processes, the book presents a number of critical commentaries on the modern practice of education. It is also guided by relevant social and sociopsychological theory from which these critical commentaries have drawn. The task here, however, is not one of translating the journal articles which academics write mainly for each other and for their graduate students. We need to understand critical pedagogy in a way that will yield sensible strategies for everyday practice.

Teachers in our schools, in institutions of postsecondary education, in the prisons, and in most other educational settings face daily frustrations in just holding the interest of their students and meeting institutional expectations. For many educators it seems ludicrous to even contemplate the notion of incorporating into their practice pedagogical strategies that do not merely sustain the way things are. Some of us in this frantic so-called postmodernist era often have a sense that we are just clinging to the wreckage. But education for social change can advance at a variable pace (which often means struggling to hold the line) and in a wide variety of contexts. Its pedagogical strategies will undoubtedly meet with resistance, but they can be sensibly enacted with careful assessment of their immediate and longer range consequences.

Opportunities for critical pedagogical practice are more clearly identifiable in some situations than in others. Yet most educational contexts afford some prospect, however slight, for a critical orientation on the part of teachers and students to shape curriculum and to resist measures which undermine the quality of education. In any event, the

Introduction

consequences of failing to introduce educational practices that hold out for a more rational, just, and peaceful world are more frightening than those which leave prevailing hegemonic interests unchallenged. (The term *hegemony* refers to the influence predominant groups—nation states, powerful ethnic groups, ruling social classes—are able to exert over others.) There is no longer any reasonable alternative than to enact a thoughtful pedagogy for transforming our schools, our communities, and ourselves.

This book is concerned with lifelong education, which is specifically addressed in Chapter 6. A critical pedagogy from this perspective places a high priority on the education of children. However, a concern with the education of children is accompanied by a concern for the continuing education of their parents, their schoolteachers, and all members of the community at large. The quality of schooling will clearly rate a high priority in any notion of community for which lifelong education is of primary concern. A critical pedagogy in this view, then, should counter the prevailing tendency to separate schools, colleges, workplaces, various institutional settings in which significant education takes place, and community-based initiatives when it comes to considering crucial concerns around educational development. Critical pedagogy is about the inter-connectedness of educational practices and learning processes in all of these contexts. So while the chapters in this book are of direct relevance to schoolteachers, the purview is lifelong education as a totality in which our schools have a crucial part to play.

Chapter 1

SCHOOLING AND SOCIETY: REAPPRAISING IVAN ILLICH

> Illich goes miles beyond everybody else and renders almost every other writer obsolete. *Deschooling Society* is a dangerous book. (Jonathan Kozol)

Schooling and the Enthronement of Expertise

Nearly three decades have elapsed since the publication of Ivan Illich's remarkable little book, *Deschooling Society* (1970). The book earned Illich a reputation as the most controversial educational thinker of the time. In a testimonial that appears on the back cover page of *Deschooling Society,* Jonathan Kozol, another doyen of alternative schooling, wrote that "this may be the most important book published in the United States in twenty years." Kozol went on to claim that "Illich is, by virtue of this book and that of his extraordinary presence, the central figure in the entire school-reform debate within the Western world." This was no small accolade from the author of a similarly thought-provoking text on the effects of conventional schooling, *Death at an Early Age* (1968). Certainly, *Deschooling Society* brought Illich to international attention and placed him at the forefront of contemporary radical educators such as John Holt (1976, 1977), Everett Reimer (1971), and Paul Goodman (1969), as well as Jonathan Kozol.

Progressive ideas on education associated with these radical commentators of the 1960's and early 1970's came under attack with the emergence of neoconservatism in the 1980's. The political ascendancy of neoconservative ideology in the Reagan and Thatcher era marked the beginning of a significant rolling back of progressive gains made for public education during the previous three decades. From this ideological perspective, the writings of radical educators that influenced educational practices in the 1960's and 1970's are held largely responsible for low educational standards, an unacceptable level of illiteracy, lack of performance, and widespread indiscipline among young people. In this view our educational institutions, along with other publicly funded services, are failing and the progressive ideas of the recent past are largely to blame. These failings in the system now provide a rationale for unrelenting budget cutbacks and for discrediting ideas primarily concerned with forms of education and publicly funded services that provide for the real needs of ordinary men and women.

We must bear in mind that the advocates of progressive educational reforms were advancing their criticisms of conventional schooling during a time of relative prosperity. Their ideas were influential during the postwar boom years which represented, especially in advanced western economies, the strongest prolonged period of economic advance in the history of capitalism. In this economic climate there was widespread expectation that funding could be made available on a continuing basis for new initiatives and reforms in education and other public services. Radical commentators could afford, without fear of appearing entirely irrational, to be bold in their criticisms of existing educational and public service institutions and in recommending costly reform initiatives.

Now we are in an era of unrelenting cutbacks in which education and publicly funded services are under seige. These cutbacks, though they are to a large extent ideologically motivated, have been well legitimated with reference to the economic downturn and a need to finance budget deficits. The pattern of the prevailing worldwide economic downturn which began in the years after 1973 became fully apparent in the 1980's (Hobsbawn, 1995) when the full force of neoconservative ideology also started to emerge. Optimistic indicators of short-term economic recovery in the late 1990's that the Clinton administration claims for the United States in no way points to a reversal of the long-term economic downturn since the 1970's. The current political claims about economic recovery in the United States ignore the extreme unevenness of how the benefits are experienced by the population at large. Problems associated with widespread unemployment in the inner cities, especially among young blacks, Hispanics, and other members of America's underclass, persist. Meanwhile, as a *New York Times* editorial (August 20, 1997) makes all too clear, an increasing number of working class and middle class white-collar occupations which appear in employment statistics are temporary and part-time.

Schooling and Society: Reappraising Ivan Illich

These occupations include neither the benefits nor the security that went with full-time jobs in better economic times. Short-term and much publicized reports on economic recovery in these times can be deceiving. They mask the reality of the global economic situation to which all our destinies are ultimately tied. And even in the richest countries such as the United States, overly optimistic reports on short-term economic trends overlook the actual experience and economic prospects of large sections of the population. It is with these conditions in mind that we must view the expansive critical commentaries of progressive educators whose ideas were spawned during a period of economic boom which many mistakenly believed would be indefinitely sustained. For those now concerned about the quality of access to education, cuts in school budgets, bigger classes, and the harmful effects these current developments have on teaching, any advocacy of deschooling as a progressive measure must appear whimsical to say the least.

In the mid-1990's, educators are finding it increasingly difficult to provide the highest quality education for all their students. Their plight is that of workers in other areas of public service. They are required to work with fewer resources in an era when publicly funded services in the interests of ordinary people are being systematically undermined. In such circumstances educators and public service employees who are seriously committed to their work would seem to be better preoccupied with making a case for what they do rather than in revisiting ideas about a deschooled society. Even so the ideas from radical commentaries on education from the 1960's and early 1970's, especially those of Ivan Illich, remain instructive for us. For Illich shows what the situation in our schools can tell us about the regulatory practices, norms, and institutions of today's society. At the very least a critical engagement with Illich's ideas can help us make the case for a progressive transformation of our educational institutions and public services. And the case has to be made by educators and others to counter the harmful effects of continuing cutbacks in our educational institutions and essential public services which are central to the development of a just society.

Illich does not like schools. He thinks society would be better off without them. They serve to make people dependent and incapable of organizing their own lives. Schools get in the way of relevant learning which fosters personal competence and peoples' capacities to develop genuine community. Professional educators teach their students to become dependent on experts who, in turn, reinforce the dependency. This tendency does not seem to be a problem for most educators because of their own dependency on the professionalized expertise of others. Dependency on professionalized expertise is the fate of men and women in today's society. The schools play an important role in conditioning people to be consumers and clients rather than producers of their own experiences, work, and community life. Thus, the capacity for independent critical thought and collective action is undermined at an early age. For most of us the stage is set in our schools for a lifelong dependency on professionalized expertise, guaranteeing a widespread sense of permanent inadequacy from which politicians and bureaucrats derive their reason for being.

Though compressed, the overview is a fair account of the position staked out by Illich in *Deschooling Society*. The book is important because it exemplifies the work of radical educators during the 1960's and early 1970's. However, Illich goes further than they in treating the school as a metaphor for society at large. The school, then, as far as Illich is concerned, represents much of what is wrong with modern life. Schooling is so pervasive that "not only education but social reality has become schooled." Education has become virtually synonymous with formal schooling and, since the latter functions to erode personal autonomy and the values of community, society as a whole needs to be deschooled. This radical objective calls for the elimination of people's dependency on experts—on licensed lawyers, doctors, dentists, real estate agents, architects, as well as on certified schoolteachers. Illich connects schooling with the ideology of expert (exclusive) knowledge and the cult of professionalism.

The tendency Illich decries is associated in the schools with the notion that "teacher knows best." Many, perhaps most, educators would want to distance themselves from this clear-cut assertion about the authority invested in their role. Yet the claim is insightful. "Teacher knows best" is implicit (from the standpoint of students) in the way knowledge is disseminated, in the design of curriculum, as well as in the way class time and the entire school day are organized. Teachers as individuals may not see themselves as having any real say in the structuring of these events, taking them for granted as the way things are or the way things should be in our schools. Such uncritical acceptance of their role on the part of educators allows the notion of "teacher knows best" to prevail as a means of structuring our schools and colleges according to bureaucratic interests (which tell us what is appropriate for the good order of the institution) as well as for teaching us dependency on experts.

From the vantage point of the mid-1990's educators might well be inclined to assert that from their experience "teacher knows best" no longer carries much weight with their students and the public at large. As evidence teachers can point to growing indiscipline in the schools, the influence of popular media (especially television) on young people, and a decline in the status of teaching within today's society. In this regard, any criticism of the enthronement of expertise inherent in "teacher knows best" would now seem to be outmoded. However, there are still expectations that teachers have a significant responsibility in addressing the ills of today's society. That these expectations exist, unreasonable though many of them may be, is clear from the criticisms which are leveled at teachers about their inability to deal with these social problems, especially with regard to the behavior of young people.

These are times, then, for educators to acknowledge the shortcomings of the "teacher knows best" view while they struggle for new ways to establish the moral leadership within society which their work entails. Progressive educators who remain convinced that education is a key to the transformation of society need to identify strategies that will improve our schools and colleges in the interests of the vast majority of ordinary people. That is what this book is about. Education for the people, for the transformation of society, means staking a large claim for publicly funded education rather than opting for a deschooled society.

Yet Illich's *Deschooling Society* is a relevant starting point to begin a discourse on reschooling for a more just society since so much of his criticism of modern schooling is on the mark. And his focus on the school as a metaphor is revealing of the extent to which modern institutions take over and condition our everyday lives. We are schooled to dependency on these institutions. So the solution for Illich is to seek alternative arrangements—to deschool society.

Activist Priest and Radical Intellectual

Among the well-known writers who shaped the critical discourse on conventional schooling during the 1960's and early 1970's, Illich is undoubtedly the most preeminent. He has been influenced by the work of Paul Goodman, John Holt, Jonathan Kozol, and Elliot Reimer, but it is clear that they all acknowledge the paramount significance of Illich's project. As a polemicist and a theoretician he has been the standard-bearer for the radical critique on schooling and education that came out of the 60's and early 70's. Illich's theoretical and research work on education, and the concerns he relates to education, have informed his brilliant polemical writing. The scope of his intellectual work and the radical commitments it addresses has earned Illich an international reputation. And his perspective is far more internationalist than those of most radical educators of his time.

Illich was born in 1926 into very comfortable upper-middle class surroundings. The father was a wealthy German aristocrat. Illich's mother was Jewish. Despite the relatively cosseted circumstances of his early childhood and the influential position of his father, Illich was to experience the painful effects of racist prejudice as an adolescent. Because he was the son of a Jewish parent, Illich was expelled from school in his native Austria.

The role played by the school in this monstrous violation of Illich's humanity cannot be overlooked. It was no doubt a painfully relevant event in his early development. Despite Illich's privileged middle-class background, he suffered from social injustice at an early age within the context of the school. It would be convenient, and ill-conceived, for us to downplay the wider contemporary social significance of this kind of school experience by relating it to Illich's special circumstances as a Jew growing up in a time when the forces of racism were rising with the fascist tide in central Europe.

Violations of human rights are still being played out in our schools, colleges, workplaces, and other social institutions on a daily basis. Whether large in consequence or seemingly trivial, the way these violations are being addressed within our schools today has a significant impact on wider social learning processes as well as individual experience. Racism, bullying, and numerous other forms of discrimination and abuses of power are both socially constructed and psychologically reinforced. They are amenable to change through education. Social justice can be learned. It can be taught. Accordingly, teachers who are oblivious to the daily instances of social injustice in schools are walking about their workplace in blinders and overlooking crucial pedagogical responsibility. And how many teachers are aware of what is going on and choose to do nothing about it?

As a child Illich traveled a great deal throughout Europe with his parents. His privileged family circumstances enabled him to enlarge on his intellectual capacities at an early age. He can certainly look to his own childhood experience to confirm that significant learning takes place outside of school. Illich developed an aptitude for learning foreign languages which subsequently added authenticity to his reputation as an internationalist. This proficiency in languages is further reflected in the attention Illich pays in his research to the connection between linguistic forms of communication and human experience.

Schooling and Society: Reappraising Ivan Illich

The urge to understand and make oneself understood, the aspiration to express one's views on crucial matters, and the commitment to speak in support of those who are silenced through oppression are significant aspects of an internationalist pedagogy (see Chapter 9) which aspires to make a difference in the world.

During Illich's early formative years, the fascist German state emerged with its barbaric cult of efficiency, tied to a racist ideology, which found its ultimate expression in the concentration camps of Belsen and Buchenwald. At the same time the hopes of international socialism were experiencing a crushing setback as the realities of Stalin's brutal bureaucratic dictatorship, exemplified in the Gulag, took hold. It is clear enough that we can, and should, look to fascism and Stalinism for chilling examples of the concerns which pervade Illich's adult work regarding the repressiveness of centralized control. Nevertheless, by the age of 18 Illich had decided to become a priest within the supremely hierarchically structured Roman Catholic Church, a powerful international institution whose accommodation to the fascist state has yet to be adequately researched.

Before taking up his first priestly assignment with a New York City parish in 1951, Illich had completed an impressive period of academic studies. His studies were in depth, but not narrowly confined like those of the modern academic specialist. Illich was awarded advanced degrees at the University of Florence (in crystallography), the Gregorian University in Rome (in philosophy and theology), and a doctorate in the philosophy of history at the University of Salzburg. Like many advocates of alternative education, Illich himself is well credentialed. His academic background gives credence to his ideas and brilliant polemics on conventional schooling.

In his New York parish Illich worked energetically with both the established Irish parishioners and newly arriving Puerto Rican immigrants. He was particularly successful in working on behalf of the Puerto Rican community. His community activist commitments were accompanied by a fairly orthodox orientation to Roman Catholic theology. In this regard, there is more than a touch of the priestly patrician in Illich's approach to leadership. As for his colleagues in the Church, it is clear that he caused offense with what appeared to some of them as overzealousness and clear-cut ambition on his part. Fortunately, Illich enjoyed the support of influential men in the Church, especially Cardinal Spellman, who admired his leadership ability, organizing skills, and sincere intentions. These are the very qualities that we should expect to find in competent educators.

It was through Spellman's influence that the Church assigned Illich to diplomatic missions in South America. In 1955 Illich was appointed vice-rector of the University of Puerto Rico and in the following year, at the age of 33, he became the youngest monsignor in the United States. Thus, Illich experienced remarkable success in scaling the ladders of hierarchical institutions.

Subsequently, Illich fell out with influential men of the Church. Though still a loyal institution man himself as far as the Church was concerned, Illich was outspoken in his criticisms of colleagues. In 1960, the Bishop of Ponce ordered Illich to leave Puerto Rico. After that the forces aligned against Illich within the Church gained momentum, increasing in effectiveness after the death of Cardinal Spellman in 1967. The circumstances leading up to Illich's interrogation at the Holy See in Rome reveal the seediness that can emerge in Church politics and organization. In this regard the Church is little different from secular institutions. As Illich himself must have understood from the success he enjoyed in the earlier stages of his career, a clear understanding of organizational political machinations (realpolitik) is just as crucial for those who seek to make progressive changes as for those who are concerned more with career advancement.

In any event, it is clear enough that criticisms of Illich's work were instigated through petty politics and professional envy. As an upshot of the Vatican's inept handling of the spurious censure motion against him, Illich decided in 1969 to resign from his priestly responsibilities. This move did not constitute a complete break with the institution. Far from it. Illich assured Church superiors that he would continue with his daily breviary and maintain his vow of celibacy.

For a short time, from 1960–61, Illich was appointed to the faculty of Fordham University. He has continued to maintain connections with the university context, and much of his work is directly addressed to academics and educators. Back in South America after the brief spell at Fordham, Illich embarked on a 3,000 mile hitchhiking trip to find a suitable missionary training center. (This initiative took place before Illich's serious difficulties with the Church began to unfold). He eventually chose the small town of Cuernavaca, close to Mexico City, for the new Center of Intercultural Formation (CIF). Eventually, CIF became established as the widely known Center of Intercultural Documentation (CIDOC). The center attracted scholars and intellectual activists from around the world. In addition to lively, well-informed discussions about the desirability and efficacy of institutional alternatives, and about the significance of language and culture, a substantial body of research was accumulated at CIDOC. Much of this research informs the publications of Illich and other progressive thinkers on education who attended CIDOC during its short but highly productive life span.

Inevitably, CIDOC came under attack from Illich's enemies in the Church. The center was censured by the Vatican in 1968 during the Holy See's investigation of Illich, and clerics were banned from participating in CIDOC's activities. (Some clerics defied the ban.) Though the ban was partially lifted, intellectual activities gradually wound down at Cuernavaca over the ensuing years. Perhaps this eventuality was not entirely inappropriate in view of Illich's ideological stance against institutions. Even before censure by the Vatican, CIDOC's success was heading along the path towards institutionalization.

Since leaving the priesthood and withdrawing his energies from CIDOC, Illich has continued to work as an independent scholar and writer on the issues he and others had so keenly addressed during the short but influential time of his mission at Cuernavaca.

Home Schooling and the Anti-Expert Motif

There is no doubt that Illich has provided inspiration for people who seek to reduce their dependency on formal institutions and on institutionalized groups of experts such as doctors, lawyers, real estate agents, and teachers. The home-schooling movement is a case in point. Children who are home schooled tend to do as well, and often better, with conventional academic work than their peers in school. Their daily lives out of school can be rich in the kind of learning opportunities that are difficult to provide, especially in a spontaneous fashion, within conventional schools. And arguments often advanced by professional educators that home schooling cannot do a proper job of socializing children are difficult to sustain.

Even if they have not read the likes of Illich, Holt, Goodman, Reimer, and Kozol, home-schooling parents can counter such arguments, with just cause, by pointing to the harmful aspects of much of the socialization that does go on in schools. John Holt's work with home-schooling parents, in particular, indicates that the socialization of their children is qualitatively superior—less competitive, more caring, and more practical—to what is happening in many schools. This is why schoolteachers and professors of education can be found among supporters of the home-schooling movement. It is not difficult to build a case for the merits of home schooling, especially for children who receive plenty of thoughtful parental attention, when the problems of modern schools come under scrutiny.

Similarly, the vision of Illich and other contemporary prophets of deinstitutionalized lifestyles seems to be realized by people who take more responsibility for their own health care, legal transactions, consumer choices, and so on without relying on professionals, bureaucrats, or corporate experts. Placing a priority on the care of oneself, one's immediate dependents, and one's community can be viewed as a practical, satisfying, and ethical alternative to dependency on the professionalized services of modern institutions.

There is no doubt that conventional institutions themselves can be influenced by examples of seemingly radical alternatives to mainstream perspectives and practices. Witness the growing rhetoric about preventative medicine among doctors and a heightened concern for teaching law students about ethics. But for all this, there is a disconcerting naivete in the prevailing trendy advocacy of alternatives to formal institutions and with the entire Illichian tendency which espouses a deschooled society, purged of reliance on designated experts.

The Commons, Vernacular Values, and Tools for Conviviality

Illich's brilliant insights go well beyond the analysis offered by other critics of conventional schooling. The concerns he has about the encroachments of professionalizing and bureaucratizing tendencies on our everyday lives are illuminated through searching metaphorical studies. His instructive metaphor of "the commons" which provides a critical concept for describing modern conditions is a good example of this critical work. The commons recalls for us a time when large tracts of land were freely available for the use of ordinary people, "in common," to graze their animals, to collect wood and edible plants, and to just enjoy. Common land belonged equally to the entire community with which it was associated.

With the onset of the modern era, the commons of medieval times have been largely converted into private property or into areas for which access is governed by official regulations. Land is now a primary resource for development rather than for the free use and enjoyment of the *common people* who possess no special rank or privilege over other members of their community. Under modern conditions, the land is no longer part of the *commonweath*. For Illich the erosion of the commons is a compelling symbol for the way vital, health-sustain-

Schooling and Society: Reappraising Ivan Illich

ing aspects of everyday life are severely damaged by the effects of modernizing development.

The valuable dimensions of everyday life originally embodied in the commons are also, according to Illich, represented as "vernacular values" in idiomatic forms of ordinary language. He is referring us here to the *straightforward*, nonmanipulative language of the common people. Illich recounts how language both shapes and is shaped by human experience. Modern languages, in their written and spoken forms, have developed systematically to reflect the interests of the state so that we experience the world in line with its norms. (We can transgress these norms but we cannot realistically will them away from our everyday experience of modern society). Hence, formerly meaningful linguistic expressions of the common people, and the vital aspects of everyday life (vernacular values) they defined, disappear in the modernizing rationalization process. Thus, modern languages tend to differ from the indigenous languages they replace.

In referring us to the significance of vernacular values, Illich holds out the possibility that we could retrieve ways of being that are free of bureaucratic interventions, dependency on professionalized expertise, and the obsession with modern technology.

In his book *Tools for Conviviality* (1973), Illich attempts to envision an alternative to advanced technocratic society and the modern mode of production. He refers prophetically to this work as "an epilogue to the modern age." Technology, as "tools for conviviality" rather than the means for profit and exploitation, should be designed first and foremost to meet the everyday practical needs of ordinary men and women. In this regard, the values of technology should match the values of the commons. These values are vernacular values. So Illich is not against technology per se. He just believes that it should be simple to use and readily accessible, free from the monopolistic control of profit-seeking industrialists and bureaucrats. (Illich identifies the telephone as a possible example of convivial technology, so long as its use is not mediated by a centralizing authority.)

Illich's critique of monopolistic forms of production suggests that technology, modern machinery in its various forms, is designed to suit the vested interests of industrialists and professional organizations rather than the immediate needs of ordinary men and women. This critical insight would apply to the so-called "user friendly" desktop computers and the technology of the Internet. They are still designed according to a notion of user friendliness which leaves control of the way computers are developed and deployed largely in the hands of the corporate sector. In this regard, user friendly refers to a marketing strategy.

For technology to be genuinely user friendly (convivial), it would have to be liberated from the control of special interest groups which tend to determine the way modern tools of various kinds are designed, the manner in which they are used, and their accessibility. In this view, modern technology steers the activities, the taken-for-granted perceived (often spurious) needs and, ultimately, the destiny of ordinary people in today's society. The ongoing momentum of technological rationality is closely associated with overproduction (with unemployment as a major characteristic), and waste, and a critical depletion of the planet's nonrenewable resources.

According to Illich, technology that is shared in common, rather than owned or designed to serve the needs of manipulating vested interests, is conceivable and has a potential to release powerful creative learning capacities currently suppressed within our modern and modernizing societies. In such societies teaching devices are largely manipulative and, in Illich's view, add unnecessarily to the cost of learning.

Illich is more explicit and utopian in his vision of a communist society than either Marx or Engels. Marxism is more circumspect than Illichian prophecy about how the withering away of the state and the replacement of capitalist modes of production (both corporate and bureaucratic) will manifest themselves. Despite his instructive insights into the harmful consequences of development under capitalism, and the way these effects are reproduced in our institutional arrangements, Illich's notion of abandoning modern institutions for communitarian alternatives is at best naively premature. In this regard, Illich's vision is akin to the escapist utopian initiatives of the past which his work invokes.

Twenty years, and more, after Illich's seminal works such as *Deschooling Society* and *Tools for Conviviality*, it is apparent that the call for abandonment of modern institutions by progressive thinkers and activists serves to concede additional power to the vested interests upholding bureaucracy, corporate industry, and monopolistic professions which Illich abhors. For a critical pedagogy at this time, it is important to recognize that future prospects for the kind of society Illich envisages require ongoing social transformation from within modern institutions and conventional workplaces, not their abandonment.

It is not surprising to discover that Illich is widely regarded as a founding figure of the ecology movement. Nor is it surprising to learn that his ideas around "sustainable development" have been nicely co-opted within the conventional discourse of such corporate entities as the World Bank and into the political speeches of those politicians who have followed in the wake of Margaret Thatcher, Ronald Reagan, and George Bush. The duplicitous message from these sources is that the environment is a matter of concern to them and so is the need for unfettered industrial expansion. Illich now deals with the contradiction by coming flat out against the concept of development.

Illich's unwillingness to consider the various forms development and underdevelopment can take appears whimsical. His critical analysis in this regard leaves out on a limb those worried about massive unemployment in advanced economies and starvation conditions in much of the world. What kind of idiocy would deny the need for economic development in African countries like Rwanda at this time?

Illich has acknowledged that his critical observations about schooling, learning, and education in general in *Deschooling Society* owed much to the contributions of contemporaries such as Goodman, Holt, Kozol, and Reimer. In fact, these American educational critics have written with considerable clarity on some of the issues with which Illich has been concerned. Goodman, especially, examined the situation in the schools and colleges more thoroughly than Illich. However, the scope of Illich's critique is broader, appealing to the mood of the 1960's and 1970's by holding up a large number other social institutions to scrutiny and in suggesting that the whole of modern culture should be deschooled.

Although Illich has expressed some regret that his name is so closely linked with *Deschooling Society* while his subsequent work has been overlooked by comparison, the book earned Illich an international reputation as the leading critic of modern schooling and chief advocate for noninstitutionalized alternatives. *Deschooling Society* is his chief claim to fame. Regardless of any reservations Illich now has about some of the solutions he advanced in *Deschooling Society*, the text remains a preeminent reference among the body of literature which uncovers the shortcomings of schools and many other modern institutions.

Illich's Alternative

So what are the solutions advanced by Illich in *Deschooling Society*? Illich wants to take away the money now allocated to state supported education and health care as a way to stop a further increase in the dependency inducing effects of these institutions. For public education he favors a system of tuition grants along the lines suggested by the prominent right-wing economist Milton Friedman. This idea envisages channeling funds to individual beneficiaries allowing them to buy the schooling of their choice. Up to the allotted amount, people should be able to select, at any time in their lives, the kind of instruction they want from the institution of their choice. They will have a vast number of "definite skills" from which to choose. The state, according to Illich, should disestablish the monopoly of the schools, providing an example to be followed in undermining the authority of other institutions which currently tend to enjoy a monopolistic position in the provision of professionalized services to the public.

In calling for state intervention to end the monopoly of schools and other influential institutions within today's society, Illich cites the initiative taken two centuries ago to block the emergence of a single church monopoly in the United States. Accordingly, Illich thinks a bill of rights is needed in which the first article will affirm that "the State shall make no law with respect to the establishment of education." However, he does believe that a law should be made forbidding the selection of staff or students to educational institutions based solely on their experience with a specified curriculum. (There is a hierarchy in the Illichian scheme for institutional redundancy, it seems. He wants to settle accounts with the Church and education before dealing with the law.) This legal stipulation is not envisaged as a replacement for relevant tests of competence. But it would do away with "absurd discrimination" in determining eligibility. Illich goes even further along this particular tack. He insists that any inquiries into a person's previous formal education for the purpose of selection should be forbidden just like "inquiries into his political affiliation, church attendance, lineage, sex habits, or social background." Illich is very much in favor of legislation, centralized planning, and state policy initiatives to tear down the barriers of formal schooling.

Skill centers are a part of Illich's alternative pedagogical scheme. These centers would be staffed by instructors who want to share their skills with anybody who wants to learn. The idea is that prospective students would purchase their training with educational credits granted for a lifetime in the form of an "edu-credit card." For this purpose, every citizen is to receive an edu-credit card at birth. Students as customers will determine the merits or otherwise of the skill centers in terms of the quality of services purchased. The exercise of individual choice and purchasing power are central features of Illich's strategy to overcome the current monopoly enjoyed by licensed teachers.

Illich suggests in his critique of teacher monopoly that teenagers who have access to appropriate resources are better than most certified schoolteachers at introducing their peers to scientific subjects.

According to Illich, skill centers should be established in workplaces, with the support of employers and workers, and in other strategic locations throughout the community. Providing "we open the market" for learning, remove the constraints of conventional curriculum, and match "the right resources with the right student" motivated in "an intelligent program," Illich claims his centers would lead to a vast expansion in "skill learning."

Involvement in formal schooling, including universities, is a "central social ritual" from Illich's viewpoint. Only by detaching themselves from this ritual can people bring about radical social change. Illich points out in his critique of institutions that many "self-styled" revolutionaries are products of institutional processes. Given this conditioning, even liberation is viewed as an institutional process (presumably through an organized party or revolutionary collective). In short, Illich believes that liberation from mandatory schooling is a precondition for freeing oneself from the compulsions of a consumer society. There is some irony in this claim, bearing in mind the Illichian scheme to undermine mandatory schooling through the exercise of consumer choice.

The educational revolution Illich has in mind depends on "a new orientation for research and a new understanding of the educational style of an emerging counter-culture." It is not clear whether this important new orientation is supposed to emerge within an alternative structure, described as "an educational network or web," or whether it is to provide the necessary insights for bringing the alternative structure into being. Accordingly, Illich refers to this new orientation as a "two-fold inversion." In any event, the new orientation is intended to help us see through "conceptual blind spots" which currently obscure a total vision of Illich's educational structure. The structure itself lies within "a conceptual blind spot." Focusing attention on this blind spot, however, would constitute a "true scientific revolution."

Illich points out that the new educational institutions he has in mind are to serve a society which does now exist. But in a chapter entitled "Learning Webs," he does list the aims of a good educational system. As already implied in his advocacy of the voucher system, Illich's educational system would ensure that those who want to learn can gain access to the learning resources they need during the entire course of their lives. People who have certain knowledge they want to share should be given help in finding those who want to learn from them. Learners should not be subjected to mandatory education. And official assessments made on the basis of whether or not they hold diplomas should not be allowed.

The Illichian scheme of lifelong education for the people by the people would be facilitated through skill exchanges, reference services, and peer-matching arrangements. Relevant technology, sensibly oriented to people's learning needs, would become more readily available to the public. Practical responses to essential learning needs, for which the necessary institutional infrastructure and resources have existed for some time in advanced industrial societies, would emerge on a regular basis. Over 25 years later, actual instances of these recommendations are more in evidence, though not yet commonplace.

As for the role of the educators (Illich defines them as "the professional personnel"), they "would be much more like custodians, museum guides, or reference librarians than like teachers." Hence, the vocational commitment of teaching is to be replaced by functionary roles which are being made increasingly superfluous through the deployment of "user friendly" technology.

Illich's criticisms of conventional schooling, the monopolizing tendencies of professions such as teaching, and the growing dependency of ordinary people on experts have been instructive. Yet the overly romantic nature of his vision is revealed in the solutions he offers. A measure of utopianism is undoubtedly necessary to sustain any revolutionary project. (And Illich acknowledges that his ideas are for a society which does not now exist.) Accordingly, having identified some of the forces and institutional structures ranged against the emergence an alternative system, Illich is right to offer us some hopeful strategies for a more emancipatory pedagogy.

Yet Illich's ideas are fanciful. There is a disconcerting naivete in the advocacy of alternatives to formal institutions and with the entire Illichian tendency which espouses deschooling society. Further, Illich's practical alternatives can appear pedestrian. What is so novel, after all, about notions of skill exchanges, reference services, and peer matching? Formal and informal arrangements such as these, whatever names we put to them, have existed for a long time. The real importance of Illich's work is in revealing that practical forms of people learning from each other are increasingly undermined because of the growing dependency within modern society on professionals and other designated experts.

It is in the scheme to do away with the schools and other public services, and this is the key feature of his polemic, that Illich's analysis falls short. He does not account sufficiently for the economic, sociopolitical, and historically determined conditions within which schooling and other public services are provided. A critical analysis which exposes the failure of schools can be neatly accommodated by status quo interests while it puts pressure on professional educators and others whose careers are bound up with formal schooling. This additional pressure makes it more difficult for educators to make a case for their work in a climate which, all too often, encourages a clumsy form of "teacher bashing."

The ascendancy of a neoconservative political agenda during the past two decades, and since the publication of *Deschooling Society* and other radical texts against conventional schooling, has clearly provided conditions in which antiprogressive attacks on educators and publicly funded education and other social services can flourish. In this regard, deschooling ideology fuels the rationale for cutbacks in funding to public education and other social services on which the majority of ordinary people must still rely.

Illichian criticism of schools does provide useful support for people who are unhappy with the performance of schools and want to opt for alternatives such as home schooling. However, though many politicians and bureaucrats might welcome criticism that undermines the status of teachers, the state under prevailing conditions cannot sensibly afford to countenance demands for the abolition of the schools. Whatever else it achieves, schooling is integral to the system of social control (imagine closing the schools in New York for 6 months or more) and to the reproduction of prevailing sociopolitical, economic, and cultural conditions.

Instances of resistance to oppressive social arrangements do take place in the schools on a day-to-day basis and are identifiable in the purposeful activities of many committed teachers as well as in student attitudes. (The nature and relevance of school-based resistance to dominant ideology will be addressed in subsequent chapters.) Yet the modern school is an important location for reinforcing processes of social control which sustain existing relations—along lines of class, gender, generation, and race—within society as a whole.

Accordingly, a radical deschooling of society, and not merely a tendency of more people seeking small-scale private alternatives to the mainstream provision, presupposes a political and social revolution of a kind not envisaged by Illich. And such a revolution cannot even be seriously contemplated if those who have the critical insight to conceptualize an alternative society abandon strategic institutions such as our schools, colleges, and universities. These institutions would be necessary sites for contestation in a period of significant political and social change.

In the end, Illich is no revolutionary. That is why his idea for revolutionary change in education is defused by suggestions for the kind of alternatives that do not threaten the present order of things. The cry for deschooling is merely a radical gesture. It does not emerge from a realistic appraisal of the conditions and forces governing our everyday lives. In these regards, Illich's proposals are neither as practical nor as sophisticated as those of early 19th century progressive utopian thinkers like Charles Fourier, Robert Owen, Pierre-Joseph Proudhon, Claude Saint-Simon, and Wilhem Weitling. Their utopian perspectives on human emancipation, less narrowly confined than those of Illich, at least took more realistic stock of the prevailing political and socioeconomic conditions of their times.

Even if the radical demand for abolishing schools is left aside, suggested alternatives to public schooling for ordinary people are problematic. Home schooling is a case in point. Though the trend toward home schooling has increased in recent years, it remains on the whole a privileged option for people of middle and upper class backgrounds. And while John Holt's work, in particular, confirms that children learn very effectively without being subjected to conventional school curriculum, typically they have home environments where there is respect for cultural and intellectual activities and where the parents are seriously committed to home schooling.

It is clear that the arguments often made by many professional educators that home schoolers cannot be properly socialized are not tenable. Given the attention of caring adults, home schoolers usually have the opportunity to participate more fully in community life than their peers in schools. What the critics really mean is that home schoolers are not adequately socialized into the regulatory norms of everyday life in schools. In this regard socialization is really a problem for the schools, not the home schoolers. Children who learn at home are likely to become just as adept, perhaps more adept, as children who attend state-supported schools when it comes to dealing with the constraints modern society places upon young people. Yet there is critical sense in which privileging the home over the school as the context for the formal education of children has been overstated by advocates of home schooling. The family as an institution is also often the site of repressive practices.

In any event, professional educators need not be unduly concerned that the increasing popularity of home schooling will lead to a significant reduction in school enrollments. Most adults do not have the energy and other resources to keep growing children at home every day. Among those who do, only a tiny minority (which includes professionally trained educators acutely aware of the schools' limitations) will seriously consider home schooling as anything but an occasional option, along with intervals of conventional schooling, for their children. Accordingly, while the home-schooling phenomenon can be viewed as a critical reminder of our schools' shortcomings, it hardly poses a threat to the continuing existence of state schooling. Home schooling presents no significant challenge to the status quo.

Even so, the notion of home schooling itself, and the Illichian educational ideas it exemplifies, should not go unchallenged. Although there are notable exceptions, it is the middle-class nuclear family, with a male head as major breadwinner, which can best afford home schooling. It is a far more difficult undertaking for single parent families (those on welfare in particular), families of minority ethnic groups, and working class families in general. Home schooling, then, tends to be a privileged option for people who are relatively well endowed in terms of disposable income, discretionary time, and formal education. The home-schooling tendency draws away the very people who know what is wrong with our schools and are the most likely to have the kind of resources to effect desirable change.

In turning their backs on the schools, then, and in restricting their focus to the private sphere of the nuclear family, parents of home schoolers reject prospects for progressive changes in public education. They merely affirm the privileged rights, in an idiosyncratic way, for a minority who have the ability to seek escapist alternatives. In this view, home schoolers are privileged dropouts. At best they manage to confirm the overly utopian nature of Illich's deschooling thesis. Home schooling turns out to be reactionary rather than progressive. As with the entire Illichian scheme, home schooling's individualistic and privatizing tendencies play right into the hands of a prevailing political ideology which is intent on undermining slightly progressive initiatives that were made in state-provided education during the 1960's and early 1970's.

What proponents of home schooling consistently overlook is that nuclear families are not exempt from the pressures and negative effects of modern life. These effects on young people, which are brought to public awareness as they are manifested in the schools, also bring stress to modern families. Pathologies experienced in our schools are generated in our homes. Taking on responsibility for home schooling only adds to the burden. The notion that the family can insulate its members, even young people, against the harmful influences of modern life is itself neurotic, raising unreasonable expectations about the home environment. It is hardly surprising, then, that the most prominent advocates of home schooling, and the abolition of conventional schooling, include in their ranks male intellectuals such as Illich and Holt who have had no direct responsibility for bringing up their own children.

An attempt to account for the problems confronting the modern family, in its various forms, is beyond the scope of this chapter. The point to be made here is that the modern family is subject to the same pathologies as the modern school. Accordingly, it is not reasonable to identify the family as a favored location with sole responsibility for educating children in today's society. Support for people's rights to provide for the formal education of their children from the home should be accompanied by an understanding that the community at large (not just parents and state school employees) has a legitimate stake in the education of our children.

The privatized, and occasionally idiosyncratic, aspects of home schooling are potentially even more harmful than the deleterious effects that Illich and others have associated with contemporary professionalized schooling. Like modern schools, modern families can use all the support they can get from caring schoolteachers, adult educators, and other trained providers of public services to the community.

In the final chapter of *Deschooling Society*, Illich claims that "the mood of 1971 is propitious for a major change of direction." Since that time there has been a deepening crisis within the school systems and an erosion of teacher autonomy. The kind of prepackaged curriculum that Illich deplores is more pervasive than ever, and is deployed on teachers and students in a top-down fashion. A political ideology which favors more direct government intervention into the affairs of schools has gained ascendancy in many advanced industrial democracies. Teacher autonomy in the classrooms and curriculum development have been major targets of interference by government which, at the same time, increasingly invokes the merits of a "hands-off" policy on behalf of business and industry. Thus commercial interests and initiatives have, in actuality, been promoted at the expense of public education.

During the past two decades the quality of education available to ordinary people has been in a state of decline. (And the same is true of other public services.) The high number of school dropouts, an increase in the incidence of illiteracy, incidents of violence in the schools, overcrowded classrooms, and reduced funding are but a few of the most significant examples of a serious decline in the quality of the educational provision. Under these circumstances, it becomes clear that rhetoric on home schooling and abolishing schools serves to reinforce plans to rationalize education and other public services, as they become increasingly vulnerable to criticism, in line with a reactionary political agenda.

If home schooling is thought to be progressive and can gain acceptance within the prevailing political climate, the same tendency applies to privatized fundamentalist religious schools and their narrowly conceived prescriptive curriculum. Since learning in such situations is characterized as requiring facilitators, or classroom custodians, whose pedagogy is steered by standardized curriculum packages, it becomes reasonable to think in terms of hiring staff in the privatized sector of education who do not have to be paid according to professional qualifications. The curriculum takes precedence over the role of educator.

In publicly funded education, especially in the postsecondary sector, the practice of hiring people without formal qualifications on a part-time basis, and for a much lower rate of pay than that of formally qualified teachers, is on the increase. Since Illich made his prognosis in 1971, teaching as a vocation has been seriously impaired and the bargaining rights of teachers eroded. Teachers at all levels of the educational system (from kindergarten through to the universities and adult education in general) are becoming rapidly *deskilled* and *demoralized* (an issue to be addressed in Chapter 2). And that is not all right.

It would be unreasonable to make Illich and other advocates of the deschooling theme responsible for the current problems in state-funded education. However, it should not go unremarked that in *Deschooling Society* Illich singles out for praise the ideas of Milton Friedman who has been a leading supporter, among academic economists, of neoconservative policy formation. In any event, it turns out that Illich and other gurus of alternative, privatized education were the harbingers of a neoconservative political ideology that has eroded the autonomy of schoolteachers, adult educators, and university academics. This is an ideology responsible for the cutbacks in the quality of publicly funded formal education and social services available to ordinary people at a time when the gap between the very wealthy and the poor is widening.

Education for progressive democratic social change is not going to be realized by good people turning their backs on our schools and other public service institutions. The relevant struggles in these times are around strengthening these institutions for the majority of the people. Schoolteachers, adult educators, and other community service workers are in a position to play a critical role in opening up our educational institutions for genuinely democratic, emancipatory learning. With this end in view, the criticism of conventional schooling made by Illich and others remains instructive while their reactionary utopian ideas must be regarded as problematic.

Against Deschooling

Illich's own ambivalent relationship with the Church highlights the contradictions and practical difficulties associated with a call for the abandonment of conventional institutions in favor of loosely structured alternatives. Despite the efficacy of Illich's critical insights, there is much within our conventional institutions which continues to meet the needs of ordinary men and women. The power of vested interests within existing institutional arrangements which work manipulatively to steer the destinies of ordinary people are not monolithic. Institutional regulations and enactments representing powerful vested interests are often challenged, sometimes undermined, and occasionally modified. Even within the Catholic Church, which has so much influenced Illich's personal development and critical thought, the Vatican's powerful bureaucracy does not entirely get its own way in the face of oppositional strategies emanating from some of the clergy and laypeople.

We can witness, for example, the work of Catholic liberation theologists in South America. They continue to work as politicized priests in Latin America's virtual dictatorships, often under very dangerous circumstances, despite the Vatican's disapproval. Their activist work on behalf of ordinary men, women, and children oppressed by the state (including direct violence inflicted on the people by the police and the militia) and corporate interests often takes place on the streets of cities like São Paulo, Lima, Santiago—in settings idealized by Illich. Yet these activist priests continue their struggle to transform the institutional norms and structures of the Church from within.

In contrast, Illich's affirmation of his continuing attachment to the trappings of priesthood, even as he abandons the vocational obligation the role entails, can be viewed as the expediency of one who hedges his bets. At a basic psychological level, Illich appears to be acknowledging that what are essential needs for him reside at the heart of a very highly structured, paternalistic institution. In this regard, his polemics against the schools and other institutions constitute a displacement of an unresolved difficult relationship with the Church.

These points need to be made because the ideas popularized in *Deschooling Society* still exert an influence on progressive thinkers among the adult population who have lost all confidence in our schools and publicly funded institutions as places where struggles for social justice, worthwhile learning experiences, and service on behalf of the majority of ordinary people can be advanced. To a very large extent it is the radical elements of the new right, traceable in Thatcherism, Reaganism, and religious fundamentalism that have understood the significance of the schools (especially) and other publicly funded institutions for carrying through their reactionary social reforms. From this ideological perspective, exemplified in the United States of the mid-1990's through the populist rhetoric of politician Newt Gingrich and broadcaster Rush Limbaugh, reasons for cutbacks in our publicly funded institutions are advanced on the basis that they have grown too large through liberal largesse. At the same time, the state is urged to make major ideologically motivated interventions in the way our publicly funded institutions are structured.

No matter that a major aspect of this new right-wing rhetoric calls for less interventionism on the part of government, the restructuring taking place in our schools and other publicly funded institutions represents an attack on the interests of the working class and the growing underclass of unemployed and people on welfare. However, restructuring within our publicly funded institutions is taking place in accordance with new right-wing political ideology and the momentum for such change is sustained by a legitimate concern for economic factors. Critics, with their minds still on the expansionist era of the 1950's and 1960's, who simply deplore the prevailing tendency to connect education and the public services directly to economic concerns fail to fully appreciate that the struggle for progressive social change and the cause of social justice have a lot to do with the state of the economy.

Accordingly, it makes sense for educators and activists who are concerned about preserving important aspects of our publicly funded services to deal with economic issues in conjunction with their focus on cultural, political, and social concerns. In this regard, the curriculum of our schools and other educational institutions should be geared more directly to the world of work, a theme enlarged upon in Chapter 5. The real struggle is not about whether or not educational curriculum and our publicly funded institutions should be tied to economic interests; it is about in what forms and in whose interests the connections should be made.

In these times an increasingly significant amount of educational innovation—and hence the opportunity for creative learning—takes place in business and industry. At the same time business influences are becoming more discernible in the way our schools and other publicly funded institutions are organized. This tendency is not part of a conspiracy, but it is not going to go away. Business interests are not being adequately served by publicly funded institutions. Where the state is seen to be abandoning its role in this regard, the business sector is assuming responsibility. The relevant response for critics of this trend is not to opt for the fatalistic stance of deschooling society. They should accept that the quality of education and public service cannot be realistically divorced from the world of work and economic development. The struggle for social justice takes place within an economic arena.

It would be a mistake to overlook existing initiatives, however small in scale, that are intended to resist the deployment of repressive, technocratic, curriculum and management practices in our educational institutions. Similarly, protests about the ongoing cuts to other publicly funded services indicate that there is already a basis for advancing sensible alternatives to the prevailing ideological schemes for downsizing and restructuring our institutions. Even though alternative progressive visions for our schools and other public institutions have yet to emerge, growing concern about current forms of ideological restructuring confirms that it is premature to simply accept assertions about the end of the welfare state and the abandonment of our educational institutions, other public services, and government to the ethos of the marketplace.

If progressive antihegemonic initiatives concerning the fate of our schools and public institutions are to gain ground, however, the already pervasive influence of business and industry must be taken into account. There are benefits to be gleaned (not the least from the emphasis on efficiency, performance, and communications technology) as well as harmful effects to be countered. And while education and social services for profit are already well entrenched, schools and other public institutions in some form are still needed by business corporate interests for whom the anarchistic tendencies of a deschooled society would be ultimately dysfunctional. The critical struggle of our times is around how our schools and other social institutions are being reconstituted, not about their demise.

Illich on Research

Illich attaches importance to research *on* education rather than *in* education. This distinction he makes is important. For Illich, research in education remains confined to the norms and interests of the experts. Even when purporting to identify the needs of learners—through formal needs assessment questionnaires, for example—the researcher *in* education orientation frames the investigation in terms of the professionals' view of reality. It is as though they know already, from the way questionnaires are framed, how the everyday life of ordinary people in our schools and other institutions should be constructed.

For Illich, then, research *in* education takes too much for granted. Fundamental presuppositions of the investigators remain unquestioned. A shift to a research *on* education, on the other hand, calls for an investigation into how educational practices and institutions are connected to the norms and institutional arrangements in other socially important settings (for example, medical care, social services, the prisons, public transportation, women's work). For a critical pedagogy, the broader purview and deeper insights afforded by an approach which emphasizes research *on* education as envisaged by Illich assume considerable significance.

Illich's distinction between research *in* education and research *on* education points us to the shortcomings of research by experts that is so narrowly confined that it overlooks relevant connections to other areas of commitment and social realities. In this view, research *in* education reinforces a tendency toward a confining exclusiveness. The profession becomes increasingly less receptive to creative ideas and new developments within society as a whole. Educators tend to define their role through a spurious professionalized, inbred discourse which tends to set their work apart from other important areas of everyday social life.

This tendency toward mystification and isolation from practical everyday life is even more apparent in conventional professions such as medicine and law. Research *on* the professions can serve to counter and uncover the negative consequences of inbred and cultish norms which are characteristic of professionalized practice. In this regard, Illich emphasizes a way of looking at education and other professionalized dimensions of society that will challenge spurious claims for a monopoly on specialized knowledge based on inbred research and exclusive practice.

Clearly, research *on* education is not intended to provide blueprints for practice or professionally self-serving techniques that reinforce an aura of special expertise. Such developments, including curriculum design, testing and evaluation, and strategies for management, become subject to a critical analysis from the perspective of research *on* education that does not take it for granted that they are in the best interests of students, educators, and society at large. And research *on* education helps educators toward a better understanding of themselves as practitioners. Similarly, research in the Illichian sense *on* medicine, *on* social work, *on* law can lead practitioners to an understanding of the wider social implications of their professionalized interests.

Even so, Illich's animosity toward schooling and the professions has led him to force a separation between the notions of research *in* and research *on* that is misleading and, ultimately, dysfunctional for a critical pedagogy. A more dialectical sense of the distinction between research *on* and research *in* than the one offered by Illich envisages an interrelationship between the two. Both of these perspectives should be of concern for researchers when investigating educational (as well as other social, cultural, and political) activities.

Research *on* education can illuminate what it is we do and what it is we are as practitioners within a wider social context, whereas the research *in* education dimension returns us towards a reflection on practice. Thus research *on* practice is complemented by the affirmation of a normative moral and political turn toward vocational practice. Without Illich's notion of research *on* education, an understanding of implications within a wider social context tends to be ignored. The absence of his research *in* education, though this may not be Illich's intention, allows us to ignore the need to engage systematically with what we should be and what we should do as educators. A critical theory of (educational) practice incorporates both forms of research identified by Illich. From this critical perspective, Illich sets up for us a false and unhelpful dichotomy.

So if research *on* education strengthens our capacities to investigate what it is we do and what it is we are as practitioners, the turn to research *in* education through reflection on practice after the distancing stance (of the spectator) of research *on* education affirms a moral and political commitment toward vocation. And it is here that we part company with Illich for whom the notion of vocational commitment, because it implies a connection to formal institutional arrangements, is problematic.

In accordance with Illich, a critical pedagogy eschews the kind of research *in* education which fixes a privileged *professional gaze* on others as individualized learners or clients. In this regard, the research *in* education dimension should focus rather on our practices and our roles as practitioners. However, while crediting Illich with making a significant distinction between forms of research in the realm of education, one must wonder why he has not incorporated this insight in the case of the Church where he has more experience. Research *on* the Church, its norms, practices, and bureaucratic structures would just as readily lead to the Illichian insights into the effects of institutional arrangements on the construction of everyday reality as research on education.

Why the displacement by this former churchman from the domain of the Church to education? What is so sacrosanct about the Church, and its medieval priestly trappings, as an object of research as opposed to modern secular institutional forms? Research *on* the Catholic Church might tell us more about how feudal forms of organization still manage to flourish in modern times. The same can be said of the modern university which retains vestiges of feudalism in the way it conducts its internal affairs and in its way of communicating a mystique about university life to the larger society.

While he avoids vocational commitment to either institution, Illich has operated successfully within both the Church and the university. He addresses intellectuals of both contexts, as well as a broader intellectual audience, when he castigates modernity and yearns, sometimes quite openly, for conditions of everyday life experienced in the medieval village. This romanticized rejection of modernity and idealized invocation of the past might well be viewed as the indulgence of elitist and well-nourished intellectuals. Community-based alternatives to conventional institutionalized programs, as the liberation theology priests of the urban barrios well understand, entail grappling with the conundrum of development in a modernizing political economy where the rich minority still takes nearly all. Antidevelopment discourse which romantically invokes the values of feudalism and the medieval village—a fairly brutish existence for most people—is surely indicative of a reactionary, antiprogressive view of the world.

Although Illich is inclined to invoke a sentimental notion of the past, there is a connection between deschooling tendencies described in this chapter and postmodernist analysis currently in vogue within the critical discourse on education. The connection of postmodernist thought to Illich's call for deschooling society is worth noting at this juncture. The postmodern analytical approach of *deconstruction*, drawing on contemporary literary criticism which is skeptical of all authoritative claims about what constitutes good form and content, highlights the same kind of concerns as Illich about conventional social practices and institutional arrangements. In this regard, taken for granted authoritative claims which are normally advanced to legitimize existing institutions (such as schools and prisons) come under scrutiny. These claims are no longer taken for granted from a postmodern perspective. The origins for their authority are shown, through an anarchistic process of deconstruction, to reside in prevailing relationships of power. In this view, authoritative claims that establish assessment (evaluative) criteria in our schools and other institutions are revealed as stemming from the will to power. As with the discourse on deschooling, postmodernist deconstruction focuses our attention on how professionalizing tendencies, bureaucratic initiatives, and conventional management practices are fundamentally manipulative plays to achieve and maintain power.

A postmodernist deconstruction of the medical profession, or the Catholic Church, or the university (in which these institutions are read critically as "texts" in the manner of literary criticism) will show how they have developed according to the logic of patriarchy; that is, in the interests of a privileged class of men with regard to how acceptable practices and norms of the institutions are ordered and legitimated.

Postmodernist deconstruction and the agenda of Illich's *Deschooling Society* are nicely linked. However, for those who still see our institutions as places for learning and struggle toward a more just society, the connection forges a dangerous liaison. Although they illuminate the spurious claims on which repressive claims for power and privilege are based, both deschooling ideology and postmodernist deconstruction serve to undermine the institutions in which a *reasonable* case can be made to develop educative strategies towards human emancipation.

Reinvesting Our Schools

Illich's work represents for us much of the radical critical commentary on conventional schooling which emerged from the 1960's and early 1970's prior to the neoconservative onslaught on publicly funded education. The major insights of Illich's project, and the serious manner in which they are presented, remain relevantly provocative for a critical theory and practice of education. Along with other radical commentators on education (and on society in general) whose work he has inspired, Illich highlights the ways in which our institutions and conventional approaches to education and the provision of social services are failing ordinary men and women. His critique of the schools extends to society as a whole. From this viewpoint all of society is a vast school. Rather than acting on the possibilities it offers for human development, however, Illich recommends abstention, and withdrawal to a private sphere. In this regard his deschooling dogma plays into the hands of neoconservative ideology which idealizes the cult of individualism and privatization in its quest to remove constraints on the free enterprise market. Publicly funded education and social services have been severely mauled in this process.

In rejecting the hopeful potential of modernizing development, including the public's interest in formal education that is part of this development, and in calling for the abandonment of our major institutions, the radical critique of Illich, and that of his contemporaries, is now passe. The overriding message for the abandonment of modernity and its institutions is dysfunctional. From here on, a critical pedagogy for our times must do without intellectual chatter and far right-wing ideology about the "end of history," romanticized yearnings for the mud of a medieval village, or leaps of faith into some postmodern nonreality. Men and women are still acting purposefully to advance community interests and their own development within our institutions. Human history evolves within our institutions, even if not under conditions of our own choosing.

In these times, the challenge for those who retain realistic hopes for a more just society is to protect and enlarge on aspects of our institutional arrangements which will further this aim. The challenge entails acknowledging that our schools and other public institutions are already politicized and accepting the need to engage in realpolitik as a means to counter repressive policies. Authoritative claims about the end of social support and progressive initiatives associated with the welfare state should at least be debated rather than accepted as a done deal. At the same time ways can be found to make our schools and other institutions in transformation more accessible to the community at large as forums for public debate. The role educators have to assume in making it clear that these forums are accessible to the public within the context of lifelong education will be enlarged upon in Chapter 6.

As for the discourse on development, tied as it is to education, educators and other intellectual activists committed to critical pedagogy should embrace the concept rather than abandoning it to corporate moguls, bureaucrats, politicians, and the media. Development of some kind or another is an inevitable part of historical and social learning processes. The challenge for critically informed educators and other activists for social justice is to *re*-present the discourse on development as the arena for struggle about which interests define development and whose interests should be served.

Just as development in some form or another is inevitable, so is the retreat to a romanticized past, implicit in the Illichian deschooling scenario, inevitably blocked. There is no way home to the medieval village even though some privileged remnants of feudal order are discernible in the Catholic Church and the university. Similarly, there is no way out to an idealized (postmodern?) future without engagement and struggle for social justice with what we now have in our schools, colleges, workplaces, and other institutional arrangements.

Educators have a critical role to play in revitalizing this contemporary ongoing struggle for social justice in the wake of unrelenting rollbacks to past gains made in education and public services for the majority of ordinary men and women. There are of course no guarantees as the radical intellectuals of postmodernism have understood in their eagerness to embrace and celebrate their discourses on irrationality. (Barbarism remains an option well within the realm of human experience as the 20th century draws to a close.) But a pedagogy of hope emanating from reasonable aspirations is surely preferable to a radical discourse on the abandonment and rejection of all the human project of modernity has achieved and has still to offer. It is reasonable for us to be concerned with the continuing development of our schools and ourselves.

Chapter 2

THE DESKILLING OF EDUCATORS

> The extent to which the process of living in any day or hour is reduced to labelling situations, events, and objects as "so-and-so" in mere succession marks the cessation of a life that is a conscious experience. Continuities realized in an individual, discrete form are the essence of the latter.
> (John Dewey)

In contrast to Illich the position taken in this chapter is that educators have too little authority rather than too much, and that what influence they do possess is being eroded by a process which literally deskills their work.

The Dimensions of Deskilling in Schools

People rarely, if ever, have complete control over their own conditions of work. However, the amount of autonomy workers can exercise over their labor varies greatly from one situation to another. Even in extremely coercive situations where the denial of autonomy is explicit—under slavery, for example—there are opportunities for some limited measure of self-expression and the practice of skillful work. Such opportunities for skill development, though they may be slight, are probably discernible in all forms of human endeavor. It can be argued that the creative potential involved in determining the conditions of work, influencing the form it takes, and the *careful* development of skills is a central defining characteristic of normally wide-awake human beings (those capable of reflecting on their experience).

The expression of ourselves through work becomes inextricably tied up with the human condition—of what it is to be human, a theme which will be addressed in the Chapter 5, Education and Work. Accordingly, the incidence of deskilling is a critical problem for educators to tackle in terms of their own work and that of their students.

Deskilling occurs when the amount of control we exercise over our work is reduced. Although concerns around the issue of deskilling will be enlarged upon in Chapter 5 and subsequent chapters, this chapter deals specifically with how it diminishes the work of educators.

Much of this chapter deals with the role of schoolteachers and the effects of currently escalating initiatives toward deskilling their work. However, the connection between the diminishment of teachers' skills and those of other educators, public service workers, and wage workers in general will also be addressed. Part of the task of critical pedagogy in these times is to show how developments in one sphere of society are experienced in others. The notion that events experienced in a particular institution, community, or society can be understood in isolation from what is going on elsewhere reinforces the fragmentation of our everyday lives in the modern world. This fragmentation provides advantageous conditions for tendencies toward deskilling which can only be effectively resisted through a firmly held sense of solidarity among various occupational groups.

Since most of us are busily preoccupied with the pressing demands of day-to-day living, it is not easy to take time out for reflection on how seemingly singular events and experiences in our lives, and in the lives of others, are relevantly interconnected. Unhappily, a failure of ordinary people to appreciate the big picture—to view society as a *totality*—means that bureaucratic, political, and corporate initiatives which diminish human creative capacities go relatively unchecked. Such initiatives are widely regarded as an inevitable aspect of the way things are and the way things have to be.

Herein lies the challenge for schoolteachers and adult educators. In attending to the way their own work is being deskilled they can be more effective in drawing attention to the pervasiveness of deskilling throughout society as a whole. The Illichian discourse on deschooling has not helped prospects for making a convincing case around the value of teachers' work. However, Illich's insights can be helpful for educators in other regards as was shown in Chapter 1. In making it clear that social learning processes are shaped (to the advantage or otherwise of ordinary people) in a wide variety of institutional and community-based situations, Illich lays out the wider context in which

The Deskilling of Educators

educators should view the relevance of their work. Either acquiescence or resistance by teachers to the deskilling of their work will have implications beyond the classrooms and the school board offices.

In the past a widely held idea of teaching as vocation has implied that teachers enjoy a significant amount of freedom in the way they organize their work. Teachers who were recognized as being good at their jobs could expect to conduct their classes and organize the curriculum without undue interference from administrators. They did not count on their work being directed by bureaucrats and steered by prescriptive curriculum guides. This perspective on teacher autonomy does not exactly portray the way things were—it is undoubtedly a romanticized viewpoint—but it is important to understand the nature of bureaucratic incursions into curriculum formation and classrooms which have taken place during the past two decades. The significance of these incursions assumes larger proportions if the message they convey to students about who controls the work environment is taken into account. If teachers allow their work to be impoverished by outside interference, what chance is there for other ordinary working people to resist the deployment of deskilling initiatives?

The deskilling of teachers occurs as the curriculum becomes more standardized and as their worktime is more strictly arranged to meet bureaucratically conceived specifications of what education should be about. Thus teachers' work is restructured to meet administrative requirements. In this restructuring process the work of teachers is diminished. It becomes easier to move teachers around from one position to another, or to simply replace them. From a bureaucratic standpoint, there is less need to be concerned about highly qualified and experienced replacements. Teachers become dispensable. They can be substituted, with a minimum of fuss, just like the standardized curriculum models which many teachers are obliged to deploy on their students.

In this regard, the predicament of teachers is akin to that of other public service sector workers, and workers in general, at this time. Like workers from other sectors, teachers are significantly represented in the unemployed, surplus labor force. Teachers are becoming *proletarianized* despite the misguided view many of them still hold about themselves as being privileged members of an established profession. And, to the extent that they reinforce this view, teachers' unions are doing their members a grave disservice. This misperception regarding their status is largely a circumstance of teachers in economically advanced countries. In developing nations, teachers tend to be clearer about the proletarian status of their work.

Taylorism and the Cult of Efficiency

In the 20th century, deskilling is associated with the name of Frederick Taylor (1967). He was the efficiency expert whose studies on time and motion in American factories of the 1920's gained him an international reputation. Taylor's project was to demonstrate how breaking down factory work into a series of simple measurable tasks would increase productivity on factory assembly lines. The initiatives of Henry Ford in automobile manufacturing had already established the significance of assembly line production. Taylor took the logic of Fordism to a further stage of development. His systematic approach was enthroned within the industrial world under the auspices of "scientific management." However, a consequence of Taylorism for workers was a loss of jobs and an increase in unskilled labor. Workers could now be trained quickly to complete the simply defined, and repetitive, mechanical tasks required of them in modern factories.

Taylorism entailed a sharp differentiation between the conception of work and its execution in the form of predetermined tasks. Organizing and planning work increasingly became the preserve of management who assigned the monotonous tasks of mass production, which made small demands on intellectual capacities, to unskilled workers. Management was thus in a much better position, in the wake of Taylorism, to control the work processes and the entire system of production. The system, especially in larger factories, required lower echelons of management—foremen and clerical workers, for example—and a number of semiskilled workers. Lower management and office workers did have to think, but not too much, about the significance of their work, while semiskilled workers were expected to be a touch more resourceful than unskilled workers. So there are levels of deskilling in the world of work according to Taylorism. However, the separation of the conception of work from its execution is a central feature of the deskilling process.

The cult of efficiency began to pervade educational as well as industrial settings, especially in the United States, during the 1920's. Taylorism in the schools influenced ideas about educational administration, the physical layout of classrooms, approaches to discipline (subsequently defined as "classroom management"), and the curriculum. Some administrators were pleased to claim that their schools were run like factories. After all, the task of schooling was to prepare young people for the workforce.

From the outset, Taylorism in the schools has met with opposition. Though never decisive, this dissatisfaction with the Taylorist agenda

The Deskilling of Educators

is located in the resentment and, sometimes, active resistance by some teachers to the top-down deployment of prescriptive curriculum. Debates between humanists and behaviorists about the aims of curriculum, the role of the teacher, and the learning processes are a manifestation of this struggle. Behaviorism, exemplified in the work of B. F. Skinner (1976), is akin to Taylorism. It extols the merits of efficiency and accountability, systematic manipulation of learners' attitudes, and control of the educational environment. Humanist educators oppose behaviorist pedagogy because they claim it impedes the freedom required for creating relevant strategies to suit the needs of individual learners in a particular educational context.

Behaviorism as Ideology

Behaviorism provides the *technical rationality* for curriculum initiatives associated with deskilling. As well as determining the shape of curriculum development, behaviorist orientations are *instrumental* in influencing classroom practices and teacher training.

At a slight risk of oversimplification (a central characteristic of behaviorism itself), behaviorism can be said to perceive human action in terms of *reaction* by individuals to stimuli from the external environment. "Neobehaviorists" attempt to accommodate criticisms of behaviorism while maintaining its overall agenda. Their attitude in this regard is both puzzling and contradictory. For in its logical form, behaviorism eliminates consideration of autonomous purposive action on the part of the individual. It is a closed system that does not logically allow for creative variations. Thus, behaviorists are narrowly preoccupied with stimuli from the environment and the direct observable responses *caused* by these stimuli. By altering the intensity and/or the frequency of a specific stimulus under controlled conditions, human behavior can be *systematically* manipulated and *objectively* observed.

For the behavioral psychologist, reports on human activity—the data—are restricted to *observable facts* which are *publicly verifiable* in *precise* terms. These data constitute behavior. They are perceived by behaviorists as the empirical basis of a scientific approach. In this regard behaviorism aspires to ape what behaviorists characterize as the methodological approach of the natural sciences. This aspiration itself is problematic since what behavioral psychologists claim as the scientific basis of their work in education is not readily observable in the way natural scientists go about their work in the laboratories. Apart from this misrepresentation on the part of behaviorism there are, in addition, the serious difficulties entailed in the very attempt to attach what might reasonably be referred to as the "human sciences" to the methodology of natural science laboratories.

In any event, according to the behaviorist standpoint, anything that can be usefully said about human action can also be represented precisely in the form of observation statements. Preferably, these observation statements should be couched in terms that are amenable to measurement. From the "scientific" data of behaviorists we can get the numbers. Subjective experiences, ideas, concepts, inspirations, and daydreams are viewed as excess mentalistic baggage until they can be reduced, objectified, and represented as precise observational statements.

According to behaviorism, the meaning that is lost to the reductionistic process is thought to be no loss because it has no relevance to the task of making us more efficient in our dealings with the "real world out there." Hence the difficulties encountered by educators who become frustrated by the absence of *contextual meanings* (the practical stuff of the "real world out there") from behaviorist curriculum design, program development, and standardized testing. The standard response that a certain number of precisely defined observation statements can be added on to take care of any significant absences of subjective experience merely confirms the depressing durability and sterility of behaviorism. "Just tack on two or three modules for social studies to take care of aboriginal and feminist needs. And perhaps it's time now for a unit on ethics." This is the kind of outlook on curriculum development that typically emerges from a behavioristic orientation.

It is the logical positivistic dimension of conventional natural sciences that behaviorism seeks to deploy onto the study of human action. The pseudo-quantification that is a central feature of the behaviorist tendency endows an aura of authority on those who draw from behaviorism for their expertise.

Behaviorism in education implies that there are clear-cut identifiable deficiencies that are amenable to either special treatment by the expert or correction through the deployment of expertly designed learning materials. Within this behaviorist orientation, the capacities of teachers to construct relevantly practical learning situations where precisely determined beginnings and endings are not immediately discernible, are judged as superfluous.

The behaviorist tendency to sideline these capacities for practical judgment is what constitutes behaviorism as a powerful ideological

The Deskilling of Educators

force for deskilling educators and their students. Behaviorism is primarily about controlling the learning environment. It is not about endowing teachers and students with capacities for autonomous critical judgment, aesthetic appreciation, imaginative work, and spontaneous activities which, given a chance, can emerge relevantly within any educational context.

At the level of theory and research, the pervasive influence of behaviorism creates obstacles for a complete study of purposeful action and the structures of meaning in educational settings. In classroom settings and around the planning of curriculum, the effect of the behaviorist agenda has been to undermine teachers' confidence in the value of their own experience as the primary source of designing the framework and content of education. Ultimately, this diminished confidence manifests itself as a reluctance to undertake the kind of personal and collective initiatives which could affirm the autonomous role of teacher as educational practitioner. With behaviorism, the necessary skills come embodied in standardized curriculum packages, testing formats, "learning by objectives" course guides, and centralized curriculum designs.

The oppositional "humanist" discourse to behaviorism in education, such as that advanced by Carl Rogers (1969), upholds the importance of *intentionality* (purposive action), *meaning in context,* and creativity for both teachers and students. The personal experiences of everyday life are relevantly incorporated into the curriculum. Thus, teachers and students are enjoined through the pedagogical process to explore the meaning and authenticate the value of their own experience. Unfortunately, the debates between behaviorists and humanists (exemplified in the recorded confrontations between Carl Rogers and B. F. Skinner) are more marginal than in past decades. Further, to the extent that humanist discourse in education has escaped co-optation into "neobehaviorist" frameworks, it is now widely associated with antiteacher ideological discourse about the legacy of 1960's classrooms where students were allowed too much freedom to "do their own thing." (Many humanist educators recall education in the 1960's, despite its shortcomings, as a short period of progressive experimentation.)

The humanists in education are right to invoke philosophical and theoretical analysis to support their claims about the relevance of subjective experience and autonomous action. Yet they have not taken adequate account of the objective material conditions that teachers must contend with on a day-to-day basis as they experience the potential of their own agency. This shortcoming of the humanistic perspective is also apparent in Illichian ideology which is firmly in the humanist camp arraigned against behaviorism.

Behaviorism legitimizes very real bureaucratic and corporate interests which are largely, though not entirely, antithetical to the liberal humanistic orientation in education. A behaviorist orientation is ideological through and through despite the legitimizing claims advanced about its scientific objectivity. Behaviorism has an *intentionality*, a purpose, all of its own. (Otherwise, how do behaviorists account for themselves? How does Skinner explain Skinner?) So, while they should continue their oppositional critique of behaviorism, taking it into the realm of politics and economics, erstwhile humanists in education now need to accept that behaviorism and its deskilling effects have to be countered through a struggle for power and resources within our educational institutions.

In contesting the ideological agenda of behaviorism that seeks to restrict their attention to the manipulation of learned behavior, teachers can widen the scope of vocational practice.

There is more to the differences between behaviorist and humanist orientations than is represented here. The critical issue at stake in addressing these different viewpoints is enlarged upon throughout this chapter and in Chapter 6.

Standardizing Education

During the past two decades, since the radical ideas of Illich, Holt, Reimer, and Kozol first made their mark, educational policy formation in advanced western economies has served quite systematically to deskill the majority of teachers in the formal school systems and in postsecondary education. Directives to teachers about the nature and design of curriculum have increased. Thus, many schools and institutions for adult and continuing education are now obliged to use standardized prescriptive curriculum formats which are designed according to behaviorist criteria described in the previous section. These formats are invariably deployed in a top-down fashion and have a clear-cut tendency to diminish the teacher's role in the educational process. The educator, in such circumstances, is turned into a classroom *facilitator* or *manager* of learning resources where the educational process is shaped and steered by learning packages. Packaging begins to preempt teaching.

Standardized curriculum formats are readily amenable to computerization. Because computers have the capacity to keep students busily

The Deskilling of Educators

engaged with programmed learning formats on an individual basis (that is, as solitary learners engaging with a computer program), they can define the entire instructional context. In this regard Illich's talk about replacing teachers with facilitators or custodians is no longer that far off the mark. The claims to expertise about which Illich complained are actually being rapidly undermined in teaching and other public service jobs.

At the same time that curriculum is becoming more standardized and prescriptive, the changing role of educational administrators further undermines the importance of teaching. The management role of administrators takes precedence over educational leadership which calls for moral and practical judgment rather than just bureaucratic competence. Even in small schools, principals and headteachers are often described as managers of resources. These resources comprise plant and machinery (the school), and "human resources" (children and teachers). In institutions of adult and higher education, especially in North America, educational administrators are increasingly characterized as corporate executives. And many of them seem to relish the designation. Executive offices and reception rooms reflect aspirations to bring corporate business style into our colleges and universities, marking a separation between the status of educational administrators as corporate style CEO's and faculty.

Even while it detracts from the role of teachers, the growing emphasis on educational management also signifies an area of reskilling to serve bureaucratic purposes. Teachers who want to advance are faced with the prospects of a radical shift in their vocational commitment. One advances into management, not into the position of headteacher. And as the gap between administration and teaching widens, the technocratic imperatives of management in our educational institutions override concerns for those ethical and practical aspects which are being diminished. Teachers, like any other employees, are resources to be managed. They pass on to their students this management orientation through strategies for "classroom management." Accordingly, the educational setting is made amenable to the top-down deployment of standardized curriculum, the design of which has been separated from the role of educators.

The bureaucratic deployment of curriculum stems, in part, from a legitimate public concern to ensure that important topics and issues are being adequately addressed in our educational institutions. Thus there is much talk in educational circles about implementing core curriculum and measurable standards. However, major curriculum initiatives tend to originate with politicians, bureaucrats, and educational experts appointed by politicians and bureaucrats rather than from among teachers and members of the public. So it is reasonable for us to wonder about whose interests are really being served.

Privileged members of society, in particular, have a vested interest in advocating for curriculum which supports status quo interests. It is not surprising that Prince Charles wants English children to learn about the historical events that legitimate prevailing social structures. Margaret Thatcher, the most nationalistic of recent British prime ministers, recognized the importance of educational curriculum as a medium for inculcating her particular view on what kind of history should be learned. In this regard, her forceful contributions to the debates about a national curriculum virtually preempted the role of her minister of education. Neither Prince Charles nor Mrs. Thatcher would agree with the view, widely attributed to Henry Ford, that "History is bunk." Both the prince and the prime minister understand that ideological concerns are attached to the way history is taught and to what or whose history is taught.

Even if Henry Ford did not understand the advantages that accrue to status quo interests through the teaching of officially sanctioned history in state-supported schools, industrialists do have a stake in the way young people are prepared for future employment. Industrialists want to select from a large pool of prospective employees who have achieved at least a minimum level of competence in reading, writing, and mathematics. And, understandably, employers want people who come with attitudes, or "learned behaviors," which are congruent with the requirements of modern workplaces. The right attitudes induce punctuality, attention to detail, respect for designated authority, a penchant for hard work, and an acceptance of the competitive ethos. The actual extent to which education reproduces these requirements is debatable. Representatives of employer interests are continuously complaining about the failure of our educational system in this regard. Still, it is clear that the business sector has a vested interest in what kind of learning takes place in the classrooms.

The ascendancy of neoconservative political ideology during the 1980's coincided with a significant increase in the amount of outside interference in the affairs of schools and colleges. Although this tendency has not been confined just to those political economies where neoconservatism gained the ascendancy, bureaucratic interventions in education became most marked under the administrations of Reagan, Thatcher, and Bush. While giving much more leeway to business interests under the banner of free enterprise, neoconservatism has also emphasized that education must be made more accountable to the government's version of public interests. The message is that education needs to run according to criteria associated with the business world. This politicized discourse of efficiency provides on the one hand a rationale for cutting back on educational budgets. On the other hand, it paves the way for the implementation of more directive, standardized curriculum formats within schools and institutions of adult education. Even the universities are being put under direct pressure to undertake academic programming which is more in line with business corporate interests. These developments will be enlarged upon in Chapter 5. The concern here is with how their manifestation in curriculum formation and deployment undermines the autonomy of teachers' work. Even though the most radical aspects of neoconservatism are losing credibility, public supported education in general and the autonomy of teachers' work, in particular, remain under siege.

A notable example of bureaucratic-style curriculum development is found in the competency-based education (CBE) movement. Competency-based education originated in the United States. The CBE movement has also gained considerable momentum in Canada, Britain, Australia and, with minor adaptations, in a number of other countries. Its proponents claim that CBE meets demands for efficiency and accountability in public education. It is particularly appropriate to dwell on CBE in the context of any current discussion around deskilling in education. For CBE is virtually paradigmatic of the way a spurious discourse on skills training actually functions effectively to deskill teachers and students alike.

Competency-Based Education

Proponents of CBE have undoubtedly enlisted a useful term to enthrone their latest manifestation of behaviorism within the conventional discourse on skills training. Who, after all, would want to decry any reasonable aspiration toward the achievement of competence? According to the *Oxford English Dictionary*, the term *competence,* or *competency,* indicates "a sufficiency of; sufficiency of qualification; capacity to deal adequately with a subject; a sufficient supply; a sufficiency, without superfluity of the means of life." The co-optation of the term to dress up behaviorist curriculum is no paltry achievement.

The lexicon of CBE now includes some interesting semantic variations. There is reference to "minimum competency," "failing competencies," "assigning competencies," "a portion of a competency," and an "isolated part of a competency." In its ideal form within CBE discourse, a competency statement is the same as a behavioral statement. Overall, the notion of competence now constitutes an impressive cover presentation for the ideology of behaviorism, the cult of efficiency, and the discourse on skills training.

During the past two decades a massive amount has been written on competency-based education. By the early 1980's, the CBE movement had reached bandwagon proportions in part of the United States. Many advocates clearly view CBE as the curriculum panacea for our times. Others are enthusiastic but more measured in their advocacy. In *The Case for Competency-Based Education* (1978, pp. 18–28), professional educator Dr. Dale Parnell insists that CBE stresses results. "It emphasizes the specific knowledge or skills rather than *how* or *how long* it takes to learn them." In contrast, "the emphasis of traditional subject matter disciplines is upon what is to be taught" and it has little direct bearing on "the competencies required of an individual to cope with modern life." For Parnell the learner-centered orientation "is probably the most basic and powerful characteristic in a competency-based educational philosophy."

Parnell goes on to describe CBE as "a clear policy demand." His perspective presents a contrast to that of Illich and the other deschoolers: "There is nothing basically wrong with the American school system except fuzzy goals." In requiring separately defined outcomes as a central feature of formal curriculum, the CBE system obliges schools to be accountable for ensuring that specific officially approved *content areas* are covered and the results measured. CBE is concerned with "real-life orientation" and makes up for the fact that "the schools have not kept in synchrony with the times and the real-life needs of a changing society." (And yet "there is nothing basically wrong with American schools".... ? No doubt the demise of "fuzzy goals" will take care of that circumstance.)

While articulating its standards through precisely defined objectives, CBE still allegedly guarantees "flexibility" which is highlighted as a major characteristic. (The precise number of competencies needed to guarantee "flexibility" are not specified by Parnell. Fuzzy goals?)

According to Parnell the case for CBE is strengthened by evidence of its adoption well before the time he was writing about the phenomenon. In 1974 CBE was a requirement for schools in 34 states and "several others are considering the addition of a state-level competency-based graduation requirement." Subsequently, CBE has spread outward from its emergence in American public schools to adult education, and to various professional associations, throughout North America and beyond.

The Deskilling of Educators

Despite the development of a massive apparatus around formal needs assessment, program evaluation, and individualized testing, there is no convincing evidence that CBE guarantees improvement in *actual performance*. The causal connections (which would be consistent with the behaviorist paradigm) between CBE and actual performance have just not been established. And it is over two decades since CBE as a curriculum panacea came on line.

The emergence of CBE in the state of Florida presents an instructive case in point. In that state the commissioner of education was convinced that raw data obtained from initial testing constitute a reliable indication of a significant increase in actual performance. In an article entitled "Good News from Florida: Our Minimum Competency Program Is Working," which appeared in the May 1979 edition of *Phi Delta Kappan* (p. 650), the commissioner insisted that "the statistics speak for themselves: we are finding those students who need help and providing them with the help they need."

Opponents of Florida's mandatory system of CBE, which was among the first and most widely publicized in the nation, were castigated by the commissioner for believing that it "is somehow unfair to insist that future regular high school graduates know how to read with understanding and do functional arithmetic," (p. 649). The commissioner of education based his optimistic claims predominantly on the percentage increase in the number of senior students acquiring acceptable scores over a 12-month period between the first statewide mandatory standardized test and the follow-up test.

In announcing that "the statistics speak for themselves," the commissioner of education made no attempt to establish that the test results mean that students were reading with more understanding and were better at arithmetic as a result of mandatory CBE. There is no convincing reliable research in Florida, or elsewhere, to confirm that students become more literate or numerate as a direct consequence of a mandated CBE curriculum. Clearly, improvement in CBE test scores obtained within the confines of the CBE framework itself can be demonstrated. It would be remarkable if that was not the case. The point is that a causal connection between the deployment of CBE (rather than other approaches) and actual performance has not been established.

Even from the outset CBE was not without its eminent critics. Lawrence Cremin, in an interview with Kevin Ryan for *Phi Delta Kappan* (October 1978, p. 115), pointed out that "there are lots of new ideas and some of them are very deleterious—for example, competency-based teacher education." The president of Teacher's College, Columbia and well-respected educational historian further explained that "what started out as a well-intended effort to connect professional preparation with reality became an unstoppable movement toward a particularistic definition of outcomes with respect to anything in the professional curriculum." Despite Cremin's prognosis, the trend toward the direct application of CBE to teacher education has, so far, been uneven. But teachers have no reason to be complacent in this regard. Elsewhere, in *The Transformation of the School: Progressivism in American Education, 1876–1957,* Cremin (1961) gave ample evidence that the crusade for deterministic criteria has manifested itself before in the history of American education. (For example, laundry lists of "minimum essentials" were in vogue over 60 years ago.) The ongoing crusade for standardized prescriptive school curriculum is about accommodation and deskilling rather than progressive change. From this perspective the reemergence of technocratic curriculum under the banner of CBE should have come as no surprise.

The CBE model can be characterized as a systematic attempt to break down curriculum into measurable components. By learning to reproduce the behavior prescribed in each component, students are supposed to acquire competence as they progress through curriculum booklets in a step-by-step fashion. In this regard, the logic of CBE invokes the principles of behaviorism; the overall approach parallels that of Taylorism in the workplaces of the 1920's. A leading exponent of CBE, William Spady (1978), defines the system in these terms:

> . . . a data-based, adaptive, performance oriented set of integrated processes that facilitate, measure, record and certify within the complex of flexible time parameters the demonstration of known, explicitly stated and agreed upon learning outcomes that reflect successful functioning in life roles. (pp. 7–8)

From this compressed, though overarching, definition it can be noted how closely the language of CBE is aligned with the aspirations of "scientific management" in business and industry.

In the main, CBE curriculum is neatly prepackaged into standardized modules. Although the modules are still largely produced in print form, they are also amenable to computerization. Either way, learners tend to spend much of their time responding to multiple choice questions and "fill-in-the-blank" formats. The CBE curriculum model is deliberately prescriptive and consistently simplistic. Yet these characteristics find favor with many administrators and teachers (CBE virtually dispenses with the need for class preparation) which largely explains why CBE or variations on the model remain very much in vogue. In addition to its deployment in many secondary schools and in teacher education, CBE has been incorporated into professional education (nursing, in particular), university graduate level programs, adult basic (literacy) education, and technical-vocational education.

Critical appraisal of CBE draws attention to how the model supports greater bureaucratic control in education. And, with regard to claims by its advocates that CBE promotes individualized learning, critical appraisal reveals how individualization, CBE style, reinforces the experience of anonymity and serial, one-dimensional thinking in learners. Accordingly, learners' capacities for acquiring communicative competence become impaired. This is a serious setback because communicative competence is a critical requirement in attempts to achieve rational noncoercive decision making within and among groups. The fostering of communicative competence in learning situations becomes central to any educational endeavor which is sustained by aspirations for genuine participatory democracy. This pedagogical task is difficult even in the most favorable circumstances. Curriculum formats such as CBE make it virtually impossible.

The notion that any educational situation can realize its full potential on the basis of a predetermined, prescriptive recipe is antithetical to humanistic learning approaches presented in the social psychology of theorists like Eric Fromm (1969) and Carl Rogers (1969). From a humanistic perspective, the artificiality and prescriptiveness of CBE fail to acknowledge that every pedagogical situation is different and needs to be dealt with on its own terms. Attempts to confine a complex activity like education through a standardized laundry list of behavioral statements, or competencies, serve neither the interests of learners nor those of teachers who have a real sense of what their vocation is about.

Much of the initial skepticism about CBE stems from its excessive reductionism. Even for those of us who have not had occasion to dwell on the artificiality entailed in breaking down aspects of human experience into standardized units, there is something odd in the notion that there is a definitive list, with a precise number of competencies (291), which fully represents the teacher's job in adult basic education. Where do these competencies come from? Why 291? Why not 1291? Why not 91?

For those already wedded to a behavioristic model, a curriculum format which specifies, in the most economical terms, major categories, sub-categories, competency statements, partial competencies and so on, carries with it a convincing aura of authority. In this regard, the important findings of *pragmatist* educational philosophers such as William James (1971) and John Dewey are being overlooked. James's warning that "out of no amount of discreteness can you manufacture the concrete" (p. 247) is on the mark. Dewey makes a convincing case in *The Quest for Certainty* (1960, p. 61) that "solution by the method of partition is always unsatisfactory to minds with an ambition for comprehensiveness." The futility and potentially harmful consequences of attempting to deal with the complexity of human activity from a laundry list approach are also highlighted in Eduard Lindeman's classic, *The Meaning of Adult Education* (1961). Lindeman reminds us that "the falsest view of life, as in the fable of the blindfolded men and the elephant, is one which rests upon some particularism as its point of reference" (p. 172).

In reality, initiatives are doomed to failure that attempt to define within an all-embracing curriculum format all aspects of competent performance pertaining to a particular occupation or field of knowledge. However all-embracing the CBE system may appear to be, there will always be concerns of relevance left out of account. It is misleading, then, to imply that the deployment of a competency-based system will ever provide the rational means for guaranteeing competent performance. In *The Creative Mind* (1946), Henri Bergson makes the inevitability of this circumstance eminently clear when he asks us to acknowledge that "in life—there are no sharply drawn situations; nothing happens as simply or as completely or as nicely as we should like." Genuinely competent teachers must surely be prepared to work from this practical understanding of what everyday life is about.

While the epistemological and ethical shortcomings of CBE can be made readily apparent, there are vested interests concerned with its efficacy in terms of social control and the role it plays in sustaining existing relationships of power. For these interests, philosophical concerns around CBE are relevant only insofar as they effect its legitimation. Given the tendencies, which Illich so much deplores, toward the centralization and standardization of vital dimensions of everyday life, it becomes apparent that prepackaged standardized curricula have enormous potential to foster large-scale bureaucratic and political control over the learning styles of ordinary people.

In this regard, Marshall McLuhan's (1967) text, *The Medium Is the Message*, becomes instructive for a critical pedagogy. To what extent do students and teachers weaned on prepackaged curricula such as CBE simply acquiesce in the diminishment of their capacities for free debate and critical inquiry? Are they aware of the erosion of their ability to deal in an autonomous way with unexpected—that is, nonstandard—problems that inevitably occur in their everyday lives?

The appeal of CBE to our need for certainty is hard to counter. When considered apart from real life situations, CBE models suggest in abstraction that there is a predetermined course to be followed. This impression can be reassuring even though, as Dewey demonstrates in *Human Nature and Conduct* (1957, p. 179), projects of action are constantly in the making and remaking as their defects and useful aspects come to light.

A further appeal of CBE formats has to do with how their deployment facilitates a situation where learners become immediately busy. Forethought and significant teaching are not required. Just open the package and off we go. The appeal here is to what might be called *the busyness syndrome* which satisfies our urge to be occupied regardless of the quality of attention required. The individuating experience which characterizes the relationship between learning package and the learner dispenses with the need for teachers to encourage group discussion and, thus, another vital learning capacity is diminished.

Although critical appraisal of CBE, particularly in adult and continuing education, shows how the model represents the interests of commerce and industry, CBE proponents have been unable to establish that their favored pedagogical format is tied to significant improvements in reading, writing, numeracy and workplace performance. Employers are more inclined than ever to complain about deficiencies in these areas. However, the CBE phenomenon continued to gain momentum during the 1980's, and continues to prevail in one form or another, despite the absence of any substantive response to the concerns of its critics.

There is an explanation for the persistence of the CBE model and the prevailing technicist approaches to curriculum development it exemplifies. CBE is *relevantly* located within current forms of capital accumulation in advanced industrial and in developing societies. It is in line with government policy formation which places a high priority on serving the needs of employers under current economic conditions. From this perspective, technicist curriculum formats such as CBE habituate learners to the kind of low skilled jobs most likely to be available despite misleading rhetoric about newly emerging highly skilled work. The deployment of prepackaged, standardized modules reinforces a tendency toward the separation of conception from execution, which is a central feature of deskilled, fragmented work. CBE's pedagogical logic and structure are antithetical to notions of skillful work and integrated occupations. Although the CBE system cannot guarantee competent performance, it endeavors to instill attitudes employers find desirable in a readily accessible surplus labor force. In this regard, it is not difficult to discern which interests are being served by CBE.

Within educational institutions where CBE is deployed along the lines spelled out by its major proponents, the interests of administration are served at the expense of teachers. Administrators become increasingly separated from teachers. Educational administration is focused sharply upon the task of managing the institution—corporate style—and away from educational issues. While CBE enables administrators to gain tighter control within the institution, they behave more like bureaucrats or corporate executives than headteachers and educational leaders. Within the CBE system, then, the institution's communication processes are converted into rigidly formalized communication protocols and teachers come under stricter surveillance to serve bureaucratic demands for greater accountability.

During the implementation phase of a CBE format, the autonomy of teachers is eroded as they are co-opted or coerced into accepting their role as facilitators of a curriculum system imposed upon them. Competency-based education intentionally deskills educators as well as learners. While teachers become more easily replaceable, learners are prepared to anticipate a working life of mobility between low-demanding (low-paying) jobs and periods of unemployment.

The CBE movement, then, provides a graphic case study of the way educators are losing whatever control over their work they still possessed. The appropriation of teachers' work through the medium of technicist curriculum restructures the relationship of teachers to their students, to administrators, and to the learning processes. As far as their students are concerned, teachers tend to become mere facilitators of learning or classroom custodians. At the same time administrators tend to treat teachers as employees to be managed rather as than colleagues or co-workers with whom consultation on educational concerns is to be valued. In this context learning processes, shaped by a bureaucratic application of standardized curriculum, are being defined in terms of narrowly conceived predetermined outcomes. Accordingly, the diminished role of teachers within our institutions begins to resemble that of the unskilled worker in the increasingly automated industrial workplace.

The undermining of teacher autonomy by CBE, and similar curriculum formats, is pervasive and hard to counter. The deskilling effects do not merely shape curriculum design. They also serve to determine the structure of the timetable, spacing arrangements, and communication patterns. An entire college can be constructed to meet

The Deskilling of Educators

the unitized bureaucratic logic of CBE. Institutional communication protocols set up around the CBE model reflect its bureaucratic intent, interfering with prospects for spontaneous discussions, the establishment of convivial relationships, and collective action. In such circumstances, communication is hierarchically structured.

As with so many bureaucratically conceived initiatives which require a facade of worker participation for legitimation, CBE is often presented by its advocates through a spurious needs assessment process. Educators slated for CBE are formally requested to provide their knowledge and skills in designing curriculum modules according to CBE formatting requirements.

In the very process of designing CBE modules for their subject areas, then, teachers are drawn into a process bent on deskilling them. Some will, of course, quickly spot the advantage to be gained by becoming converts, and may make career gains at the expense of their coworkers.

Those teachers who are concerned enough to discuss CBE in a critical vein are at first enjoined not to waste time philosophizing, to treat obvious flaws as a challenge, and to get on with the job. Continued skepticism from teachers will meet with claims that they are "traditionalists." According to CBE ideology, CBE is progressive and proponents of CBE are progressivists. Other approaches to teaching and learning tend to be stigmatized as "traditional" (that is, not good), and teachers who remain skeptical of CBE are "traditional" (not good). Critics may point out that CBE is behaviorism in its latest clothing and therefore not novel, and that it manifestly fails in educational terms to do what it claims to do. They will be dismissed as academics from the ivory tower with their heads in the clouds. Meanwhile, academics themselves need to be alert to the possibilities that CBE will gain a foothold within the university. At this time, academic autonomy in teaching, curriculum design, and program development are not immune to initiatives which promote increased standardization and bureaucratic control.

Continued opposition, however well founded, from teachers in institutions where CBE has a hold will lead to censure of one kind or another from management via communication protocols and, ultimately, to dismissal. The bureaucratic logic of CBE renders it immune to direct opposition from individuals even though, or simply *because*, evidence of its shortcomings and controlling agenda is apparent to other teachers who are still not devoid of critical appraisal.

There ought to be a lesson for teachers' unions and faculty organizations in all of this. In the face of top-down initiatives such as CBE, these employee organizations should drop pretentious aspirations about professional status (it is no longer in the cards for schoolteachers and other public service educators—if it ever was) and focus on the struggle for their members to be *substantially* involved in the formation of curriculum.

In preparing future members to protect themselves against deskilling tendencies, the unions should make more effort to exert an influence within colleges of education and other areas of the academy which are themselves under siege in these times. The pundits promoting deskilling initiatives such as CBE are not at all coy about recruiting naive or opportunistic academics to act as legitimizing consultants.

At a basic level of organizing resistance, though, there is a need for teachers' associations to be well informed about strategies required to protect members' interests in combating coercive, deskilling tendencies in our educational institutions.

Other forms of top-down skills-based (so-called) curriculum initiatives may appear less obtrusive than CBE. But their deleterious effects work in the same vein, to the detriment of teachers, as those which characterize the CBE model. The argot of bureaucratically imposed skills-based curriculum ("core curriculum," "common essential learnings," "outcomes-based learning") are accompanied by ideologically inspired rhetoric about "accountability" and "global competition."

The conventional dogma is that publicly funded education is virtually the culprit for all of the present economic woes of modern society. Hence, according to the conventional political agenda, educators need to be brought to account at this time through centralizing educational policy initiatives.

Teacher Autonomy via Curriculum Formation

Many educators are disturbed by the increasing momentum of educational policy initiatives which deskill the teaching role. Others accept the situation fatalistically or just do not care to understand the nature of the forces which are eroding their status and the value of their work. It is more than enough for many teachers just to fulfill their demanding job requirements as they are currently defined. A growing number of teachers are diagnosed as suffering from mental exhaustion or burn-out and are eager to settle for early retirement. Under such circumstances it is not surprising that some teachers can find merit in prescriptive standardized curriculum packages which define their

The Deskilling of Educators

tasks for them, induce a measure of certainty into the teaching function, and create an aura of meaningful busyness around the educational process.

It seems to many teachers that education gets the blame for all the major ills of society and is confronted with unreasonable expectations to provide the solutions. Why should they even pretend to take on such an impossible responsibility?

Intellectual gurus of alternative education have denigrated the vocation of teaching and written off the schools, while academic educators of a critical persuasion suggest that teachers should be agents of resistance within the schools. Unhappily, many academic advocates of teacher resistance are often as naive as the intellectual deschoolers. Both tend to underestimate the full force of government and corporate interest in maintaining public education as a primary location for social control and the reproduction of the prevailing arrangements of power relationships. In any event, during the past decade or so educational policy formation has not been reticent in its incursions into public education and the work of teachers.

Given the circumstances described in this chapter, how might teachers begin to gain more control over their work? The criticisms launched by the advocates of alternative education against formal schooling, official curriculum, and the conventional role of teaching are still prevalent. Accordingly, the writings of Illich, Holt, Goodman, Kozol, Reimer, and others are important sources from which today's educators should draw for critical reflection upon the nature of teaching as a vocation. Because the gurus of alternative education did not adequately account for the sociological, economic, and political dimensions of schooling, they overlooked altogether the significance of schools and other publicly supported educational institutions as locations for fostering some potential for social and political change. The radical, ideologies of the New Right certainly recognized this potential as they launched their assault on "progressive" education during the 1980's. The deschooling advocates also failed to acknowledge that teachers can be agents of such change. However, rather than resenting what the deschoolers have said about public education, teachers could invoke them as a justification for changing curriculum development into a more genuinely democratic process.

The prospects for such an initiative around curriculum development, which will be further explored in the chapters which follow, depend upon the willingness of teachers to participate significantly in determining the nature of curriculum and in public discourses around education. As the shortcomings of top-down curriculum deployment become increasingly apparent, educators can derive opportunities for retrieving more control over their conditions through the democratization of curriculum.

Relevant Connections: Teachers as Intellectual Activists and Workers

The parallels between what is happening with educators described in this chapter and the experience of working people in society as a whole are significant for a critical pedagogy. Teachers can play a role, as activists and intellectuals, in making the connections between the democratization of curriculum and prospects for a more genuinely democratic society.

Educators can also make their ethical contribution to the struggle toward a more just society through a clear understanding of how the impoverishment of teachers' work is reflected in the deskilling tendency which pervades modern society as a whole. Such an understanding establishes a rational basis and source of knowledge from which teachers can identify sensible strategies for resistance.

For teachers who reflect critically on the effects of so-called skills-based curriculum characterized by CBE, it should not be difficult to identify with industrial and office workers whose labor is reduced to monotonous repetition of a small set of measurable responses. The drastic reduction in creative thought processes entailed in conventional workplace circumstances is nicely manifested in the experience of curriculum such as CBE. In both the conventional workplace and in educational settings the effects of deskilling represent work as *abstract labor* which can be readily brought under the control of management.

The absence of real substantive content in skills training curriculum, masked by a preoccupation with precision and the aura of busyness, is in line with modern industrial society's need for a large reserve army of temporarily unemployed semiskilled workers. For these workers no substantial education and training are required. This reality runs counter to a pervasive ideological discourse about upward mobility and equality of opportunity for all. Thus, it is in the interests of the state and employers for a significant proportion of the workforce to have relatively low expectations about advancement.

Even the menial labor that needs to be done becomes dubiously legitimized through the argot of skills training in standardized curriculum and in workplace initiatives for personnel management. Through skills jargon, the natural vagueness of such menial work becomes subjected to the techniques of job classification which facilitates the interchangeability of personnel.

For most unskilled and semiskilled workers under modern conditions only brief on-the-job training is really required. However, modern workers do need to be amenable to taking on new jobs at short notice, accompanied by a willingness to learn them quickly. Further, after a short training period, they must adapt to busy, largely unimaginative work at a fast steady pace. The conditioning for these requirements is to be found embodied in standardized curriculum formats. Accordingly, the very concept of skill in both the conventional workplace and educational settings has been radically devalued.

In advanced industrial societies, then, we are witnessing the prolongation and spread of an increasingly superficial education for ordinary people, combined with the reduction of work to simplistic monotonous tasks which are increasingly being taken over by automation. Through the deployment of standardized curriculum, education and training are about making sure that the majority of workers can simply carry out the work schedule and acquiesce to the conditions (low-grade employment and job uncertainty) that the modern economy has in store for them.

Although the existence of a large reserve of semiskilled and unskilled workers is a requirement of the modern economy, in recent years it has become apparent that employers also need more workers who are able to think creatively about their work and take initiatives in the workplace. In this regard, skills-based standardized curricula are inadequate. So is the short-term, low-level, on-the-job training with which such curriculum formats are ideologically linked. (The issues around education and work will be enlarged upon in Chapter 5.)

The trend toward deskilling then, though powerful, is not monolithic. This is good news for educators committed to a critical pedagogy that relates their work to developments in society as a whole. The technocrats in education do not have it all their own way.

Within our schools, adult education institutions, colleges, and conventional workplaces the unavoidable need for a degree of upskilling is now associated with a discourse around *critical thinking skills*. This focus on critical thinking skills is problematic, from the perspective of critical pedagogy, in that it calls for a commodification—a prepacking—of notions about critical thought. The artificial reconstruction of critical thought into critical thinking competencies that will match the requirements of a wide variety of occupations is absurdly reductionistic. Accordingly, it is up to a critical pedagogy to demonstrate that mere variations on the familiar behavioristic theme of technocratic standardized curricula will not suffice.

It is through a critical appraisal of how deskilling degrades our own work, and in the course of devising strategies to revalue the craft of teaching, that educators can help ordinary working people like ourselves to realize their creative capacities for autonomous work. This critical task, it must be understood, is most difficult. The following chapter invokes a more telling metaphor than Illich—that of the prison—to emphasize what educators are up against when they question the prevailing conventional discourse and draw attention to the social structures and norms that hinder the emergence of genuinely democratic emancipatory learning processes.

Chapter 3

THE PRISON AS METAPHOR

> Shades of the prison-house begin to close
> Upon the growing boy. (William Wordsworth)

This chapter is about prisons. Its purpose, however, is not to report on the various formal education programs delivered to inmates. Rather, the intent is to examine the prison experience with a view to discovering what it can tell us about schooling, learning processes, and mechanisms of social control "on the outside." The prison walls and the act of incarceration define a context which is instructive for the development of an emancipatory pedagogy. Within the prison setting, the obstacles and contradictions confronting a critical pedagogy are starkly apparent. In this regard it is appropriate to invoke the critical insight of Max Horkheimer, a leading figure of the Frankfurt School of Critical Theory which will be considered in Chapter 4. In his essay on "Institute Activities," Horkheimer had this to say:

> An intensive analysis of a single relation or institution that is particularly representative of the prevailing pattern of reality may be far better able to develop and grasp the nature of pattern than would be an extensive compilation and description of assorted facts. (Bronner & Kellner, 1989, p. 266)

Herein lies the significance of focusing on the prisons as a critically informative context for revealing how social reality is represented in our major institutions.

A thought-provoking article in the *Manchester Guardian Weekly* entitled "Sentencing System Blights Land of the Free" reported on imprisonment in the United States:

> The criminal justice system has increasingly been used as the main vehicle through which America handles its social problems, a catch-all de-

vice which scoops up drug users, the mentally ill, the homeless, and other social "failures", and puts them out of sight and out of mind into the prison system. (Walker, 1991, p. 10)

The article points out that the United States has the world's highest known rate of incarceration:

> The American Gulag boasts 426 prisoners per 100,000 population, well ahead of South Africa (33 per 100,000) and the [former] Soviet Union (268 per 100,000). The rate in Britain, which is notorious in Western Europe for its incarceration rate, is 97 per 100,000.

No room for complacency here. In the United States the large number of males who are either in prison or out on parole provides the basis for a major industry. Building prisons is big business.

These inmates may be "out of sight and out of mind" but the experiences they embody are discernible in our schools and other institutions, and in our everyday lives.

Recent statistics on falling crime rates in typically high crime rate areas of the United States such as New York City do not register a significant improvement in the overall trend or in the social conditions associated with high rates of crime and the growing incidence of violent antisocial behavior that goes unchecked in our schools, on our streets, and in our workplaces. Rather, the statistics are indicative of short-term politically motivated initiatives which allow additional powers to the police at the expense of civil liberties (Associated Press, 1997). Such initiatives, relying on a greater show of force by the police, do little to offset the culture of fear in urban areas. Thus, claims for a significant reduction in crime rates at this time are, at best, misleading. By the same token, it is premature to anticipate any meaningful reduction in the high rate of incarceration.

In a recently published text, *Thinking Critically About Crime* (McLean & Milovanovic, 1997), the authors raise critical questions about the ideology of crime control as well about the validity of official reports on sentencing rates and other crime statistics. The book, written from an international perspective, is particularly critical in its assessment of current crime control research in the United States.

For most people on the outside prisons are viewed as serving an important function. Adequately designed institutions are necessary to secure habitual and dangerous criminals. A prison sentence removes convicted criminals, for a specified term, from further opportunities to violate "law-abiding" members of society or the rights of property ownership. The term of imprisonment also satisfies requirements for a rationally determined form of punishment. Apart from meting out

The Prison as Metaphor

a just measure of punishment, there is a widely held expectation that the prison experience should induce in the convicted offender an inclination toward more socially acceptable behavior. Prisons are supposed to be *correctional*.

Prisons become a special focus of public attention when a generalized concern about rising crime rate is agitated by media coverage. Reports of riots or spectacular hostage takings are very effective in drawing public attention to the existence of these ugly institutions. Right-wing politicians, in particular, are inclined to invoke a spectre of the prison as a way of gaining public support. They want more offenders locked up for longer periods of time. The implication these politicians seek to convey is that they are more attentive to public safety than their political opponents. Even liberal and social democratic politicians in the 1990's have adopted the "get tough on the criminal element" rhetoric. This gambit was used to considerable effect in George Bush's presidential campaign. The image of a revolving prison door was repeatedly broadcast on television during the campaign. Mr. Bush's Democratic opponent was thus labeled as being soft on criminals. It is significant that the successful Democratic candidate to defeat George Bush in the next elections did not make the same mistake. Clinton wanted it made clear that he was also tough on criminals. The image of the prisons can be brought to public awareness as a very powerful image for conditioning mass response.

From a somewhat finer critical point of view than the one envisaged by Presidents Bush and Clinton, the prison as metaphor provides us with useful insights into the ways modern educational practice and social learning processes in general are shaped by institutionalized imperatives. While the image of the prison is not so immediately present to most people as that of the school, the mechanisms of surveillance and control the prison embodies are present in various forms throughout society as a whole. Thus, for the poet, William Wordsworth, "shades of the prison-house begin to close upon the growing boy" (Wordsworth, 1904/1950). The metaphorical intent of Wordsworth's image obliges us to recognize how repressive aspects of prison experience are manifested in everyday living on the outside. In this regard, the social theorist Max Weber characterized modern society as an "iron cage" within which there is virtually no escape from administrative control over our lives.

An important educating task for those committed to the notion of a critical practice is that of heightening public awareness about the larger function of prisons in modern society. Why is it that they contain so many young adults from deprived socioeconomic backgrounds and minority groups? Black and Hispanic Americans in U.S, prisons, black Englishmen (and women) in English prisons, and Native Canadians in Canadian prisons. Are people from these groups more genetically disposed than the population at large to commit injurious acts? If not, what are the material conditions and societal norms which induce so many of them, compared to the population at large, to be apprehended for committing offenses against other persons and property?

These are but a few of the critical questions which, if they are examined rather than being taken for granted, bring out important contradictions existing within modern societies where ideas about democracy and equality of opportunity are so frequently invoked. Prison educators who do not take such questions for granted are more likely to adopt an involved critically informed orientation to teaching inmates, curriculum formation, and the nature of their role within the system.

Prisons exist as a crucial means of social control, especially over groups of people at the bottom end, or on the margins, of society. These are the groups for whom opportunities for economic advancement are clearly limited. During economic depression, these limitations become even more apparent and there is a tendency for the prison population to increase. The justice system is widely regarded as the bulwark to counter individualistic acts of aggression against people and property; pressure is siphoned off to the prisons.

In totalitarian regimes, the standpoint on crime and punishment is more clear-cut. Political dissenters as well as those caught committing offenses against people and property are often imprisoned without proper recourse to careful legal procedures. But in both western style democracies and regimes which tend toward totalitarianism, prisons reify a notion of deviance and, thus, play an important role in conditioning people to conform with socially acceptable behavior.

Mechanisms of surveillance and control are all pervasive within the hostile and anomic environment of the prison. These mechanisms are sustained by the guards ("corrections officers") who are responsible for the movement of inmates and other personnel within the institution. Inmates are subject to frequent unannounced security checks and, to the extent that they are never sure when they are being observed, become their own guardians. The design and operation of the prison are intended to inculcate self-surveillance.

Although security measures are immediately apparent in the prisons, they signify a technology of power that permeates modern society. These are connections that have constituted a major focus of

Michel Foucault's work, particularly in his book *Discipline and Punish: The Birth of the Prison* (1977). Foucault draws on Jeremy Bentham's concept of the panopticon which was first adopted as a progressive innovation for prison construction in England during the 1830's. The principles of the panopticon call for an architectural design which results in prisoners and staff being under continuous observation from a central location. The assumption is that conformist behavior follows from a sense that one is always being watched. Further, because panoptic arrangements are such that breaks in the system of surveillance cannot be detected by those it is intended to observe, complete surveillance is still assumed even when no one is watching. Thus, there is a tendency for the objects of panoptic surveillance (prisoners and staff in the prisons) to shape their behavior—in a sense, supervising themselves—as if they are being watched at all times.

It takes only a slight shift in critical awareness to recognize how panoptic strategies of surveillance and control, in some form, are systematically brought to bear in schools, hospitals, business and industrial locations, the family, and many other spheres of everyday life. The prison system, then, can be regarded as a paradigm case for the identification of how existing systems of control and power relations are sustained within society as a whole. An understanding of these power relations—of their negative and positive effects—is integral to any educational practice geared towards the realization of genuine participatory democratic action.

Offenders are sent to prison not just for punishment; they are sentenced to treatment and correction as well. In fact, a correctional ethos, alongside the idea of deviance, has been enthroned within the modern penal system. The purpose entailed in "corrections" is to rectify deficiencies in behavior, preparing inmates for eventual return to "normal society." Hence techniques of surveillance and control are intended to have a normalizing effect on inmates. The notion is that, in the case of convicted offenders, correctional strategies normally associated with institutions on the outside, such as the family and the school, have not been adequately internalized. Inmates are antisocial because they have not learned to behave properly. As institutions such as the school and the family experience greater difficulties in fulfilling their normalizing roles, the spectre of the prison looms larger over society as a whole.

The rationale for overlaying the notion of offender to be punished with that of delinquent to be corrected has been accompanied by an abstract concept called the "criminal mind." This concept has proved useful in the development of an entire body of professionalized knowledge, such as the discipline of criminology, besides constituting a major preoccupation of modern psychiatry. Thus correctional discourse has the authoritative support of experts and is well entrenched. Even inmates during formal conversations with people in authority readily lapse into the professionalized argot of criminology, psychiatry, and psychology when describing what they have come to characterize as their own delinquency. And they can identify soon enough what this professionalized discourse says is needed to transform them into "responsible citizens." Inmates learn that parole board decisions are also steered by the language of the correctional ethos and, sensibly enough, present their appeals in line with what parole board members expect to hear from adequately reformed prisoners.

Yet the failure of the correctional project to transform convicted offenders into law-abiding citizens is apparent. Prisons provide a setting where inmates are likely to be drawn further into criminality. This tendency of incarceration to reinforce criminal tendencies is well understood among prison employees despite the continuing deference given to official discourse about the correctional mission. Natural aging is a more significant factor reducing the probability of recidivism in a former inmate than any correctional strategies experienced in prison. Yet the vast setup to treat, correct and, hence, infantilize criminals as delinquents remains firmly embedded in the penal system as a normalizing technology. Diagnostic testing, psychiatric assessment, and extensive documentary processes are deployed to get a fix on individual offenders through "expert" definition of their psychological deficiencies.

Although convincing claims cannot be made that correctional strategies and techniques reduce the incidence of criminality or the rates of recidivism among those who have served time, the durability of the correctional ethos remains intact. Its pervasiveness serves to illuminate how formal learning processes are determined within society as a whole and the extent to which they are geared to the restriction of our creative capacities from early childhood. In this regard, the poet Wordsworth was surely on the mark.

A major justification for providing formal education and training programs in the prisons themselves is that these initiatives will help correct deviant behavior. From this standpoint, criminality is envisaged as being typically caused by psychological deficiencies that are amenable to fixing by an educational approach based on the techniques of behavior modification. The idea is that this approach—sometimes called "the medical model"—will lead to a reduction in the recidivism rate and the successful rehabilitation of former prisoners in "normal society."

Within this pedagogical framework, prison educators manage to provide opportunities for inmates to take part in a variety of programs. When the budget provision—which can be reduced virtually at whim in accordance with economic and political pressures—permits, some prisons offer courses at the university level and in the fine arts along with regularly scheduled classes for basic literacy and the trades. As an alternative to the mechanistic behavior modification rationale, the case for a more creative and wider range of educational programming is advanced on the grounds that it keeps inmates meaningfully occupied and contributes to their moral development. The correctional ethos, however, remains the guiding principle and formal education within the prisons is clearly accommodative to the overriding system of surveillance and control. Even so, politicians, bureaucrats and members of the public enjoined in the current "get tougher on criminals" rhetoric are convinced that discipline and punishment are more effective control measures, and hence more appropriate, than education. Their position is reinforced by the demonstrable failure of rehabilitative programs in the prisons to reduce the rate of recidivism. The case for the provision of education programs in the prisons has to be advanced and defended on different grounds. It is a social justice issue. Why should prisoners not have access to formal educational programs like other adults regardless of whether or not this education is rehabilitative? Being committed to prison is the punishment.

Although prison education is carried on under dismal circumstances and requires endorsement in terms of dubious correctional criteria, it does manage to provide worthwhile learning experiences for many inmates. Often prison education programs are superior in quality to the kind of educational provision in the social settings from which many inmates come. There is a good chance that inmates will encounter within prison education program teachers who have a strong sense of vocational commitment. At the very least prison classes constitute one of the few areas within an otherwise hostile institution where civil discourse can occur. Thoughtful discussion enhances communicative competence. In an institutional setting where communication tends to be brutalized or shaped by bureaucratic protocols, fostering dialogue around relevant issues is a worthwhile educational activity. It allows some potential for the practice of critical pedagogy.

In addition to the formal provision for education, a significant amount of informal learning takes place in the prisons. Some of it, as already noted, serves to draw inmates even further into the ways of criminal practice. There are many instances, however, of inmates who undertake self-initiated learning projects to improve their educational level while in prison. An impressive array of creative work in the form of poetry, prose, fine arts, and crafts has emerged from the prisons. It is perhaps ironic that revolutionary activists and political theorists formulated some of their major work from inside prison. Notable figures such as Antonio Gramsci, Rosa Luxenburg, Mohandas Gandhi, Malcolm X, and Nelson Mandela spring to mind. Even in this most systematically coercive of institutions, then, emancipatory forms of education that are genuinely transformative can arise to offset both the bureaucratic apparatus for constant surveillance and the attendant anomic conditions of prison existence. A pedagogy of hope, slight though it may be, is discernible within the prison walls. This circumstance in itself is the source of a critical, emancipatory practice of education. Adult educators working in the prisons are in a position to foster the process of self-education while carefully avoiding any inclination to bring it under the control of the formal system.

Yet it is the correctional ethos of the formal system, so enthusiastically invoked to legitimize our prisons, which is most pervasive throughout other institutions, especially the schools. However, as a symbol of the various structures and techniques for social control, the prison as an institution is instructive for educators who believe that a critical pedagogical practice has a part to play in the realization of a genuinely democratic and just society. The prison serves to demonstrate how effectively bureaucratic techniques of control and surveillance are being deployed, especially when supported by an officially sanctioned correctional ethos which endeavors to shape learning processes. There need be no illusions about the immensity of the difficulties confronting educators whose pedagogical practice raises fundamental questions about existing relationships of power which are sustained through our institutions. If instances of emancipatory educational practice can be located in the prisons, however, there is a good reason to believe that critical pedagogy in institutions on the outside can signify something more substantial than the rattle of academic radical rhetoric within a Weberian iron cage. Certainly, a critically oriented pedagogy needs to counter the nostalgia associated with the call for deschooling society by affirming that locations exist within our institutions where the struggle around emancipatory practices for a more just society can be waged.

From the perspective of a critical pedagogy we need to envisage a future society without prisons, not one without schools.

Chapter 4

DIMENSIONS OF CRITICAL PEDAGOGY

> Criticism [as critical reflection] can only be conducted in a community where there is determination to learn rationally from each other. (McTaggart & Singh)

Although the analysis on deschooling and the prison as metaphor help to show how modern society is overly managed by experts and bureaucrats, the tendency to give up on important institutions like schools and colleges should be countered from the perspective of critical pedagogy. In the light of this critical perspective, it is irrational to abandon institutionalized locations where prospects, however slight, still exist for critical discourse and for struggle toward more genuinely democratic participatory initiatives. While carefully avoiding a temptation to exaggerate the transformative potential of such prospects, those committed to a critical pedagogy can be realistically involved in enlarging the *sites* within our institutions where genuine, noncoercive dialogue and reasonable opposition to oppressive bureaucratic controls can emerge.

Connections to Critical Theory

Critical educational practices are linked to critical theory. Critical theory provides the rational means for understanding institutional norms and practices. Based on this understanding it holds out prospects (without guaranteeing them) for progressive social change through *contextually relevant* political strategies. From a critical theory perspective, educational institutions are viewed as *sites* where status quo bourgeois values and existing arrangements, particularly with regard to class, gender, and race, are largely reproduced. While these values and arrangements are nevertheless contestable, both the formal and *hidden curriculum* reinforce attitudes that prepare lower-class students for future work at the lower end of the job market (see Chapter 5). Educational institutions serving largely middle-class clients tend to inculcate higher expectations. The *hidden curriculum*, in this sense, is made up of those unstated objectives around important attitudes, beliefs, and values that are taught particularly in our schools, but also in other institutions. In his book *Ideology and Curriculum*, Michael Apple (1986) refers to the *hidden curriculum* "as the tacit teaching to students of norms, values, and dispositions that goes on simply by their living in and coping with the institutional expectations and routines of schools day in and day out for a number of years" (p. 14). Thus, the *hidden curriculum* "socializes people to accept as legitimate the limited roles they ultimately fill in society" (p. 32). This socialization process, however, cannot be left to its own devices. Hidden or otherwise, it does not suffice to guarantee status quo arrangements.

From a critical theory standpoint, conservative and even liberal educational initiatives of the progressive kind are largely responses to crisis situations which threaten the status quo. They are seen as gestures to bolster existing social relationships of power within the larger society for which students are being prepared. Rather than engendering equality, justice, and genuine participatory democracy, educational institutions are viewed as a means for the reproduction of social class structures which sustain privilege and exploitation. During the high tide of neoconservatism there has been little evidence of even token progressive educational initiatives to counter this tendency. On the contrary, it has been reinforced through the political ascendancy of the far right. Thus, the problem for critical pedagogy during this period has centered around coping with the radical right-wing assault on gains made in the educational provision for ordinary people since World War II.

The social reproduction role of education under bureaucratic communist (or state capitalist) regimes—such as the former U.S. S. R., eastern European countries, and China—and within most totalitarian dictatorships is more apparent and overly determined than in western nations. In western corporate capitalist economies, the role social reproduction plays in schooling and adult education (to the continuing advantage of privileged classes) tends to be partially obscured. Yet the tendency is always discernible. During the past decade or so, it has become more obvious that education is shaped by a business corporate ethos. Thus, from a social reproduction critical analysis, the major function of schooling and formal education is seen as being determined according to the needs of a commercial-industrial nexus. These needs are met in the form of an accessible compliant workforce and a people hooked on the goods and services it provides.

Closely related to the critical analysis on the connection between education and business is concern about how conventional schooling and modern adult education practices are increasingly defined by a technocratic rationality. This tendency constitutes a *cult of efficiency* and manifests itself, for example, in the development of prepackaged standardized checks, and bureaucratic approaches to educational leadership. The driving influence of technical rationality and the cult of efficiency in modern society has been a central concern for Frankfurt School Critical Theory.

Frankfurt School Critical Theory

The work of the Frankfurt School critical theorists—in particular that of Max Horkheimer, Theodor Adorno, and most recently, Jurgen Habermas—has provided educational commentators with a social critique from which to analyze the consequence of an overriding preoccupation in education with the application of technique. Such critical analysis focuses on the structure of educational institutions and pedagogical practices in general. It eschews the narrow professionalized, psychologistic preoccupation with examining students to explain individual differences and personal inadequacies which are identified as reasons for failure. Rather, investigations of educational practice informed by the Frankfurt School tradition of critical theory are concerned with what gets in the way of prospects for realizing genuine participatory democracy.

The Frankfurt School of Critical Theory had its beginnings in Germany during the 1920's. It took the form of a research center for leftwing, middle-class intellectuals who had lost all confidence in Moscow's version of state communism under Stalin. At the same time, they were alarmed by the rising tide of fascism and sought initially to investigate the historical, political, economic, and social-psychological conditions which could account for its emergence. This led to the publication of *The Authoritarian Personality* (Adorno, 1950) which remains remarkably instructive as a social-psychology account of how and why fundamentalist movements promoting racism, religious and political intolerance, and stigmatizing visible minority groups are able to garner substantial support from the population at large.

Apart from Max Horkheimer and Theodore Adorno, the works of prominent 20th-century intellectuals such as Walter Benjamin, Leo Lowenthal, Eric Fromm, and Herbert Marcuse are associated with the first generation of Frankfurt School Critical Theory. As a result of persecution from the Nazi regime (the founding members were leftist and predominantly Jewish), the institute carried on its work in the United States during World War II. After the war, the institute was reestablished in Frankfurt. Many of the critical theorists following in Frankfurt School tradition—including its most prominent contemporary exponent, Jurgen Habermas—have since left the institute to carry on their work in other contexts. Frankfurt School Critical Theory is now making its impact on research in many disciplines, including educational theory and practice, throughout North America and elsewhere.

Like conventional social science, critical theory is concerned with the important task of describing the current state of affairs in a matter-of-fact way. However, it seeks to go beyond a mere description of *what is* to setting out *what ought to be*. This emancipatory project necessitates a systematic disclosure and analysis of contradictions within contemporary social structures. In the opening paragraph to *An Essay on Liberation,* Herbert Marcuse (1969) provided this overall definition of critical theory by which its scientific character could be sustained while holding out the prospect for revolutionary social change:

> By logical inference from the prevailing conditions and institutions, critical theory may also be able to determine the basic institutional changes which are the prerequisites for the transition to a higher stage of development: "higher" in the sense of a more rational and equitable use of resources, minimization of destructive conflicts, and enlargement of the realm of freedom. (p. 3)

Central to the work of Adorno and Horkheimer is a critical analysis of instrumental, or technical, rationality and the way it defines our modern over-administered society. Instrumental rationality, already identified by Max Weber as an inevitable pervasive restricting force of modernity, refers to a way of everyday living in which questions of *means* (a preoccupation with strategies and tactics) take precedence over *ends* (a concern for what ought to be done) and where *facts* are treated as separate from *values*. Adorno and Horkheimer, to a large extent, set the stage for their successors in seeking to show how the enthronement of instrumental rationality in modern society shapes individual consciousness and, hence, learning processes. Their work reveals how what appears on the surface to be common sense strategies and tactics for action ("let's cut the talk, and get on with it in the most efficient way") cover up for particular interests which benefit from cutting short democratic discourse. Accordingly, *the cult of efficiency* is invoked in a way that is inimical to aspirations for human emancipation. Thus, a major task of critical theory is the identification of taken-for-granted strategic actions—forms of decision making—which run counter to the achievement of a genuine participatory democracy. Transformative pedagogy informed by critical theory seeks to locate and to make problematic such repressive strategies within an educational context so that the privileged interests which they serve become more apparent.

Adorno and Horkheimer (1972) became increasingly pessimistic about the prospects for significant social change toward human emancipation. For them, "critical theory became resignative; it could at most unmask unreason at the heart of what passed for reason without offering any positive account of its own" (McCarthy, 1985, p. 176). Adorno turned to *autonomous art* as the primary location for learning experiences through which the overwhelming effects of bourgeois commodification and mass culture could at least be held at bay. This decisive move to the aesthetic dimension is currently reflected in a somewhat more optimistic pedagogical orientation toward art and cultural criticism in which "art becomes a laboratory, the critic an expert" (Habermas, 1985, p. 201). Shorn of the pessimism and the touch of elitist individualism that characterize his later work, Adorno's focus on the aesthetic dimension is still instructive for critical pedagogy. An emancipatory potential can be found in making music together, literature, painting, dancing, and other art forms where creativity is not entirely influenced by market forces or bureaucratic stipulation.

Like Adorno, Herbert Marcuse (1978) placed a high value on the aesthetic dimension as an integral aspect of critical theory. Yet he never gave in to the despondency of Adorno and Horkheimer. Nevertheless, while recognizing the importance of establishing reason at the core of critical theory, Marcuse was unable to link rationality, in theoretical terms, directly with the cause of human emancipation. As a consequence, Marcuse (1966) holds the position of Adorno and Horkheimer about *the eclipse of reason* in the struggle against the unrelenting pervasiveness of a wholly administered society. His appeal is to resistance through negation:

> The critical theory of society possesses no concepts which could bridge the gap between the present and its future: holding no promise and

showing no success, it remains negative. Thus it wants to remain loyal to those who, without hope, have given and give their life to the Great Refusal. (p. 201)

And he refers us to this stark declaration made by Walter Benjamin at the beginning of the fascist era:

It is only for the sake of those without hope that hope is given to us. (p. 201)

In his political role Marcuse inspired a whole generation of student activists during the 1960's, and there is still much that a critical pedagogy can draw on from his writings and commitments. Jurgen Habermas points to the absence of rational grounding in Marcuse's theoretical project ("his theory cannot consistently account for its own possibility"). Yet Habermas refers us directly to Marcuse's "affirmative" outlook and "to one of his most admirable features—not to give in." Recalling the vivid effects following a conversation he had with Marcuse who lay dying in hospital, Habermas paid this tribute to his fellow critical theorist:

I know wherein our most basic values are rooted—in compassion, in our sense for the suffering of others. (Habermas, 1985, p. 72)

For Habermas, however, reasons for this compelling moral position can be located in his critical social theory. He has sought to retrieve rationality for critical theory as central to an analysis of the modern condition and to the discourse on human emancipation. In his ongoing research project Habermas (1971,1984, 1987) has been at pains to ensure that his critical theory is *rationally consistent* with the emancipatory and utopian possibilities it holds out.

Like his Frankfurt School predecessors, Habermas deals with the overarching influence of instrumental (technical) rationality on today's society. His analysis informs us about how contradictions, distortions, and the repressiveness of a near totally administered society are actually reinforced by the very learning which they serve to shape. We *learn* to support the social norms and structures which block the way to a realizable potential for human emancipation. The discernment of this potential toward the realization of a more rational society (sustained by a genuinely participatory approach to decision making) is vital for contemporary critical pedagogy.

Habermas, then, goes beyond his Frankfurt School predecessors in positing a superior form of rationality for critical social science and emancipatory discourse. The basis for this development in critical the-

WE HOPE THAT YOU ENJOY THIS BOOK...
and that it will occupy a proud place in your library. We would like to keep you informed about other publications from KRIEGER PUBLISHING.

Please use this form to request future literature in up to four (4) categories.

Subject Categories

- [ ] Medical Sciences (C)
- [ ] Psychology/Sociology (E)
- [ ] Education/Communication (F)
- [ ] Anthropology/Philosophy (G)
- [ ] History/Religion (H)
- [ ] Engineering/Technology (J)
- [ ] Chemistry/Biochemistry (K)
- [ ] Mathematics/Statistics (N)
- [ ] Business Sciences/Economics (P)
- [ ] Biological Sciences (R) (Botany, Ecology, Zoology, Biology, Nature)
- [ ] Physical Sciences (S) (Geology, Geography, Oceanography, Water/Soil Management, Astronomy, Meteorology, Ecology, Environmental Science)
- [ ] Veterinary Medicine (V)
- [ ] Adult Education (W)
- [ ] Space Sciences/Physics (X)
- [ ] Public History (Y)
- [ ] Herpetology (Z)
- [ ] Other _____

Name _____
Mailing Address _____
_____
City _____
State _____ Zip _____ +4 _____
Country _____ Postal Code _____

Name
Address
City
State _____ Zip _____

Krieger Publishing Company
P.O. Box 9542
Melbourne, FL 32902-9542

Please place postage stamp here.

ory is located in an account of the human capacity for communication through language. Within the human capacity to understand and be understood through speech communication resides the basis for affirming *communicative rationality*. The detailed theoretical project of Habermas has provided us with a means to validate this affirmation.

Communicative Competence

Communicative rationality, from which genuinely democratic decision making about what should be done can emerge, is posited as balancing the interests of three dimensions of human experience. These three dimensions can be designated respectively as *instrumental/technical, moral/practical,* and *aesthetic.* Each entails a specific orientation—a corresponding "action system." Relevantly combined, they guide us in determining what it is we should do and ultimately what we should be.

What we learn from Habermas's elaborate research project on communicative action is that there is rational justification for seeking the means for reaching decisions in a genuinely participatory democratic manner. This potential is realizable in a more balanced way of understanding the world in which ethical and aesthetic considerations are not subordinated to the imperatives of instrumental rationality and to bureaucratic, or corporate, interests. In essence Habermas sets out the theoretical grounds from which reasoned reflection on alternative ways of experiencing and shaping our modern society becomes possible. Critical pedagogy can invoke his work to explain *why* the quest for human emancipation enlarged upon in Chapter 7 is a rational endeavor. The basis of this insight resides in Habermas's account of those innate learning capacities which enable us to understand each other and the world we inhabit.

A pedagogy informed by communicative rationality moves us away from a deterministic subject-object way of knowing which characterizes strategies geared to instrumental rationality. It is not a case of dispensing entirely with technical considerations. They are also a primary feature of the human experience. Rather, a situation is envisaged where otherwise manipulative strategies associated with instrumental rationality can be openly and relevantly incorporated into genuine democratic decision-making processes. This communicative context entails a deliberate intention, in the give-and-take of reasoned careful conversation with others, to change one's viewpoint on the basis of rational arguments as well as a predisposition to engage both critically and respectfully with the views of others.

Delaying recourse to manipulative strategies associated with instrumental rationality until they can be relevantly incorporated into genuine democrative decision-making processes is difficult to justify in terms of efficiency in the short term. Herein lies the challenge for those committed to a critical pedagogy who are, nevertheless, pressured to deploy strategies and curriculum formats in which technical rationality is embodied. While the notion of communicative action clearly does not envisage that the vast majority of straightforward day-to-day activities should be preceded by protracted deliberation, the *ideal speech situation* posited by Habermas is thought to invoke an idealized quest for an unrealizable state of affairs. Such criticism is advanced from a standpoint that views emancipatory practice as a careful and ongoing engagement with the obvious injustices and contradictions of everyday life. In this view there can be no "saving message" or adequate rational grounds to be derived from any comprehensive concept or theory of action. The search for a substantially grounded theoretical perspective on human action or for a guiding concept is seen as *misguided*. Yet the case for *communicative competence* in terms designated by Habermas illuminates a highly relevant task for critical pedagogy. Communicative competence can be learned, and the Habermasian project has shown that the capacities for such learning are accessible in pedagogical processes which value dialogic interaction.

Educational commentators who draw on Frankfurt School Critical Theory (see, for example, Michael Apple, 1986) view educational institutions, schools in particular, as locations for the struggles toward a more just society. They are optimistic that educators committed to a transformative pedagogy can play a significant role in these struggles. Drawing especially from the analysis of Jurgen Habermas, they see the need to develop communicative competence as an educative task. The move toward developing communicative competence is an emancipatory endeavor since it entails the identification of institutional practices, relationships of power, and attitudes which prevent genuine noncoercive dialogue. In this regard, the notion of communicative competence reinforces Paulo Freire's emphasis on dialogue as a paramount educational strategy (Chapter 7). Clearly, the growing influence of prepackaged curriculum design and other top-down bureaucratic educational initiatives can foreclose on the prospects for developing communicative competence. And so the struggle to foster a careful dialogic approach within our institutions and among ourselves assumes emancipatory significance.

Lifeworld and System

In showing how the pervasive effects of instrumental rationality shape learning processes and the course of our everyday lives, the distinction Habermas makes between the "system" and the "lifeworld" is instructive. The system represents that overriding dimension of modern life where the imperatives of technical efficiency and bureaucratic management are predominant. These imperatives "colonize" the lifeworld which sustained traditional community values. Thus, the practical activities and attitudes which characterized community-based values become progressively distorted under modern conditions. They have become shaped by the criteria of efficiency and strategic action which characterize the "system world." And with the incursion of the system into the lifeworld, we lose part of our humanity.

The subjection of lifeworld values and practical activities to the imperatives of technical rationality emanating from the system diminishes the potential for us to experience the full richness of life. This is the situation Marcuse addressed most graphically in *One Dimensional Man*. (1966).

Habermas holds out the possibility that something can be done about the restricting circumstances associated with system imperatives. He acknowledges that it makes no sense to think in terms of abandoning the system. There is no going back from the modern world to the medieval village (as Ivan Illich seems to suggest), but it is reasonable to think in terms of incorporating lifeworld values into the system. Habermas's analysis suggests that possibilities exist for introducing into our institutions the kind of practical activities, caring behavior, and ethical concerns which are still embedded in our most cherished notions of community and family life. In other words, the prevailing trend whereby the system invades the lifeworld can be resisted and reversed. The careful analysis undertaken by Habermas in arriving at these insights provides theoretical support to those who continue to hope that a more rational society, not conditioned by an overarching instrumental rationality, is achievable, and that education has a role to play in bringing it about. The insights afforded through the concepts of the lifeworld and the system are crucial to a critical theory and practice of education and will be invoked again in subsequent chapters.

Potential and Pitfalls of Oppositional Tactics

A replacement of the deschooling orientation with a view of educational institutions as locations for a meaningful critical pedagogy does not mean that our schools and colleges should be identified as the only sterling source of fundamental progressive social change. This kind of unrealistic expectation, promoted by some academic educators of the critical persuasion, only serves to overburden the critical pedagogical project. The advocates of deschooling are probably right in suggesting that, under prevailing social conditions, our educational institutions on their own are unlikely to generate from within any radical progressive educational transformation let alone create initiatives for significant democratic social change. Yet fostering critical dialogue and other carefully planned oppositional strategies to bureaucratic hegemony in educational institutions should be envisaged as highly relevant to the wider struggle for a more rational democratic society. The kind of commitment entailed by a critical pedagogy is more grounded than utopian escapism inherent in the deschooling project exemplified by Illich and others. In contrast to the call for deschooling society, critical pedagogy recognizes that it has to contend with existing power relationships in institutionalized forums where people working collectively can make a difference.

All the same, it is important not to underestimate the prevailing social and political forces which shape institutionalized learning processes. A redefinition of these processes according to the needs of ordinary people is not going to be realized solely through initiatives within educational institutions. In advanced industrial economies, especially, state and corporately defined interests are just too well entrenched. Our schools and colleges do play a substantial role in reproducing prevalent cultural patterns. This reproductive role, as already noted, undoubtedly favors status quo arrangements and runs counter to the interests of students from working class and marginalized social backgrounds. Even progressive educational initiatives are advanced from a largely white middle-class 'malestream' perspective. They tend toward maintaining the prevalent social and economic structures instead of transforming them. From this standpoint, conventional expressions of concern and occasional liberal reformist initiatives within education are seen as little more than token gestures.

Dimensions of Critical Pedagogy

As such, these initiatives merely confirm existing relationships of power within the larger society for which students are being prepared. Rather than promoting equality, justice, and genuine participatory democracy, educational institutions serve to reproduce social class structures which sustain privilege and exploitation.

The tasks of a critical pedagogy in modern industrial, and modernizing societies have to be played out alongside the homogenizing messages of mass culture. Culture critique in the tradition of Adorno and Horkheimer reveals how influential dimensions of modern life—news broadcasting, commercial entertainment, and even idealized notions of family—are experienced in prepackaged, stylized forms. The resignation of Adorno and Horkheimer can be attributed to their pessimistic conclusion that mass culture conditioning is sufficiently well entrenched to withstand any challenges from progressive critically informed initiatives for social and psychological transformation. From this depressing viewpoint, mass culture is sustained by an all-pervasive instrumental rationality according to which the most significant aspects of human activity are assessed only for their effectiveness. Ethical, aesthetic, and practical considerations are thus subsumed under the criteria of technocratic rationality. Inevitably, these criteria tend to reflect the embedded overlapping interests of the modern state, the bureaucracy, and capitalist enterprise. The work of Marcuse, Habermas, and other critical theorists reveals that these interests do not constitute an entirely unassailable monolithic bloc. Yet the social forces opposed to revolutionary social change are such that oppositional pedagogical strategies must be carefully enacted.

So while it is all right to talk about the merits of resistance to bureaucratic constraints within educational institutions, such oppositional discourse should not be invoked to legitimate idiosyncratic gestures against authority. Individualistic acts of defiance on the part of an educator can lead to marginalization or dismissal without establishing a widely appreciated ethical point or a worthwhile political gain. Apart from the hardship involved for the individual concerned, and for any dependents he or she may have, the dismissal of a lone educational critic serves to demoralize others who might otherwise be inclined, at propitious moments, to call for scrutiny of taken-for-granted management practices. Despite initial protests from some staff and students, such dismissals from educational institutions usually signal a victory for management over educators. The effects tend to be long lasting, and it is very unlikely that the real reasons for dismissal of an educator who takes a stance against repressive management practices will be a matter for the record.

Accordingly, critical educators engaged on a long-term project need to avoid becoming isolated in direct confrontations with management. This prudent approach does not mean that the nature of one's overall commitment or critical views on important issues should be disguised. Rather, occasions for public confrontation over key issues should be accompanied by an appropriate sense of timing and reasonable support. In this regard, the distinction Antonio Gramsci (1971, p. 207) makes between "war of manoeuvre" and "war of position" in the realm of civil society can be instructive for those committed to a critical pedagogy. Most often it is more propitious to put energies into forming counter-hegemonic alliances than in conducting frontal attacks on state bureaucracy.

Educators who are compelled on principle to go it alone against repressive management practices should probably be seeking out more supportive context for pursuing their commitment to a critical pedagogy. If tolerated, they are usually made to appear idiosyncratic. And, ultimately, they do become idiosyncratic. Further, the lone gadfly all too often serves the interests of repressive management practices by affording it the appearance of a liberal and tolerant approach. By the same token, the tolerated lone protester can reinforce the complacency of fellow workers already conditioned to put up with the status quo: "The administration can't be that bad; look how they put up with so and so."

A concern about the harmful consequences of idiosyncratic forms of resistance to authority, however, cannot be reasonably invoked to justify resignation in the face of repressive management practices. Rather this critical concern is intended to underscore the need for patient commitment and *systematic* collective struggle over the long haul. For critical pedagogy in these times, the struggle has to be largely about protecting and, now to a large extent, recovering educational gains made in previous decades.

Celebrating the Struggle

The identification of educational institutions as "sites for struggle" does not mean that commitment to critical pedagogy has to be a cheerless daily uphill battle. On the contrary, a relevant task for critical pedagogy is to initiate occasions for celebration within our institutions. Enjoyment—simply having fun—can be part of the educational process in the classroom and in organized extracurricular activities. In this regard, critical pedagogy has a role to play in aesthetic, cultural, and social activities which afford alternatives to prepackaged entertainment and the day-to-day soporifics of mass culture.

A sense of satisfaction can be derived from involvement in critical dialogue and carefully planned projects which challenge the top-down edicts of coercive management. There is no need to extract the capacities to enjoy, to celebrate, and to make music together from the practice of critical pedagogy. Those who are committed to critical pedagogy, and to the disappointments such a commitment often entails, need to keep in mind the cheerful maxim of the political activist Emma Goldman: "If I can't dance at the Revolution, it can carry on without me."

Postmodernism and Deconstructionist Critique

Though strongly influenced by the Frankfurt School, or Habermasian, analysis of modernity and other tendencies in critical theory, critical pedagogy draws from other intellectual currents which run counter to status quo arrangements. In particular, postmodern deconstructionist critique informs a significant amount of contemporary academic commentary on educational practice and research. Educational commentators who have adopted postmodernist critique draw largely on the work of Michel Foucault (1977, 1980). For them the task of deconstruction is to challenge any notion that we can ever have recourse to a guiding rational approach for assessing what we should do and what we should become. To invoke the argot of postmodernist perspectives in literary criticism, deconstructionist analysis undermines the authoritative claims of the *canonical text.* Postmodernist thought in educational discourse, as with social theory in general, is much influenced by its manifestation in literary criticism. The notion that we can rely upon a sterling source, or set of criteria, for evaluating ideas and the course of human action is brought into question by what amounts, ironically, to an *authoritative deployment* of deconstructionist critique. The appeal to reason inherent in all theorizing which views modernity as an ongoing project is rejected by postmodernist discourse.

The challenge posed by postmodernist thought and deconstructionist analysis to taken-for-granted authoritative criteria which guide our understanding of the world, and our everyday activities, is akin to the protest launched by Illich against institutionally based expertise and his yearnings for a deschooled society. Illich's radicalism is traceable to his resistance against the authoritative norms and regulations of the Roman Catholic Church. These *canonical* rules governed

Illich's early intellectual and vocational commitments. Accordingly, unfinished business with the Church as an institution may well be the source of powerful insights for his deconstructionist arguments against secular institutions. In any event, it is the enthronement of power in our institutions, and the accompanying designation of experts (doctors, lawyers, priests, schoolteachers) with ritualized authority, that concerns Illich and intellectuals who opt for deconstructionist critique.

Postmodernism draws largely on the philosophical work of Friedrich Nietzsche. Briefly stated, his philosophy highlights the prevalence of power relationships in everyday life and the *will to power* as the primary motivating force for both the individual and society. Within the vortex of struggles around existing power relationships, postmodernist thought recognizes the potentiality of many points of view and many voices. Hence postmodernist critical discourse is about the struggles for power "to be heard"—about the empowerment of "other voices." It provides a helpful critical orientation for educators who seek to unsettle the dominating discourses of status quo interests embodied in state bureaucracies; institutions such as schools, business and industry; and the conventional nuclear family. The adoption of this analytical orientation within critical pedagogy is intended to illuminate the efforts of disempowered groups and individuals to assert themselves against the ongoing disparities in power relationships within today's society.

In these regards, the projects of postmodernism, Frankfurt School Critical Theory and other versions of the critical theory legacy in education tend to overlap. Like critical theory, postmodern deconstructionist analysis questions the consequences of a technical rationality which determines a whole array of institutional arrangements and learning processes in the field of education. However, the postmodernist tendency offers no *reason* as to why critically oriented educators should advance the interests of disempowered groups and "other voices." The effort itself would constitute yet another example—in this instance, on the part of educators—of the will to power. From a Nietzschean viewpoint a pedagogical commitment on behalf of the disempowered, and any efforts to provide altruistic reasons for such mediation, would merit contempt. Postmodernist critique abandons the quest for identifying *rational* grounds on which to conceptualize and build "the just society." From a critical theoretical standpoint the relativism in postmodernist discourse around engendering *differences* and *other voices* is irrational and ultimately dysfunctional. For a pedagogy informed by critical theory, reasoned justification (the rational

Dimensions of Critical Pedagogy

grounding) is central to the aspirations for and the realization of the just society; the center must hold.

In a sense the academic critical commentators on education who attempt to link postmodernist thought with critical theory are placing critical pedagogy in a predicament. Deconstructionism by definition detaches any firm anchorages for rational discourse that critical theory endeavors to consolidate. Hence the advocates of postmodernism within critical pedagogy fall between two paradigms. On the one side there is a theory and practice which seeks validity in rationally grounded discourse and, on the other, a Nietzschean worldview which scorns such an endeavor. There are no sensible means to a rapprochement between the two paradigms.

Critical theory does not abandon the project of modernity. It holds out the possibility that *rationally* derived criteria of how human beings should be and should act in the world are still achievable. With regard to critical pedagogy, Frankfurt School Critical Theory is particularly useful in showing how a dependency on technical rationality is, in fact, *irrational* and unreasonable in the way it (mis)shapes the learning processes.

A satisfactory account of the fundamental differences between critical theory and postmodernism is well beyond the scope of this chapter. There is no doubt that the postmodern tendency offers important insights for critical pedagogy. However, the distinction does have to be made because attempts to effect a rapprochment between critical theory and postmodernism blunts the cutting edge of critical discourse.

In these times, what is required amounts to a rearguard action in defense of past gains. A critical pedagogy that has any relevance must make its stand from a theoretical commitment which endeavors to give reasons for why our publicly funded institutions are necessary, and for why human emancipation should be the primary goal of education.

Chapter 5

EDUCATION AND WORK

> Jobs are not big enough for people. It's not just the assembly line worker whose job is too small for his spirit, you know? A job like mine, if you really put your spirit into it, you would sabotage immediately. (Writer for a corporation, interviewed by Studs Terkel)

> It is true that the animal, too, produces, it builds a nest, a dwelling like the bee, the beaver, the ant, etc. [Yet] the animal only fashions things according to the standards and needs of the species it belongs too, whereas man knows how to produce according to the measure of every species and knows everywhere how to apply its inherent standard to the object: Thus man also fashions according to the laws of beauty. (Karl Marx)

In this chapter an attempt is made to address the issue of work in a generic sense as well as in terms of the particular forms it takes on in modern society. From the perspective of critical pedagogy, aesthetic, moral, and political dimensions of work have to be taken into account in addition to the imperatives of production and technical efficiency. Although the importance of work to our everyday lives is widely recognized it tends to be viewed in a taken for granted, unreflective, manner. In what follows we build on the concerns raised in Chapter 2 which addressed the work of teachers.

Fundamental Importance of Work

To work is to be human. Here we are referring to work as a fundamental purposive activity that distinguishes human beings, in *being* creative, from other animals. In this view, work is discernible in the primeval purposeful tendency of our earliest ancestors to identify, and ultimately shape, basic tools from their immediate physical environment, to draw water, to make fire and, subsequently to express themselves through crude drawings. As purposive activity, requiring conscious engagement with the environment, the work of human beings differs significantly from the instinctive busy foraging of other animals. This distinction obtains even when we consider the observable regularized activities of herding animals and of "busy" insects such as ants and bees as noted in the opening quote from Karl Marx. Still a sterling theoretical source for our times, Marx also has this to say about the distinction:

> Conscious life activity distinguishes man immediately from animal life activity. It is just because of this that he is a species being. (Marx, 1990, p. 113)

Although primarily concerned with the use value of labor, a Marxian worldview stems from an understanding of the paramount importance of purposive human activity on the environment:

> As useful activity directed to the appropriation of natural factors in one form or another, labour is a natural condition of human existence, a conditon of material interchange between man and nature, quite independent of the form of society. (Marx, 1989, p. 36)

Human nature, in this view, develops in the process of human interaction with the environment. In the widest sense of the term, this interaction constitutes *production*. And it is the within the *mode of production*, along with human relationships accompanying it, that human consciousness is formed. The *mode of production* refers both to the technical aspects or manner of producing and to the social system within which production takes place. The social system includes patterns of social relationships—for example, employer/employee, owner/wage-earner.

The most deeply committed ecologists, rightly concerned about the damage inflicted on the planet by human development and hubris, may argue against the anthropocentric bias of elevating production and drawing a distinction between human beings, the environment, and other animals in this way. However, their case ultimately reinforces the argument by highlighting the moral responsibility that resides with human beings to redress the harmful consequences associated with this tendency of viewing everything in terms of human values and experience. The "deep ecologists" are appealing to ethical

Education and Work 81

sensibilities and creative, productive capacities that form part of what it is to be human as the means for saving the planet.

In this ontological sense of viewing work as integral to human nature, the human capacity and urge to work autonomously precedes the development of cooperative relationships that led to various forms of communication and, subsequently, language development. There is a crucial connection, then, between the fundamental human capacity for purposive work, the establishment of relationships, the urge to communicate in a meaningful way, and the development of language competence which could be considered at length. At this juncture, however, it is sufficient that we are clear about the primary importance of work, in its various manifestations, to human experience and, hence, to any consideration of our educational institutions and the shaping of social learning processes.

When work is envisaged in the terms used here, it becomes apparent that there is overlap between work and leisure when the latter is engaged in as a creative rather than merely consumerist activity. We often derive a deep sense of satisfaction when we put something of ourselves into an activity. There is pleasure in the act of creation itself. It is simultaneously self-fulfilling and meaningful. Studs Terkel highlights the importance of self-fulfillment and meaningfulness in the introduction to *Working* (1975), where people from various walks of life "talk about what they do all day and how they feel about what they do":

> It [work] is about a search, too, for daily meaning as well as daily bread, for recognition as well as cash, for astonishment rather than torpor; in short, for a sort of life rather than a Monday through Friday sort of dying. (xiii)

In any event, for most of us, work is a vitally important part of everyday life. The kind of work we engage in, and how we go about it, to a large extent defines our identity. An absence of work in the life of an individual is usually associated with boredom, depression, and more serious psychological ailments. Without work of some kind, a person's life seems to lack purpose. Work is a crucial expression of our being, of human experience. We cannot readily imagine a society in which most of its members are not involved in some form of work. As a major dimension of the conscious lives of all men, women, and children, the world of work is of paramount concern to all educators. It should be a major consideration in curriculum formation, the planning of educational activities, and in institutional design. Further, the extent to which the world of work already defines individual experience and social learning processes needs to be continuously appraised as the critical context for lifelong education (Chapter 6).

The Distinction Between Work and Employment

In our society, the notion of work is automatically associated with jobs and employment. However, although wage-related employment is a major priority, the previous section has emphasized that there is more to the world of work than earning a living. The narrowness of our typical conception of work as employed labor can be gleaned from the discussion on "The Fundamental Importance of Work" in the opening section of this chapter. Again it is worth quoting Studs Terkel for a broader perspective:

> Perhaps it is time the "work ethic" was redefined and its idea reclaimed from the banal men who invoke it. In a world of cybernetics, of an almost runaway technology, things are increasingly making things. It is for our species to go on to other matters. Human matters. (xxvii)

Clearly, going on "to other matters" cannot entail giving up on conventional productive employment at this juncture of human development, but Studs Terkel reinforces his argument with this critical insight from Ralph Helstein, president emeritus of the United Packinghouse Workers of America:

> Learning is work. Caring for children is work. Community action is work. . . . . .the problem is going to come in finding enough ways for man to keep occupied, so he's in touch with reality. (xxvii)

The appeal here is for us to exercise our imagination about present and future trends in the development of work and leisure. This critical appraisal of current and future directions in the world of work is in itself a crucial pedagogical task.

Whether or not we agree entirely with Terkel's insight, educators in particular need to be aware of the distinction between work that, in the main, is done for its own sake and the sort that is done only in return for a wage or salary. The former implies relative freedom of choice, or self-directedness, whereas the latter, while it often includes a dimension of satisfaction and self-directed initiative, is associated with bosses and the regulatory norms of a particular trade, business, or profession.

For most of us, then, work that is performed for wages still takes priority over the kind of work undertaken for its intrinsic value, which

Education and Work

we designate as *leisure* or *recreation*. As a consequence of what Terkel refers to as "the work ethic," we are inclined to assess our own worth, and that of our peers, in terms of performance and status in paid employment. Other activities tend to be devalued within mainstream society.

This state of affairs is also reflected in the different emphasis given by the formal system of education to each of these two spheres of work. For instance, when a comparison is made with the resources allocated to developing job skills in the area of adult and continuing education, educational initiatives not clearly connected to prospects for paid employment are sure to be seen as less valuable. This imbalance between the two dimensions of work can be viewed from a liberal humanistic perspective as being partly responsible for the inordinate amount of stress-related illness in modern society, a tendency which imposes a major obstacle to the development of creative human potential. The privileging of paid work over unpaid work is nowhere more clear than in the devaluation of women's unpaid domestic labor. Unfortunately, then, unpaid labor, and those who perform it, are rendered invisible and undervalued when compared to people who "actually work" and have "real" jobs.

In what follows, the reference is mainly to the relationship between employment and training in advanced industrial economies, some of which are faring better than others in terms of economic performance at the present time. Elsewhere, in the developing countries, the situation is typically one of high unemployment, low wages, minimal access to education and training and, for the vast majority, a daily preoccupation with hand-to-mouth survival. However, in light of the slowdown in worldwide economic expansion, the onset of free-trade agreements and moves toward realization of a global economy, the majority of employees and the unemployed even in advanced economies have been losing their bargaining in the job stakes over the past two decades. It is not surprising in these circumstances that the predominant discourse on work is shaped by a preoccupation with job acquisition and job creation. While recognizing the force of this imperative, a critical task for educators at this time is to sustain a larger purview on the meaning of work and, in particular, of its significance as the means through which human creative capacities and human potential are realized.

There are many straightforward pedagogical strategies that can be devised to draw people's attention to how the distinction between work and jobs manifests itself in their lives. At the classroom level, they could be asked to calculate how many hours per month they spend in work for remuneration and to describe the main skills required for their job. By the same token, they could be invited to estimate the number of hours per month spent in leisure activities where they are *active participants* rather than *passive consumers*. It might be illuminating to have them reflect on their reasons for participating in such leisure activities and the validity, if any, of drawing any distinction between passive consumption and active participation.

Given the increasing enrollments in adult and continuing education classes, it might be useful in some circumstances to have people begin to reflect on the distinction and relevant connections between work and employment by listing programs, courses or workshops they have taken to improve their chance of employment, to promote leisure activities, or to gain knowledge for a volunteer activity. Added relevance to the exercise might be derived by asking participants to account for any overlap in the lists they generate.

Of course, competent teachers whose imagination and sense of initiative have not been undermined by the process of deskilling (Chapter 2) are well capable of generating meaningful pedagogical approaches that avoid the *business syndrome*. It is in teacher work that the difference between mere busyness and real work becomes clearly discernible.

The Difference Between Work and Busyness

How often do we hear the complaint from students and employees that their teachers or bosses are giving them meaningless tasks just to keep them busy? Who among us have been so fortunate to avoid the infliction of "busy work?"

Even though such complaints are not always justified, it is evident that our schools, colleges, and workplaces are the settings for a great deal of mere "busy work" ("make work") which does not seem to have much legitimate purpose. At some time or other, most of us have experienced the frustration of having to perform humdrum tasks, the only purpose of which is to keep us busy. When imposed to excess such busy work serves to dehumanize the nature of creative potential of purposive human activity. In this regard, the distinction made in the opening section of this chapter between work of human beings and the activity of other animals becomes blurred. Thus, we are often commended for being as "busy as bees."

It is important, then, for educators to recognize the difference between meaningful productive, creative work and mere busyness. We think of work as being accompanied by some kind of outcome, or satisfaction, which can be judged worthwhile to some degree even when there may not be a tangible product. When a sense of satisfaction or the prospect of a worthwhile outcome is not apparent, we tend to talk in terms of "make work." A tendency to engender meaningful work rather than busy work is the hallmark of the competent educator who thereby resists prevailing institutional initiatives which are apt to deskill her or his own work.

By and large, the only people who gain satisfaction, or utility, from "make work" are those who have a vested interest (usually about maintaining current relationships of power) in keeping others preoccupied or busy, regardless of whether there is a positive outcome for the learner or worker. Sometimes we are liable to submit to "make work," or mere busyness, because having something to do—whatever it is—seems preferable to the aimlessness and accompanying uncertainty of having no immediate project to engage us. Accordingly, in facilitating, planning, and administering programs for their students, educators need to make a conscious effort to avoid the temptation of imposing the kind of "make work" which so often manifests itself, as Illich rightly observes, in the public schools and in other areas of everyday living.

Evidence of busyness does not guarantee that those involved are performing effectively or that they are engaged in a meaningful learning activity, although it might serve the interests of those responsible for the imposition of busy work. Certainly, the "busyness syndrome" runs contrary to any pedagogical aspiration toward the encouragement of critical thought, which is a key attribute of creative work.

Education, Training, and Employment

The preceding discussions about the importance of work to human experience and the distinction between work and jobs suggest that the normal taken-for-granted notion of work as corresponding to paid employment affords only a limited perspective on people's productive capacities. Yet, even though we can agree that there is much more to the *meaning* of work, employment for remuneration remains a key concern in the everyday lives of most people in developed and developing economies. Most of us become acutely aware of this fact when faced with the prospect of unemployment. Having a job is a fundamental "bread and butter issue." Consequently, it is reasonable to expect our educational institutions to incorporate some focus on preparation for employment and job skills into the discourse on curriculum.

In addition to technical-vocational courses in schools and the programs designed for job preparation which are available within formal adult and continuing education institutions, business and industry provide an enormous amount of training for employees at all levels. Many educators in our schools and colleges do not appreciate the extent of education and training that goes on within business and industry, professional organizations, hospitals, provincial and federal governments, the military, and so on. New terms such as human resource development (HRD), continuing professional education (CPE), and organizational development (OD) have emerged in recent years to describe the vast range of education and training activities that take place within these various institutions. So far, these developments have had only a peripheral impact on program development and curriculum discourse in formal educational institutions. This circumstance, however, is beginning to change as the direct influence of business and industry in education and the social learning processes continues to expand.

In economically developed and developing countries continuing attempts to tie in the educational system more closely with the economy, and hence the interests of business and industry, are a major feature of the discourse on education. Such attempts have been resisted from a liberal humanist orientation which aspires to preserve an integral pedagogical space for the teaching of traditional academic subjects apart from the needs of the economy, the interests of business and industry, and the influence of a marketplace ideology.

From a liberal humanist perspective, then, education tends to be regarded as a worthwhile activity which imbues students with civilized values and capacities for practical reasoning. In this way education develops people who accept civic responsibilities, earn a living, and make an appropriate contribution to society while enjoying some of "the finer things of life." In this liberal humanist view, technical-vocational classes are tolerated, at best, as a marginal add-on to the curriculum, a kind of diversion for less able students who find it difficult to focus serious attention on academic subjects.

Even a more pragmatic, less academically based approach to the role of education—that is one which acknowledges the relevance of technical-vocational instruction as part of the curriculum—does not necessarily seek to establish clearly defined ties with the interests of business and industry. The views of John Dewey, whose pragmatist philosophy guided his influential views on education, are instructive on this matter:

> The kind of education in which I am interested is not one which will adapt workers to the existing industrial regime; I am not sufficiently in love with the regime for that. It seems to me that the business of all those who would not be educational time savers [sic] is to resist every move in this direction, and to strive for a vocational education which will first alter the existing industrial system, and ultimately transform it. (Dewey, 1977)

Regardless of the ongoing legacy of a liberal humanist perspective in education and the widespread influence of Dewey's insights on educational philosophy, students, parents, and teachers hold strong expectations about the connection between the attainment of educational qualifications and job acquisition. Students who apply themselves to school work are more likely to gain the educational qualifications which will eventually afford them access to better paying, more prestigious jobs. Those who do not take school work seriously enough and drop out, or fail the examinations, will probably have to settle for less skilfull, casual jobs, or the prospect of unemployment.

The chances of participating successfully at this game are stacked in favor of the middle and upper classes, but students of all classes understand what is at stake. Aspirations about the future, life styles are shaped around this understanding about the tie in between school work, educational qualifications, and job prospects.

This situation prevails even though the heavy concentration on preparation for examinations shapes the curriculum, teaching practices, and the learning experience for students in ways that are inconsistent with creative pedagogy. At best, the extent to which examinations and, hence, educational qualifications, are reliable indicators of educational achievement and learning potential is debatable. The debate has been around for a while. In these times, it is running in favor of an ideology which advocates the legitimacy of examinations and educational qualifications as indicators of competence and potential. This is the case even though the overlap between conventional qualifications attainable from large sectors of the educational system and the actual skill needs of the job market are not that substantial. The transmission of skills and job-related attitudes from the educational system to the job market is, at best, uneven.

Even though the transmission of actual skills and attitudes from the educational system to the job market is not significantly substantial, educational qualifications are used by many employers as a means of selection. In this regard, the educational system does provide a *significant* credentialing service for the employment sector. Yet, not only are these credentials no indicator of competent performance (Illich is right on this), educational qualifications are not significantly related to degree of success in an occupation (Collins, 1979, pp. 19–20). Many of the skills which are relevant to both actual performance and occupational success (these two outcomes do not necessarily coincide) are not as a rule taken into account by educational qualifications. However, these qualifications do serve a purpose because they are administratively convenient to employers and they work to the advantage of those best placed to succeed at school work and pass examinations.

In their major work on how education serves to reproduce the existing relationships of power in society, Bordieu and Passeron (1977) account for the inherent inequalities in the school credentialing system. They explain how it is geared toward the *cultural capital*, in the form of knowledge and communication skills, which upper and middle class children experience through their family life. These children are already predisposed to do better in school than children from working class and under-class (welfare) backgrounds.

In many respects, then, it can be argued that schools reproduce the social relations of the workplace and society as a whole (Bowles & Gintis, 1976). Expectations are kept more or less in line with the social control requirements of the state and the needs of employers. A major function of schooling in this view is to socialize students in line with prevailing attitudes around class, gender, and race. Thus the schooling of young people instills in them the roles they are expected to play within these social stratifications. A significant aspect of the stratification process which takes place in schools is the development of expectations about future employment prospects.

An understanding of how the schools function to shape roles and expectations is particularly important at this time. It unmasks the contradiction of populist rhetoric which continues to enthrone the principle of equality of opportunity while legitimizing cutbacks in publicly funded services to the welfare class and others living under the poverty level. This contradiction is compounded by a (mis)perception that when such people have access to welfare they are not disposed to compete for the low-paying unskilled jobs that are available. With the recent stipulations in the United States, representing a withdrawal of a significant 1930's New Deal provision for the poor, that welfare support to individuals must be ultimately contingent upon

Education and Work

their acceptance of whatever employment is available to them, populist rhetoric has been turned into social policy.

No doubt the effects emanating from unequal access to *cultural capital* and from the way educational institutions serve to reinforce the social relations of the workplace and society as a whole can be exaggerated. Clearly, these tendencies do not block all prospects for advancement to people from lower class backgrounds. Nor do they guarantee success for the children of the upper and middle classes. But these insights about the unequal distribution of *cultural capital* and the function of the schools in reproducing existing social relations seriously undermine aspirations toward a society of equal opportunity, especially with regard to the connection between education and employment.

At the same time it is apparent that there are formal initiatives within the educational system to help students understand the world of work. Although the quality of service offered to students is variable, career counseling is now a fairly normal feature of the curriculum. However, in view of critical insights into the way schools reproduce prevailing patterns of social relations of the workplace, the notion that existing career education programs help young people participate meaningfully in decision making about their lives must be called into question. Given the way opportunities are structured, via the attainment of educational qualifications and accessibility to jobs, most people have to settle for what they can get. At best, students gain a more informed understanding of how the game is played and confirmation of the normative limitations on what jobs they can expect and on what roles they can play in society. Where career counseling is inadequate, or absent from the school curriculum, already disadvantaged students can be further disadvantaged.

When career education extends to actually *learning about work*, there is an opportunity for students to focus on their future roles as workers and citizens. *Learning about work* becomes more relevant to the lives of students when educators are able to include actual workplace experience into the curriculum. It is important to ensure that work placements are carefully planned and not perceived as a source of free labor for participating employers. And it is usually feasible, where there is a will, to invite employers and trade unionists (an acceptable liberal balance) into classes on *learning about work*.

Unfortunately, such organized initiatives undertaken on a regular basis as part of the curriculum are still the exception rather than the rule. Further, even in educational institutions where creative approaches to teaching about the *world of work* are prevalent, it is increasingly difficult for teachers to explore with their students critical questions about the unequal distribution of wealth as it relates to employment, or to examine how the claims of capital (represented by the interests of employers) run contrary to the interests of workers and the unemployed.

Although the educational system continues to provide selection criteria for employers through the allocation of formal qualifications, the practice of promoting the acquisition of specific occupational skills—through technical-vocational courses, for example—has diminished in the schools. The same is true of modern universities up until very recently. Historically, prior to the industrial revolution, universities in Europe were important in providing the educational background needed for high level officials and clerics. Apart from technical institutes, and technical programs in postsecondary colleges, the main consensus has been that specific job preparation is best left to the employer. This view has been more pervasive, for example, in countries such as Britain than in the United States.

To support this preference for the workplace as the site for specific job training, the opinion is often advanced that the provision of substantial vocational training in schools constitutes an unwarranted drain on resources. In addition to the liberal-humanist privileging of conventional academic subjects, there is a concern that technical-vocational programs in schools tend to restrict prematurely the occupational choices of students. Further, in these times specific job skills taught in technical-vocational courses are likely to become quickly outdated. To the extent that this is the case, technical-vocational programs as presently constituted in our educational institutions would seem to serve neither the interests of students nor employers. Within this particular line of debate, there also exists a reasonable viewpoint that if employers seek employees who are amenable to the prospects of retraining for a number of different jobs (some of which do not yet exist) during their working lives, then let employers take on the responsibility for workplace training.

In light of the references in preceding paragraphs to how educational institutions tend to reproduce existing social relations in the workplace and society at large, there is substantial evidence to suggest that technical-vocational programs are to a large extent limited to lower attaining students who are steered toward low-level jobs. In this view, the existing low expectations of students are further reinforced by narrowly defined job-training courses in schools and colleges.

Yet, technical-vocational, job-related programs provide many students with a high incentive for learning. There is a discernible pedagogical dimension to courses promoting specific job-related skills. Could it be premature, then, to sound the death knell of job-related curriculum in our schools. In this regard it is instructive to quote Alfred North Whitehead, prominent mathematician and educational philosopher:

> The antithesis between a technical and liberal education is fallacious. There can be no technical education which is not liberal and no liberal education which is not technical. (Whitehead, p. 74)

The issue raised here will be addressed in a subsequent section of this chapter on Businesslike Education.

In recent years education and training in industry, and to a lesser extent in the technical-vocational programs of some postsecondary institutions, have come under the rubric of human resource development (HRD). Leonard Nadler (1980a) describes HRD in the following terms:

> Human resource development (HRD) is the career area within an organization that focuses on changing and improving the capacities of individual human beings to contribute to the success of the organization. (p. 1)

In the *1990 Handbook of Adult and Continuing Education* the following definition of HRD is advanced:

> Human resource development is the field of study and practice responsible for the fostering of a long-term, work-related learning capacity at the individual, group and organizational levels of organizations. (Watkins, 1989, p. 427)

Although it is largely concerned with carving out a more systematically defined area of professionalized practice for those involved with training in business and industry, HRD has managed to forge connections between the conventional notion of training and adult education. To a significant extent training for business and industry and the modern practice of adult education have become merged as HRD. For Nadler, "HRD is concerned with providing learning experiences for people" (1980b, p. 2), clearly suggesting a very considerable overlap between HRD and adult education.

There is no doubt that HRD, which is also linked with the personnel management function, has become a major undertaking that emphasizes the importance of well-organized learning activities, the provision of educational resources, and the individual development of employees. Yet employer and management perspectives still remain the paramount concern for HRD. From an HRD standpoint the individual needs of employees are viewed as coinciding with organizational interests. In this regard, HRD mediates between employees and employers in the interests of the latter. Where layoffs are to occur, HRD provides *education for transition,* softening the effects of harsh reality on workers and, by the way, sparing the organization as much trouble as possible.

In her essay on HRD, which appears in the *1990 Handbook on Adult and Continuing Education* Karen Watkins (1989, p. 430) cites Perelman's study on *The Learning Enterprise: Adult Learning, Human Capital, and Economic Development* to reinforce her argument about the direct connection between education and training and job creation:

> Virtually the entire population needs retraining and new learning to be economically productive. A fifth of the present adult population is functionally illiterate. Most of the rest—including skilled workers, managers, and professionals—have knowledge and skills that technological change is rendering obsolete.... The emergence of a knowledge-based economy requires a new synthesis of the functions of training, education, and other forms of communication and learning under the single umbrella of the learning enterprise.

In this view HRD subscribes to human capital theory. Education, training, and job creation are seen to be causally connected. This viewpoint is very much taken for granted within the discourse of HRD which still lacks a critical dimension of the kind which would pose even the more obvious questions along the following lines: "Where are all the more highly skilled jobs to replace those which have disappeared?" "How much education and training are really required to prepare people for low-skilled, poorly paid, temporary jobs at the bottom end of the labor market?" "What kind of education is required to raise critical awareness about the facts of under-employment?" And "Are human resources people?"

Critical reflection on any of the above questions can be instructive, but let us take the last and most provocative question from an ethical perspective. The consequence of the "HRD" designation is that employees are categorized as just another resource along with physical and financial resources. It is as though the characteristic of *being* human (as in "human *beings*") is reduced so that human *beings* can be conveniently categorized for deployment just like plant and machinery, raw materials, and property. At one time the term "labor" was acceptable, but it is now viewed as too politicized for the discourse on

Education and Work

HRD. In business and industry the term labor invokes conflict of interests whereas HRD is concerned about consensus formation.

In its quest for consensus formation within the workplace, HRD is still more alert than traditional training methods to the autonomous needs of individual employees. Accordingly, HRD incorporates adult education strategies to facilitate a level of employee participation in decision making which accords with the overall management agenda. HRD is smarter about learning and development than industrial training methods of past decades. It prefigures a more decisive movement towards industry-driven education and training.

The Current Situation

In this section the focus is upon how economic conditions affect the employment prospects of ordinary working people. Too many people are chasing too few jobs. Despite ideological rhetoric about people on welfare who are said to be willfully avoiding employment, business is not providing enough job opportunities for a growing number of unemployed people who are able and willing to work for wages. As noted in Chapter 1 (p. 2), current statistics on the employment situation in the United States are misleading. These statistics are indicative of a short-term economic upturn within a prevailing worldwide economic downturn. They hide the reality that a high percentage of working class and middle class jobs have been reduced to a low-paid, part-time, and temporary status. More significant is the continuing high level of unemployment in the inner cities. Official statistics which support government policy always warrant critical appraisal, more so when they purport to represent the employment situation.

In Canada, where the quality of life is rated by the United Nations as the highest in the world (1996), the "hidden" unemployment rate for 1993 reported by the federal government's Department of Finance was 17%. This figure far exceeded the official rate of 11.2% and may well be even higher than reported by the Department of Finance. Unemployment, especially among young adults, is one of the major issues of our times. For older adults, even the appearance of continuity and stability in employment that marked the postwar era in industrialized nations has vanished. We are being conditioned away from expectations that we can hold the same kind of employment for life even if we are good at the job and find it fulfilling.

For business and industry as a whole (from small local enterprises to multinational corporations), the name of the game is "downsizing," which usually means the "shedding" of employees ("human resources") from the organization. The trend is of international proportions and there are no sensible expectations that the unemployment picture on a global scale will significantly improve in the near future. (The implications are enlarged upon in Chapter 8).

Though marked by minor short-lived upsurges in economic activity, which tend to be uneven and are regional rather than global in scope, the economic downturn that marked an end to the postwar boom has defied a widely held view that adequate rates of profit and levels of employment could be sustained under capitalism through monetary policies. In the command economies of the former Soviet bloc countries, the failure of the state to ensure reasonable levels employment and an improved standard of living for the majority of people has already led to the virtual abandonment of any hope for state capitalism as it existed in the former USSR. The sense of false optimism that accompanied this view about the management of business cycles has permeated the way at least two postwar generations in the advanced industrial nations have thought about their economic security. This thinking has changed under current economic conditions. The availability of secure, adequately paid, jobs can no longer be taken for granted by the majority of ordinary men and women even if they are relatively well credentialed.

Added to these consequences of the global economic downturn is the concern about a significant deterioration in economic performance of many western capitalist societies (including, for examples, the United States, Britain, and Canada). This decline is seen to be the result of a continuing reliance on an outmoded industrial development model which is based on the mass production of standardized goods. The model depends on protected national markets and is no longer adequate to meet the demands of global competition which calls for flexible systems of production and marketing. Accordingly, it is argued that prevailing structures of management and the educational system must undergo radical transformation in order for us to cope with growing technological change and increased economic uncertainty.

It is in this context that the ideological discourse at the national level about the dangers of falling behind other countries in the global marketplace must be viewed. Education and training are to be harnessed in the interests of business and industry. It is asserted that this is the way for us to improve our capacities to compete within the new economic order and avoid falling behind in the competition among industrial states. Meanwhile, corporate business is increasingly able to

Education and Work

move capital and jobs to parts of the world where people (human resources) will work for lower wages.

Yet this situation does not operate entirely in favor of corporate capitalism. In locations where there is a large pool of unemployed and, hence, low-wage workers, it is usually difficult to fill the need for crucial skilled workers. Further, industrialists often discover that people in low-wage areas do not have the kind of "work ethic" (workplace discipline) that, in the past, has characterized working class cultures in the older industrialized nations. Here again, we see the emergence of a rationale for connecting the workforce needs of business and industry and the educational system.

Worldwide economic restructuring suggests that education and training are required for new kinds of jobs that will become available, as well as for changing conditions of employment. Yet there is an imminently critical need to address the crisis of unemployment among young adults seeking paid jobs and older adults who are being laid off.

The crisis situation with regard to job prospects for younger adults is profoundly disturbing and cannot be divorced from a growing sense of malaise among younger people as the 20th century draws to a close. An increase in the incidence of violence and in the rate of suicide, especially among young people from minority groups, is accompanied by widespread pessimism about prospects for the future, cynicism about the feasibility of political action in general, as well as growing contempt for mainstream political parties. These trends are not improved by an orientation toward a consumerist social life which sustains an increasingly tacky commercial entertainment industry and a thriving drug culture. Such observations as these, readily confirmed in daily news reports, are often ridiculed as exaggerated and overly moralistic, representing a "gloom and doom" outlook, especially since they overlook purposeful activities undertaken by young adults. These reservations are not without some justification, but they also serve to mask deeply entrenched pathological problems associated with the alienation of young people from today's society.

Educators and youth workers are all too aware of the generalized lack of purpose among young adults, a situation that can be readily exploited by far right-wing organizations who seek to channel pent-up youthful energy toward race hatred and scapegoating of identifiable minority groups. In this regard, a major concern should be that the emergence of political commitment among young people will mark a resurgence of fascism. The large reserve of disaffected unemployed young adults constitutes favorable recruiting grounds for fascist organizations which contrive to exploit for their political aims the justifiable anger about lack of job prospects while focusing the blame unjustifiably on visible minorities.

From political and social, as well as economic, perspectives there are eminently sound reasons for giving high priority to the current crisis in the relationship between the educational system and the youth labor market. For those educators and other stake-holders who still have any doubt about the existing disjuncture between education and employment, and the serious implications entailed, it is necessary to insist that they are in deep denial.

Although the educational system still functions to reproduce social classes, it is not at all geared toward the transmission of skills and attitudes required in a changing political economy. There is widespread recognition that existing technical-vocational programs have become obsolete, but there is no political will among educators to undertake the radical reconceptualization required. Tampering with the existing employment-related programs by way of curriculum fads (for example, competency-based education, outcomes-based learning), which are mere variations on past learning models, will not suffice. They tend to mirror the outdated industrial model for the mass production of standardized products via fragmented work tasks. This curriculum approach is certainly not in line with employer needs in a changing economy. Nor does it foster the kind of critical thought that will enable workers to understand what is at stake in organizing to further their own particular and collective interests vis-à-vis those of employers.

In advanced economies the traditional industries which employed large numbers of young unqualified adults are in serious decline. The same goes for many industries which required skilled manual labor. At the same time, technological innovation and the emergence of "knowledge-based" industries have created some demand for more highly educated workers than in the past. Although these new more highly skilled jobs do not make up for the jobs that have disappeared, employers report that they require better educated applicants to fill the former. From the employers' standpoint, then, there is an undersupply of adequately educated recruits to fill newly emerging skilled employment (though enough educated recruits would still be insufficient to achieve a state of high employment), and an oversupply of unqualified labor.

A prominent approach to dealing with the crisis of widespread disaffection among young adults is through the development of an "enterprise culture." The officially sanctioned discourse on the "enterprise economy" is intended to generate more positive attitudes among young adults toward business and industry. While the concept of "enterprise" in this ideological context has yet to be fully articulated, the message it carries about the responsibility individuals should accept for creating or finding their own jobs, thus absolving the state and employers, is clear enough. Accordingly, the educational system has a critical task before it to explore with students the implications of the mainstream, normative discourse on employment, and the role of the state, in addition to imparting knowledge, skills, and attitudes required by business and industry under newly emerging economic conditions. Apart from the role of the state, the moral responsibility of employers and trade unions should form part of any debate around the reconstruction of employment-based curriculum in the educational system.

The effects of the "enterprise culture" have already reached the highest levels of the educational system. In the August 20, 1995 issue of *The Observer* (a prestigious British newspaper with nationwide circulation) a special supplement is devoted to what universities have to offer applicants. The long-established institutions, along with the newer universities, now "vie with one another to attract students" (Gregson, 1995). What is revealing here is the way that even one of the most cosseted and elitist university systems in the world has been forced into the marketplace. Traditional and newer universities compete with each other to sell their academic programs in terms of how they will prepare prospective applicants for the job market. This capitulation by the administrations of even traditional universities to marketplace imperatives is indicative of how the new economic reality is re-shaping formerly well-entrenched social institutions.

Although there is no going back to cosier times in the academy, as many nostalgic liberal humanists would wish, there is no reason to accept that either corporate interests or right-wing political ideology which emerged from the Reagan and Thatcher era must go unchallenged in the formation of curriculum and in the setting of educational priorities. For a start, we are still able to question this whole notion of "enterprise culture" and to ask about the extent to which graduates admitted to universities and other postsecondary institutions are finding employment in keeping with their educational achievements.

As a result of the relatively long period of economic expansion which followed the Second World War, especially in the western industrial nations, many people who now enjoy relatively comfortable living conditions had reasonable expectations that they would obtain higher status, and better paying jobs than their parents. To a very large extent these rising expectations have been realized. What has happened under prevailing economic conditions is that the children of the newly emerging postwar middle classes now find their taken-for-granted assumptions that the trend would continue have been dashed. Most of the children of this newly emerged (post–World War Two) middle-class section of society are now unlikely to exceed the economic and social status achieved by their parents. Those who remain dependent on their parents into adulthood—a growing trend—manage to maintain the trappings of a middle class lifestyle. But this is not the case for a still significant number of the mature offspring of the new middle class that opts for adult status and is obliged to depend on jobs at the lower end of the employment market, unemployment benefits, or social assistance. If these children of the new middle class opt for higher eduction, they are burdened with repayment of huge loans taken on to pay college fees. (Otherwise their parents pay for them, signifying a continued "dependence on father" well into adulthood.) In any event, a growing number of this group of young people are wondering how they are going to acquire homes and the other kinds of assets which the older generation of the new middle class managed to obtain during more favorable economic times.

The trend toward the proleterianization of the children of the new middle class is uneven and may differ within families where one sibling, for example, may be unemployed while another is on the way to a successful career in a high status occupation. Young adults from this group still have acquired the "cultural capital" which can give them a substantial advantage over lower class youth, in terms of the attitudes and overall self-confidence instilled by family experience, in the competition for low status as well as high status occupations. Yet the tendency toward the growing proletarianization of young adults is now apparent within the social group that acquired middle-class status in the postwar years. Meanwhile, the well established members of the middle and upper classes, especially those who possess substantial assets, have prospered under new economic conditions. Their children have access to privileged schooling and the educational qualifications which assure them entry to the most favorable occupations. As more and more people lose the economic security that marked their middle-class status, the gap between the high income and low income sectors of society is widening.

For young adults from lower class and underclass (welfare) backgrounds, the rhetoric about advancing in society through their own efforts (leading to well-paying employment), has acquired a hollow ring. Clearly, there are always individual exceptions where highly motivated young people "pull themselves up by their bootstraps," as it were, and manage to acquire acceptable forms of employment. But, by and large, the young adults from lower class backgrounds see through the veneer of the discourse equating individual effort with socially acceptable economic advancement, and this understanding is displayed in the high incidence of antisocial behavior.

The claims advanced here about the effects of current economic conditions on young adults from middle class and lower class backgrounds merit further research. Yet the evidence available is sufficient for educators to view the disaffection and political passivity of young adults as a critical concern in light of the way that the educational system, business and industry, and the state are failing to provide a reasonable level of employment. It would be a mistake to believe educators could stir up political activity among young adults. Political commitment emerges from a combination of conditions and social forces and cannot depend for its emergence solely on conventional pedagogical discourse even where this discourse takes a critical view of the status quo. The question for educators to ask at this critical juncture is whether or not they see themselves as playing a part in the reemergence of organized political commitment on behalf of a more just society which also engages the energies of young people.

As far as political education for young adults around the issue of education and work is concerned, a pedagogical context in which the following kinds of questions are addressed would be relevant at this time. How much has the expansion in education really got to do with giving people more opportunities to improve themselves? In what ways does the government admit, and deal with, the fact that unemployment is one of the biggest social problems of our times? How do government initiatives mask or illuminate the nature of unemployment in today's society? What function does the provision of greater "access to education," and initiatives to persuade potential "dropouts" to stay in school have on (un)employment statistics? To what extent is it true that more and more people are entering higher education because they cannot get a job? In what ways does the prospect of unemployment after graduation from a university lead students to focus narrowly on the acquisition of high grades? What is the logic behind the notion that jobs must go when profits fall? Can relevant questions be posed to challenge the view that unemployment and wage cuts are unfortunate but are consequences we have to endure according to the imperatives of a market economy? What arguments can be advanced to demonstrate that the demand for an adequately paid job as a right is eminently reasonable?

Clearly these are leading questions, and should be challenged as such within the context of critical pedagogy. Their purpose is to foster the reemergence of a political discourse among young adults about unemployment as an issue of paramount concern to their everyday lives. In the process, aspects of the culture of passivity come under scrutiny, expectations are raised, and a sense is instilled in young adults that they can make a difference to the way social problems are now being addressed. Clearly, a useful way to incorporate political education into the curriculum is to engender a critical discourse around the connections between education and (un)employment.

If the primary focus here has been on how current economic conditions affect the employment prospects of young adults, the predicament of older adults who have lost their jobs, or who are facing that possibility, should not be shortchanged. Apart from the need for retraining, there is also a need to generate a moral-political discourse, in the form of political education, around the impact of "downsizing" on large numbers from a generation of adults who had been (mis)led into believing that they had job security for life.

The new economic reality has witnessed a larger number of women entering the workforce. However, education and training have yet to address adequately the systemic disadvantages which women still encounter in the employment sector when it comes to wages, promotion prospects, and overall working conditions. A critical dimension to the discourse on the connections between education and training with regard to women's experience is needed because those inadequate gains in terms of equality that have been made are offset, especially among younger adults, where both males and females are facing a difficult job market. There is also a need for a critical educational discourse to challenge a pervasive ideological view that women of all ages, especially in times of high unemployment, should not take on jobs which would otherwise be available to men.

The disadvantages faced by most members of minority and immigrant groups are also of relevance to critically informed educational discussions on the issue of (un)employment. Yet, despite the need to widen the scope for a more politicized debate on the relationship between education and employment, it still makes sense to focus on the situation of young adults from all backgrounds as a priority. They constitute the future and the potential source of genuine commitment toward a more just society than can be realized under prevailing trends (largely favoring a business corporate agenda) toward global economic restructuring.

Businesslike Education

A prominent feature of corporate initiative in the emerging global marketplace is manifest in the way business now seeks to provide knowledge for profit. Thus, knowledge is assigned an economic value. At the same time, business values and the corporate agenda for economic priorities are becoming more influential in shaping the discourse concerning our traditional publicly funded educational institutions and in how processes of learning are structured. The overall trend is for business to take over from the state more and more responsibility for education.

There is no conspiracy behind this development as some radical academic and intellectual critics who are concerned about the emphasis on economic rather than on aesthetic, social, and political issues, want to believe. The trend toward greater business influence on education is driven by economic forces in which the commodification of education and learning is increasingly taken for granted. The commodification of education and the learning processes, nicely exemplified in prepackaged learning modules, is accompanied by a new, and a more decisive, expression of a view that education should be connected to economic development and national strategy. In this view, education is seen as essential for an individual to earn a living and for the state to sustain economic growth.

The provision of knowledge for profit is tied, on the one hand, to the enormous advances in data-generating communications technology and, on the other, to a shift away from factory-based production toward a service oriented economy which in the advanced industrialized nations accounts for about 80% of the workforce. Although these developments are often remarked upon in conventional educational settings, our schools, colleges, and universities still lag far behind business and industry in formulating an appropriate response to the imperatives of the "information age."

Employee education provided directly by business organizations has assumed a high level of significance within the global economy, whereas universities and other publicly funded postsecondary institutions have yet to redefine their roles in regard to education for employment. Meanwhile, corporate universities, of which McDonald's Hamburger University near Chicago is only one of many sterling examples, are expansive and flexible enterprises that represent an effective alternative to university-based business schools. Our schools, colleges, and universities are trailing far behind business in the imaginative deployment of new learning technologies which are becoming a prominent aspect of everyday living in the global economy.

In addition to dealing with knowledge as a resource and product and investing increasingly in employee education, modern businesses now treat their customers as learners. This approach is consistent with the notion that customers purchase products (knowledge) that will make them "smarter." Customers as learners become smarter through the use of "user friendly" technology which is intrinsic to knowledge-based products. The product actually educates while it serves consumer needs. Experience with user friendly technology, especially in interactive multimedia forms, outside of our public educational institutions is leading to a more radical transformation in learning than publicly funded education can match. In this sense, a notion of education without schooling is already operative. However, the commercialization of social learning processes obviously works to the advantage of those who can afford to buy "smart products." In this regard the gap between the haves and the have-nots is widened, a circumstance which points to the inability of marketplace education to address social justice concerns.

Because the incentives to adopt flexible and innovative systems are far more pressing in the business world, where survival is increasingly dependent on a willingness to adapt, than in publicly funded education, a case can be made to suggest that a business approach to education is necessary for any country to remain competitive in the new global economy. From this argument, support for initiatives toward privatization on a wide scale is derived. Privatized education as part of the marketplace will respond more quickly to student (consumer) demands and, hence, in accordance with the current economic priorities of advanced capitalism. The emergence of new forms of privatized education such as charter schools, which invoke the virtues of a business-oriented approach, is a manifestation of this advocacy for an enterprise culture.

The notion is that business-oriented learning incorporates the attitudes and know-how of today's information age. These capacities are exemplified in an emphasis on productivity, speed, flexibility, global economic imperatives, and attention to customer service. Where students are viewed as customers the introduction of a "user pay" policy for educational services is seen as a reasonable measure. (After all, the thinking goes, an education that one has to pay for out of one's own pocket, or from a substantial loan, is more likely to be valued). In this way, educators (as providers of services or facilitators) are more likely to be held to account for the quality of their product. Thus, there is a renewed emphasis on measurable results in education while courses and programs for which there is low demand will be quickly identified and discarded. Business practices, then, are already a feature of the newly emerging privatized educational institutions, and are being introduced into traditional schools, colleges, and universities. Here again, though, the new marketplace education does not address social justice concerns around equitable access to good quality education. Rather, business-driven education points toward a deepening of existing class divisions. Those who can best afford to pay, reap the advantages in terms of competition for jobs and the preservation of privileged status.

Toward a Critical Pedagogy of Work

A key challenge for critical pedagogy in our times is to focus attention on the central importance of work, in all its manifestations, to the everyday lives of men, women, and children. And a clear distinction has to be made between mere busy work (*busyness*), most of which can ultimately be managed by technology, and creative activity. In this regard, a critical pedagogy should make the connection between the quality of work and the quality of life as it is experienced on a day to day basis. This understanding also highlights the way capacities for creative activity provide the basis for fulfilling leisure time. Thus, *meaningful* work can be viewed as the antidote for boredom which, especially among the young, prefigures involvement in various forms of antisocial activities.

The will to elevate *meaningful* work, as opposed to busyness or exploited labor, as a central dimension of human development is critical in the struggle to combat the widespread effects of alienation within contemporary society, especially among young adults. A sharp focus in education on the significance of meaningful work begins to make sense through a pedagogical process in which we envisage ourselves as *producers*—creators—rather than as *consumers*. To this end, a task of critical pedagogy is to help us examine the social learning processes (particularly as they are exemplified in commercial advertizing and the mass media in general) through which we come to identify ourselves as consumers rather than producers. The consequences of this more passive (mis)conception of ourselves as predominantly consumer oriented on the willingness to take an active (that is, a *productive*) role in political decision making can be more effectively explored. To what extent is it reasonable to claim that the conventional election ballot for choice of government from among two or three establishment political parties has become the supreme emancipatory achievement of our consumer-oriented democracy? In what ways might we still expect more from a genuinely worker-oriented participatory democracy?

From the perspective of critical pedagogy of work, it is necessary at this time to give primary attention to the issue of *work as employment*, as the means of making a living. This emphasis means incorporating into educational curriculum a substantial emphasis on the teaching of attitudes and skills that are directly relevant to the needs of students for jobs and the demands of the employment market. At this juncture, then, despite any misgivings about the encroachments of corporate values, the employment situation for young adults should be accorded high priority in the structuring of curriculum in our schools, colleges, and universities.

It is futile to merely lament over the growing influence of business on our educational institutions. The trend is irreversible and not without its benefits, but its trajectory—as many liberal-humanist and radical critics fear—is not necessarily steered according to the corporate agenda. Clearly, the business corporate viewpoint is exerting more influence now, but only in the absence of a counter-discourse on what the connection between our educational institutions and the world of employed work should be about. Rather than just witnessing, in resigned fashion, the current demise in the significance of our publicly funded institutions, critically informed educators should accept the new economic imperatives as a challenge to struggle for a space in the reformation of curriculum around education and work.

So if the powerful influence of business corporate values on education today must be regarded as a done deal, what is yet to be enjoined is a critical debate about whose interests are ultimately best served through the conjunction between education and work—those of a privileged minority or the vast majority of ordinary men and women. To fuel a counter-hegemonic discourse on education and employment, critical pedagogy needs to invoke a reasonable aspiration that the innate competence of ordinary people to organize workplace production effectively and on their own behalf will be realized. For ultimately, there is no fundamental necessity for dependency on a privileged elite to determine the manner of production and distribution of goods and services.

At the level of educational practice, the way back to this genuinely humanistic vision of the organization of work is to inculcate within the learning processes a realization that the conception and execution

Education and Work

of work—that is the planning and actual "hands-on" performance—should be integrated. It is in the separate assignment and isolation of these dimensions of work that the origins of its impoverishment in the form of exploited labor are found. By making problematic the taken-for-granted acceptance that normally work is to be divided hierarchically in terms of its conception and execution, attention can be turned to the politics and power relationships which influence the way work is structured and allotted.

Thus, a critical pedagogy of work addresses the following concerns: the way the imperatives for efficient production are determined (particularly in regard to the division of labor); the problem of deskilling and alienated work; the inequalities inherent in the distribution of work and in the remuneration of women and minority ethnic groups; and the circumstances which give rise to the persistence of a reserve army of unemployed workers. The kind of critical perspective on work raised here has been very much marginalized, especially during the past two decades, and a real effort of will is required to refocus it in a way that can throw a different light on the discourse about education for profit outlined in the previous section. Herein lies the challenge for a critical pedagogy of work: to emphasize the importance of acquiring skills and attitudes required for employment while engendering a discourse about the politics of work which explores how, and to what purposes, unequal relationships of power are played out. This political discourse on work needs to be reengaged because, as Ettore Gelpi (former head of UNESCO's Lifelong Education Unit) reminds us:

> Marx's observations on the division of labour, a) that it increases the dependence of the worker and brings him down to the level of the machine, b) that it augments the productive force of work, the wealth and refinement of society and at the same time impoverishes the workers, are proving themselves for the most part still accurate; as also his observations on the alienation of labour. (Gelpi, *A Future for Lifelong Education*, 1979, p. 4)

Something should be said here about the roles of the professions and the unions. In the case of the professions a critical pedagogy of work would explore, in a similar vein to Ivan Illich, the validity of claims for special access to expert knowledge, exclusive (monopolistic) practices, and the rationale for licensing procedures as well as simply describing the services offered and entry requirements. In talking about the role of the professions, it is useful to draw a distinction between the meaning of "professionalism" and "professionalization." The former term is widely used in referring to the level of competence and commitment people bring to their work regardless of whether or not they are members of a conventional profession. The latter term usually has to do with the way certain groups of practitioners offering the same kind of services are able to organize themselves for their mutual benefit. Their success in this regard depends largely on the degree of public acceptance of the legitimacy of the claims for special professional status. From this perspective teachers, for example, are in a difficult position to consolidate their status as members of a profession because teaching associations do not even have the authority to grant their members the certification to practice. In this regard, it is argued that teachers' associations are more akin to trade unions.

However, while the trend toward professionalization and the availability of continuing professional education have increased, the unions and worker education have become less influential during the past two decades. The loss of power by the unions is another aspect of contemporary economic restructuring and, to a large extent, the direct result of successful anti-union tactics from employers who have gained a much stronger hand in advancing their interests over those of employees during the years of neoconservative ascendancy. In these times, then, another task for a critical pedagogy of work is to review past approaches and identify new strategies for protecting and advancing the interests of most wage earners in today's labor market.

One straightforward strategy from the perspective of a critical pedagogy at this time is to create more opportunities for unions to present their case within our educational institutions. At the same time, it is important for unions themselves to become clearer about the distinction between employee education for specific job performance and worker education which is concerned with the attainment and preservation of worker interests as opposed to those of employers. Education for workers provided by unions currently tends to ape employer education and contains a strong HRD (Human Resource Development) component. To a significant extent the unions, and intellectuals who have identified with worker education and working class struggles in the past, are now abrogating their former commitments. Thus the history of working-class contributions to economic development as well as the significance of working-class culture need to be reclaimed via a critical pedagogy of work.

A focus on the importance of work in all of its forms, including the necessity for making a living, should be *systematically* incorporated into educational curriculum from the early years of schooling. For older students, internships in conventional workplace settings should be negotiated under conditions in which employers are expected, as a

Education and Work 107

community obligation, to provide suitable placements for students while educators are responsible to ensure that the learning experience is not diminished by either exploitation or neglect. Although these conditions may not have been easy to insist upon in the past from a school-based initiative, their emergence is now favored by the way the business ethos is permeating educational institutions. In this regard, educators who work for the systematic incorporation of workplace experience into the curriculum are not pushing against the grain.

At the same time, employers, workers, and trade union representatives should have regular access to our educational institutions. This aspect of workplace curriculum, if it is to be taken seriously, cannot remain dependent on casual invitations or left entirely to the personal initiatives of one or two teachers committed to opening up their classrooms. On the contrary, a pedagogical discourse within the institution can be constructed which sets reasonable obligations on educators to make provision for regular visits from workplace representatives and on the latter to make themselves available. Clearly, careful planning and negotiation are required, but these are part of an educational process in which all parties have a stake. The time is ripe for publicly funded educational institutions to take bolder steps in organizing relevant programs for workplace oriented learning. This is a modest proposal, but could have important consequences of elevating the status of publicly funded education at a time when privatized alternatives are gaining momentum.

Colleges of education, in particular, have a chance to be pacesetters in the reconstruction of curriculum to prepare students for the world of work. Since education students tend to rate their school-based internships highly, colleges of education should make this part of teacher preparation central to the overall program. At present college of education faculty tend to regard the school-based internship experience as peripheral to their main academic interests. This attitude prevails despite the importance education students attach to the internship experience and the notorious inadequacy of college-based methods classes to prepare teachers for today's classrooms. In any event, it is timely for the disjuncture between faculty dispositions and student needs for high quality internship experience to be addressed given that colleges of education can no longer count on a high demand for certified teachers to guarantee survival.

Although establishing the school-based internship (or "practicum") as the key component of teacher preparation will in itself orient education students to the value of workplace-based learning, colleges of education also need to reconceptualize their programs for the preparation of technical-vocational teachers. At present such initiatives tend to be accorded low status and left on the margins of college of education programs in a state of decline. This is unfortunate because the fate of technical-vocational programs prefigure the future prospects for colleges of education in general. For it is around a reconstruction of technical-vocational education programs in line with new economic imperatives, and incorporating an emphasis on lifelong education, that colleges of education can make a case for their continuing relevance on today's fiscally constrained university campuses.

A critical pedagogy that does not aspire to engage educational programs with the current realities of today's workplace merely adds to the ongoing liberalistic academic lament about how corporate values are taking over our universities, colleges, and schools. Learning the capacities to become employable does not necessarily presuppose an uncritical acceptance of corporate values or the inability to evaluate concepts about how productive work can be reorganized in the best interests of the majority.

Chapter 6

REFLECTIONS ON LIFELONG LEARNING AND LIFELONG EDUCATION

The transfer from the idea of initial training to that of continual education is the mark of modern pedagogy. (Edgar Faure)

We believe that every person has the capability, the right, and the responsibility to become a lifelong learner, and that the environment should be supportive of people in this task. We believe that the opportunities to continue to learn throughout life should not be limited by location, economics, or other restrictions. (*Phi Delta Kappan* Report on Lifelong Learning)

The Lifelong Concept

The notions of "lifelong learning" and "lifelong education" are often used interchangeably. During the past 20 years or so, the growing frequency with which these terms have been deployed in conventional education discourse, usually to convey a sense of optimism about the future, has rendered the lifelong concept into little more than a catchphrase. Yet, though often bandied about without much forethought, the terms lifelong learning and lifelong education in referring us to an expansive and hopeful vision are significant for critical pedagogy in this age of cutbacks.

Though both terms will be used somewhat interchangeably in this chapter, it is useful to think of lifelong learning in a general sense as referring to the actual experience of the individual learner or of groups of learners. The focus, then, is on how psychological factors, social contexts, teaching practices, curriculum formation, and educational management techniques have a bearing on the shaping of learning experiences in their immediacy. The term lifelong education tends rather to draw attention to the nature of the commitment, policies, and forms of restructuring needed to ensure that relevant educational services become accessible to us throughout the entire span of our lives. In this broad sense, then, lifelong education is concerned with the social transformations required to create the circumstances in which lifelong learning becomes the central feature of a global learning society. This vision was nicely expressed over two decades ago by Edgar Faure and associates in *Learning to Be: The World of Education Today and Tomorrow*:

> Is not this the time to call for something quite different in education systems? Learning to live, learning to learn, so as to be able to absorb new knowledge all through life; learning to think freely and critically; learning to love the world and make it more human; learning to develop in and through creative work. (Faure et al., 1973, p. 69)

These days the term lifelong learning is virtually guaranteed an appearance in any formal or informal discussions around curriculum. As a slogan it has been useful, at the very least, in reminding us that education is not limited to what is offered by our schools, colleges, and universities. These institutions have tended to be preoccupied with a narrow view of education that clearly guides the way they conceptualize and structure the learning context. Adult education professor John Niemi has described this institutional preoccupation in the following terms:

> After all, our emphasis in education from school through university and beyond is always on **finishing** our learning, not on continuing to learn throughout the life-span. We talk of **finishing** elementary school, **finishing** high school, **finishing** college, and **finishing** our doctorates. (Niemi, 1978–9, p. 5)

However, though this institutional emphasis on finishing our learning is still very pervasive despite rhetoric about the importance of lifelong learning, there is now a growing recognition that significant learning among children and adults of all ages takes place outside educational programs given in institutional settings.

The lifelong learning concept is bolstered in educational literature by related terms such as *continuous learning, recurrent education, continuing education, and education permanente*. Then there is the largely British field of *further education* which marks off formal job training, usually in college programs for technical education and literacy upgrading, from university education for degrees, liberal adult education, adult education with a social change agenda, and recreational adult education. Thus the notion of *further education* is somewhat akin to the training aspect of human resource development which invokes lifelong learning in regard to programs for preparing employees to meet new workplace tasks.

For professionals and quasi-professionals, a rapidly expanding field of *continuing professional education* has emerged indicating that initial entry qualifications are no longer sufficient to last an individual for an entire career. Like further education and human resource development, continuing professional education is concerned with a somewhat narrow outlook on lifelong learning in line with organizational perspectives. This tendency is discernible even in the current form of worker education provided by the unions for its members. As noted in the previous chapter, trade unions, in the advanced western economies at any rate, now tend to adopt the human resource development training model in planning educational programs. At the present time, they are much less inclined than in the past to tie in worker education with a political and social change agenda.

Two decades after the Faure Report educational commentators are still calling "for something quite different in education systems." To a large extent this realization of the need for structural changes in our educational systems is being advanced around the lifelong learning concept. Lifelong learning as a feature of curriculum development which reflects the needs of changing societies is said to have a role in bringing about the integration of rapidly emerging knowledge with the already proven aspects of established curricula (Ornstein, 1994). This rediscovered concern for integration is apparent in educational literature which sees lifelong learning as a foundational concept for connecting schools and the workplace. Conrad Toepfer (1994), for example, makes the case for involving young people in exploratory curricula which will help them define occupational interests, become aware of changing workforce skills, and demand sound attitudes to work well before their senior years in secondary school. In an interview for the National Association of Secondary School Principals published in *High School Magazine* (Rensi, 1993), the chief executive of McDonald's talked about the overlapping of skills required in the McDonald's workplace with those acquired in the schools. He argued for a relevant balance between work and school, upholding in accordance with his corporate slant on the lifelong concept a view of employment as complementary to high school education. (The sources cited here serve to reinforce the commentaries made in the previous chapter about developing a more realistic connection between the world of work and education through school curriculum conceptualized within the context of lifelong learning).

Similarly, Sharratt, Gene and others (1992), in an article entitled "Vocational Education Rural America: An Agenda for the 1990's," conclude that changes in the U.S. workforce demand that vocational and academic education be integrated within a lifelong learning context to provide every student with basic skills, advanced cognitive skills, a core of academic knowledge, and new forms of vocational preparation. This article offers some specific suggestions for curriculum reform of relevance to educators in rural settings. Further useful sources of reference on this area of concern, and focusing on education in remote rural Australia (Mason, 1992; Scott, 1991) are also cast within the context of lifelong learning.

Among other trends and issues that have been tied to the lifelong learning concept in recent literature we can identify concerns for the acquisition of competence in information technology (Dahlberg, 1990; Jalaluddin, 1990; Kaufman, 1992) as well as for the need to promote creative development, emphasizing individuality and flexibility, at all phases of the life cycle (Malikova et al., 1990; Tonegawa, 1991). These themes are more or less enlarged upon in articles such as "Information Literacy for Lifelong Learning" (Hancock, 1995), "Life-centred Schools....: Or What Would Our Schools Be Like If We Really Believed in the Concept of Lifelong Learning?" (Staples, 1994), "New Basics, Lifelong Learning, Student Employment, Technology and the Arts" (OECTA, 1994), and "Living On One's Own Horizon: Cultural Institutions, School Libraries, and Lifelong Learning" (Carr, 1991).

Writing for the *Journal of Industrial Education*, and with a gaze fixed predictably on the Year 2000, Buffamanti (1994) advocates reengineering schools for "the high performance economy." For Barron (1992) the school library, furnishing "information power" to foster student thinking and commitment to lifelong learning would be a primary location for restructuring. The restructuring theme in the lifelong learning context is reinforced by articles in *Computing Teacher* (Ray, 1991) and *Electronic Learning* (Bruder, 1990) which relate the relationship of technology education to school planning and the role of the teacher.

The lifelong learning concept is now invoked, even enthroned, as the guiding principle in identifying the needs of young adults as a special demographic category, particularly with regard to the problem of "school failure" (King, 1992; Oran, 1993). References to lifelong learning occur with regularity in contemporary studies on educational philosophy, lifespan transitions, educational assessment, civic learning (citizen education), socioeconomic development, spirituality, the arts, outdoor education, the environment, and international perspectives. Such studies are not confined to publications concerned primarily with developments in our schools, colleges, and universities.

Of critical interest here are commentaries on lifelong learning that argue for the need to foster a new dialogue on the relationship between initial education and adult education (Belanger, 1991) and, by the same token, for connecting schools and community organizations (Heath, 1994). This concern will be further addressed in the section on "Making the Connections" later in this chapter. Another critical insight developed within the discourse on lifelong learning, and which will be picked up again in the next section on "The Learner and Learning," has to do with "learning to unlearn" (Rinne, 1991). This perspective offers a thought-provoking variation on the popular theme, also prominent in lifelong learning discourse, around "learning how to learn" (Smith, 1982).

The recent sources cited here are of significance in that they confirm how real substance is gradually being incorporated during the 1990's to the rhetoric on lifelong education and lifelong learning in the schools.

Given the enthusiastic endorsement of the lifelong concept since the appearance of Edgar Faure's *Learning to Be* (1973) and Torsten Husén's *The Learning Society* (1974), it is not surprising to encounter these days overwhelming advocacy for "making lifelong learning a way of life." Numerous professional associations and major educational conferences have adopted the term in their titles. It is almost two decades since a leading American adult educator of the time, Alan Knox, specified "a positive attitude toward lifelong learning" as a key proficiency for adult educators (Knox, 1979, p. 9). To the extent that this specification speaks to a commitment that can now be taken for granted among adult educators, they find themselves sharing a standpoint that claims our very existence, in all its dimensions, is a lifelong learning process.

But what has been the practical import of the mounting lifelong learning discourse of the past two decades? No doubt educators and others who do not take education for granted are more attuned to the fact that significant learning is not confined to our schools, colleges, and universities. Yet it cannot be reasonably asserted that these institutions, along with our other important public service agencies, have been systematically transformed in line with the lifelong learning concept in the years since the Faure Report and Torsten Husén's recommendations for "The Learning Society." Many seemingly impressive programmatic changes and add-ons to conventional curriculum formats may have been undertaken under the rubric of lifelong learning, but there have been no fundamental changes in the institutional structures that shape our schools, colleges, and universities.

No doubt ongoing fiscal restraint has had something to do with the reenforcement of a traditional conservatism and the development of a survival mentality in these institutions which work against initiatives for radical transformations from within. Perhaps understandably, the tendency within our institutions has been more toward accommodation to outside pressures in the hope of "saving the turf" rather than for creative, admittedly riskier, moves to bring about entirely new institutional arrangements. Clearly, something quite different is envisaged here to the now familiar kind of restructuring ("downsizing") that comes in reaction—as a perceived necessity—to budget cutbacks.

It is true that we have witnessed a widespread deployment of advanced technology to educational services of all kind in recent years. (The corporate sector is in favor of such innovation). In most western and the developing countries formal education is becoming more accessible to people of all ages and backgrounds. Organizations such as the British Open University, which was once rightly regarded as nontraditional, and educational institutions wedded from the start to alternative forms of distance education as their major commitment, have become more widely accepted. However, the approaches of even these "alternative" or "nontraditional" institutions tend to legitimize their status with the conventional trappings (formal examinations, standardized curriculum, degrees, certificates, continuing education units, and organizational designations) as our mainstream institutions. The British Open University, once spurned by most of the academic establishment in the U.K. is now very much part of that establishment. It competes rather successfully with other universities in a league table foisted on the university community by the government, having relinquished some of its founding commitments—most notably, to worker education.

These "alternative" institutions may offer something a little different in education, but they can hardly be viewed in their present form as the means for "making lifelong learning a way of life" as far as the vast majority of people are concerned. The fact of the matter is that more than a quarter of a century after the Faure Report, and despite prolific discourse around the lifelong concept, the nature and organization of pedagogy today, our formal and informal systems of education, and the preparation of teachers (especially) and other public service practitioners (in general) remain substantially unchanged.

Rather than embracing lifelong learning as a guiding principle for fundamental change our educational institutions, public service agencies, and workplaces have taken the concept on board largely as an add-on to existing approaches to curriculum formation and program design, to teaching and counseling, and to views on learning and development.

Perspectives on the Learner and Learning

Tied in with the discourse on lifelong learning is a view of the learner as being largely self-directed. This view challenges the notion that education is mainly about the dissemination of prescribed knowledge from teacher as expert to student as a virtually passive recipient. Thus, the traditionally didactic role of the teacher is replaced by a pedagogical approach in which the responsibility for learning lies predominantly with the individual learner. In the parlance of self-directed learning the teacher becomes a facilitator whose main function is to organize learning opportunities where the emphasis is on learning how to learn.

Self-directed learning, in conjunction with the advocacy for lifelong learning, has become the centerpiece of mainstream modern adult education (Knowles, 1980). For Malcolm Knowles, self-directed learning can be operationalized within an institutional setting by means of a formal learning contract drawn up between the educator as facilitator and learner as client and which specifies beforehand the nature, amount, and quality (grade anticipated) of the learning to be undertaken (Knowles, 1986).

Whether or not a formal learning contract is entailed, it is not difficult to appreciate how the pedagogical relationship implied by this notion of self-directed learning can be readily introduced into settings outside of our designated educational institutions. Self-directed learning, in the context of lifelong learning, envisages a change in the nature of the traditional relationship between doctor (or any health professional) and patient, lawyer and client, social worker and welfare recipient, and so on. In this view, the expert's role includes a responsibility for ensuring that people served have access to relevant information, adequate understanding and, thus, the capacity to work out what is entailed in their own interests. If the interrelated notions of lifelong learning and self-directed learning are taken seriously, no longer should people take the authoritative prescriptions of experts on faith, or feel reluctant to let them know what is wanted (and why). This relationship does not mean, of course, that the professional is absolved from the responsibility of carefully making the case for his or her own judgment where it differs from that of the client. But the approach becomes dialogic rather than authoritative from the outset.

There is a voluntary dimension to self-directed learning that consists of respect for the autonomy of learners (including oneself as learner) in making choices about the learning and development process that does not fit with the prevailing behaviorist orientation to learning. The ethos of behavioral psychology, with its pseudoscientific claims that the learning process can be relevantly ordered beforehand through the stipulation of measurable behavioral objectives (sometimes defined as *competencies, learning outcomes,* or *proficiencies*), is still pervasive. It remains a major feature of teacher training programs and curriculum texts. Though losing ground somewhat during the 1960's and 1970's to the "humanistic" approach exemplified in the work of Carl Rogers (1969), the behaviorist tendency has since made a comeback in the educational world. This resurgence has accompanied the demands for accountability and back-to-basics in the wake of the alleged overpermissiveness of the 1960's and early 1970's. In this present ideological context, learning by behavioral objectives can be reassuring. Administrators are provided with precise measures of achievement for their records while curriculum is organized predictably into neatly unified categories and subcategories.

Unfortunately, the behaviorist perspective has been incorporated into the discourse on lifelong learning and the conception of self-directed learning (in particular, where learning contracts are mechanistically reduced to behavioral objectives). Some educators who recognized the contradictions entailed in invoking self-directed learning while deploying behaviorist technique believe that the problem is overcome if they accept the behavioral objectives' approach as "just another tool" among others. What they overlook is the instrumental rationality that accompanies behaviorist pedagogical strategies. For with behaviorism "the medium is the message." It determines the formation of curriculum, teaching practices, organizational arrangements, and the learning process. Thus, the behaviorist viewpoint is entirely antithetical to the aspirations for voluntary, autonomous, learning that sustain any reasonable notion of self-directed learning within a context of lifelong learning.

Given the importance of this claim, some sense of how behaviorism

Reflections on Lifelong Learning and Lifelong Education

and variations on the theme subvert the emancipatory potential of lifelong learning in general and self-directed learning in particular is required. Yet, while enlarging on the short critique of behaviorism begun in Chapter 2, within the context of this chapter we can only draw the outlines of behaviorism's serious shortcomings. At least, this should be sufficient to make problematic the taken-for-granted acceptance of the behaviorist influence on educational institutions and learning processes while the concepts of lifelong learning and self-directed learning are being so widely endorsed.

Behaviorism as a view of learning has many exponents, but in modern education the behaviorist approach is largely influenced by the work of B. F. Skinner (1976). As with all of behavioral psychology, this work is indebted to the experimental projects of the Russian physiologist Ivan Pavlov (1849–1936) to legitimize claims for the scientific status of behaviorism. Pavlov's experiments were designed to elicit predictable responses from laboratory animals. By the same token, behaviorism in education seeks to achieve desired learning outcomes (predictable *responses*) through the deployment onto learners of pedagogical strategies (*stimuli*) which are precisely defined in terms of behavioral objectives. Through the process of *reinforcement* (repeating the strategies, or *stimuli*, in their initial or modified form, and applying appropriate "rewards" to learners for demonstrating desired outcomes), the specified desired behavior is learned. Thus, virtually an entire generation of teacher trainees, subject to the behaviorist approach in their methods and psychology courses learned to chorus "education is change in behavior" when asked in class to define education.

Few advocates of the behavioral approach would be inclined to argue, in defense of the scientific claims of behaviorism, that the pedagogical techniques called for by their precisely defined behavioral (learning) objectives can be regulated in the way that Pavlov applied his precise experimental stimuli to animals under controlled laboratory conditions. It is apparent that the correspondence between stimulus and response that Pavlov achieved with his laboratory animals is not reproducible in educational settings. Yet it is also apparent that curriculum development based on behaviorism can be operationalized in the sense that specified statements of learning objectives can be formulated to correspond in measurable terms with outcome statements. The question is what these measures tell us about the nature and quality of learning, the development of intelligence (learning capacities), and the role of the educator.

As for the foundations of behaviorism's scientific claims, its exponents aim to limit in their investigations all their data to publicly observable facts. These data constitute behavior and are taken to be the empirical basis of a scientific approach. According to the behaviorist standpoint, anything that can be *meaningfully* said about human action can also be precisely expressed in the form of observation statements. These observation statements correspond to actions (reactions to stimuli) that are quantifiable and, hence, measurable. Clearly, these circumstances are easier to set-up for rats in a controlled laboratory environment than they would be for students in a classroom setting or other formal learning context.

For behaviorists, our mental life, autonomous expressions of purpose, and subjective meaning must be capable of reduction to quantifiable observation statements. Otherwise the life of the mind is to be regarded as irrelevant metaphysical baggage as far as investigating human action and, hence, learning are concerned. Behaviorists, then, have adopted the approach of what is conventionally regarded as the model of the natural sciences. This model invokes a Darwinian, or the cause and effect research orientation of logical positivism, which for many contemporary professional scientists is no longer sufficient as a means for explaining the natural world let alone the everyday lifeworld of human action. In any event, from a logical positivist standpoint, behaviorism is based on the assumption that knowledge about the actions of human beings can be arrived at from their overt behavior just as the systematically controlled observation of the "behavior" of substances and physical movements provides information in the natural sciences. Too bad that the behaviorist cannot explain his or her commitment to behaviorism—B. F. Skinner cannot explain B. F. Skinner—in terms of the behaviorist paradigm.

The behaviorist agenda to achieve for the study of human action (for the "human sciences") the exactitude of the natural science through reductionistic observation statements has led to pseudo-quantification. By this is meant the (mis)application of numbers to human qualities and endeavors which are simply not amenable to quantification. The notion that exactitude to this degree is a necessary condition for arriving at the truth of the matter—for understanding psychological and social phenomena, in particular—is not justified. For as Ortega y Gasset (1964) pointed out "exactness cannot exist except in terms of quantitative objects." (p. 72). His further observation that "a truth may be very exact, and yet be a very small truth" (p. 73) also brings into question the relevance of the entire behaviorist project.

Malcolm Crick (1976), in rejecting the behaviorist standpoint that

Reflections on Lifelong Learning and Lifelong Education

any account of subjective meaning and purposeful lies outside the province of scientific observation has this to say:

> Haunted by the problem of 'other minds', equating mentalism with nonscience, psychologists in many fields retreated into a behaviorism which has left out some of the most basic characteristics of human beings. In so doing psychology cuts itself from that conceptual system out of which a realistic account of human action could have been built. (p. 96)

Clearly, the behaviorist frame of reference raises immense difficulties for thoughtful designers of educational curricula and educators who are obliged to work within its parameters in that it fails to deal adequately with human intention and meaning as aspects of purposeful action. The *agency* of both teachers and learners is undermined. Crick alludes to the limitations imposed on educators and others locked into a behaviorist paradigm in these terms:

> When watching a human being in the course of social interaction, one is not witnessing a body behaving and failing to witness a mind thinking, one is seeing a person in action. (p. 97)

At the most, the behaviorist program for the sensory observation of overt human behavior can take into account only a relatively small aspect of our psychological and social world, missing out entirely on everyday experience associated with commonsense thinking. We are referring here to those vital dimensions of experience, often taken-for-granted, that psychologist, philosopher of pragmatism, and educationist, William James (1950, pp. 221–222) refers to as *knowledge about* and *knowledge of acquaintance*. It is because these dimensions of knowing are part of the immensely dynamic mixture of familiar, taken-for-granted, everyday activities that they cannot be sensibly reduced to a finite number of clearly divided and narrowly defined observational statements.

So there is a great deal of meaningful activity that escapes the behaviorist perspective with which positivistic curriculum systems (the so called objectives-based learning, competency-based instruction, outcomes-based education, skills-based learning, and other variations on the theme) are aligned. And in spite of its insistence on the primacy of direct observation, behaviorism's status as the philosophical underpinnings is repudiated by outstanding studies in the philosophy of science. Noam Chomsky (1965, p. 206), for instance, doubts whether behavioristic investigations should be regarded as empiricism at all. The entire behaviorist program is rejected by Karl Popper (1965) as scientifically invalid. Popper explains that it is not possible to derive a set of observation statements which will each coincide with a specific sense experience. "An 'immediate experience' is **only once** 'immediately given': it is unique." (p. 94). Attempts to compile a series of observation statements which somehow coincide with 'immediate' experience are misguided and futile. So there goes behaviorism's claim for generalizability and the scientific, or theoretical, legitimation of curriculum designed according to the behaviorist model. Empirical statements in science are connected with theory and as Chomsky (1965, p. 193) makes clear behaviorism is demonstrably atheoretical.

What these critical commentaries on behaviorism amount to is that protocol statements (that is, statements which report on direct observations without interpretation and provide the basis for empirical verification) about our everyday lifeworld experience cannot possibly serve the same function as protocol statements about the natural world. The problem stems from misplaced efforts to reduce complex human affairs to a series of operational definitions and observation statements which simply cannot induce either the precision or explanatory power of operational definitions and protocol statements in the natural sciences. In this regard, as far as learning is concerned, it is true that models of competence based on behaviorism are "so trivial that it is possible to ignore them." (Chomsky, 1977, p. 50). Yet the excessive reductionism that emanates from the behaviorist influence in education has had deleterious consequences for curriculum formation, program planning, and teaching practices that should not be ignored. In particular, the fragmenting effects of behaviorism are seen in the remarkably pedestrian laundry list approach to designing curriculum (increasingly in the form of modules or learning packages that are amenable to computerization), to program planning and evaluation, and to educational policy documents ("action projects") of all kinds. Even self-directed learning, as already noted, has taken on board a reductionist method by which the learner is encouraged to specify beforehand all the particulars for a learning project.

It is surely time for us to revisit the critical insight of Eduard Lindeman who made the following observations in *The Meaning of Adult Education* (1961) about the shortcomings of the tendency which is exemplified in the excessive reductionism of behaviorism and in variations on the behaviorist theme in education:

> The falsest view of life, as in the fable of the blindfolded men and the elephant, is one which rests on some particularism as its point of reference. (p. 172)

And here is what the pragmatist philosopher of education John Dewey (1960), who was an advocate of careful planning (or rehearsing) our projects of action, had to say about the reductionistic approach:

> Solution by the method of partition is always unsatisfactory to minds with an ambition for comprehensiveness. (p. 61)

In contrast to the behaviorists, Dewey maintained that "standards and tests of validity are found in the consequences of overt activity, not in what is fixed prior to it and independent of it." (p. 73). The pundits of outcomes-based education (the most recent of recurring variations of behaviorist curriculum development) should take note.

In its February 1974 edition, *Phi Delta Kappan*, a leading educational journal, published an interview with Ralph Tyler entitled "The Father of Behavioral Objectives Criticizes Them: An interview with Tyler." (pp. 55–57). Tyler claimed that he had been widely misunderstood and that he was not using the term "behavioral objectives" as it is understood by the school of behaviorism. More recently Tyler has endeavored to distance himself further from the behaviorism of B. F. Skinner in yet another interview for *Phi Delta Kappan* (Hiatt, 1994) where he talks about teaching as a complex activity, the need for continual learning as a process of discovery, and self-directed learners. This Tylerian perspective on learning is quite different from that of his very influential text, *Basic Principles of Curriculum Instruction* (1950), which even in its more recent editions bears the stamp of behaviorism and exemplifies the reductionistic method in education.

Despite the public rejection of behaviorism by "the father of behavioral objectives," the influence of behavioral psychology in education is bolstered through its ties to the significant ideological movement in today's political climate which does not favor public funding for initiatives designed to achieve social equality through educational programming and other forms of state support for the lower classes. In this ideological context, the notion that intelligence as a measurable construct ("intelligence quotient" or IQ) is predominantly hereditary (that is, biologically determined) sits well with a point of view that asserts a causal connection between intelligence and social class position. Both are largely the result of genetic factors. Since, in this view, there are definite limitations to how much an individual's intelligence can be improved through educational or social initiatives designed to compensate for socioeconomic environmental deficiencies, it is recommended that investment in such programs should be curtailed. At the same time, the definition of intelligence as IQ (amenable to measurement and allegedly not susceptible to significant change in the context of favorable environmental circumstances) is causally connected in today's society to criminality and race as well as class position.

Much of the critical discourse on IQ, including many well-substantiated studies, shows how IQ testing is biased toward demonstrating higher performance among middle-class (IQ testing seems to be an imposition upper-class and upper-middle class people can afford to ignore) and dominant ethnic groups than for the lower classes. Thus, issues of equity and social justice arise where, for example, selection for a superior quality of education is reserved for those who achieve above average scores on IQ-oriented examinations as was the case for British children. Yet, despite critique countering the pseudoscientific claims, or "scientism," of the IQ movement which, at best, represents a very limited and limiting concept of human intelligence, IQ measurement along with the other trappings of behavioral psychology, has managed to remain entrenched in many of our educational establishments.

The publication of *The Bell Curve: Intelligence and Class Structure in American Life* (Herrnstein & Murray, 1994) has renewed interest in IQ as a measure of human intelligence. This very lengthy book, promoted as a *"New York Times* bestseller," was reissued as a paperback in 1996. For those who maintain that intelligence is genetically determined and the key factor in accounting for an individual's class position in today's society, *The Bell Curve* brings further legitimation to their position. The study exemplifies the quest of behavioral psychology to establish its status as a conventional scientific discipline (Herrnstein was a long-time disciple of B. F. Skinner). The detailed statistical tabulations and correlations are all based on the virtually taken-for-granted assumption that the measurable *ideal concept* IQ corresponds to human intelligence which behaviorists assert is predominantly determined for an individual's entire lifespan from the time of conception. In this view, then, intelligence (IQ) is not amenable to significant change through the process of lifelong learning.

By relating IQ to crime, unemployment, welfare, child neglect, poverty, and illegitimacy, as well as class and race, and drawing implications for social policy, *The Bell Curve* also reveals the connection between behavioral psychology and a political ideology which opposes publicly funded support for educational and social programs to improve the circumstances of the underclass. Charles Murray has been a prominent member of three leading ideological think tanks, the Hoover Institute, the American Enterprise Institute, and the Manhattan Institute for Policy Research. The policies he and his colleagues advocate are characterized by attacks on subsidies to the poor and on

Reflections on Lifelong Learning and Lifelong Education 123

welfare in general. During the early 1980's, at the height of the neoconservative ascendancy, Murray argued that social programs were worthless and should be abolished. He renews the attack on somewhat different grounds in the book he co-authored with Hernnstein which is a thinly veiled attempt to show the innate inferiority of blacks.

The pernicious effects of this ideology and the complicity of behavioral psychology in providing its pseudoscientific basis are amply addressed in *The Bell Curve Debate: History, Documents, Opinions* (Jacoby & Glauberman, 1995). This text is made up of a large number of contributions dealing with the inadequacy of IQ as a definition of intelligence, the spurious claims for scientific status asserted in *The Bell Curve*, and its flawed methodology. *The Bell Curve*, for all of its influence, is shown to be the most recent project of a reactionary ideology based on social Darwinism which, in itself, relies for legitimation on a pseudoscience of behaviorism. On the first page of the book the authors trace their intellectual (and ideological) lineage to the social Darwinist, Francis Galton whose work has been invoked as the "scientific" basis demonstrating that the Irish who survived the Great Famine were, like the "negro", "more generally of a low or coarse organization." The authors of *The Bell Curve* also give special mention to Henry Goddard whose work, which showed that Jews were "feebleminded," was subsequently used as a basis for the Nazi's projects in applied eugenics.

In his aptly titled contribution to *The Bell Curve Debate*, "Measure by Mismeasure," zoology professor Stephen Gould has this to say about the Herrnstein and Murray book on human intelligence:

> Intelligence, in their formulation, must be depictable as a single number, capable of ranking people in linear order, genetically based, and effectively immutable. . . . . . . The central argument of *The Bell Curve* fails because most of the premises are false. (p. 5)

It is well for educators and those who work with social programs for alleviating the related problems of crime, unemployment, welfare, poverty, child neglect, illegitimacy, and racial tension to be aware of these critical crosscurrents around the issue of human intelligence and class structure. For the position adopted here is that if we are to take seriously a notion of lifelong learning that hinges on the capacities of human beings for continuous self-development and on aspirations for a more just and rational society, we should abandon the restrictive (mis)measures of IQ testing and the prescriptive pedagogical trappings of the behaviorist agenda.

Intelligence is learned and, to some extent, it is teachable throughout the lifespan. Given this understanding, we also gain a realistic insight into the prevailing social structures, institutional arrangements, and ideological forces which still get in the way of initiatives to realize a learning society which serves the needs of the vast majority of people rather than the interests of an elite minority.

Toward a Theory of Lifelong Learning

Abandoning the behavioristic approach to curriculum development and assessment, with its emphasis on precision and quantification, does not entail a rejection of systematic, careful, planning on the part of educators. The problem for so-called humanistic education (should there really be any other kind?), which to a large extent invokes the work of Carl Rogers (1969), is that it has been linked in ideological discourse with the allegedly overpermissive laissez faire attitudes ("anything goes") of progressive educators in the 1960's and early 1970's.

It is difficult to take seriously the ideological assertions that emerged, particularly during the Thatcher and Reagan years that followed, blaming progressive educators for all the prevailing ills of society (juvenile delinquency, drug abuse, loss of work ethic, and so on). However, in their efforts to give due emphasis to the agency of students and teachers and their eagerness to loosen the grip of prescriptive curriculum formats, some educators at that time were undoubtedly excessive in their scorn for systematic planning of any kind. This tendency associated with humanistic education as the alternative to behaviorism, though not as widespread as alleged, was unfortunate. A systematic approach to learning and teaching is entirely in keeping with a respect for the agency of teachers and learners in the educational process.

The constituents of a theory of learning that stays away from ideological discourse while highlighting the significance of human agency can be derived from the work of Alfred Schutz. His seminal text in this regard is *Reflections on Problems of Relevance* (1970). This study, enlarged upon in subsequent publications, offers a systematic account of human action—and hence learning and teaching—that does not resort to the kind of pseudoscientific quantification which is exemplified in behaviorism.

The concept of relevance as it emerges in Schutz's investigations refers us to the typical events and structures that constitute everyday life (the *lifeworld*). Within our everyday lifeworld meaningful action, which is neither entirely predictable nor completely haphazard, is always constituted in a recognizable context which allows us to make sense of our projects of action. This emphasis on the relevance of *meaning in context* and the agency of individuals (the capacity for purposeful action) has implications for the way we view the situation of the learner or client, the role of the teacher or public service professional, program planning and evaluation and so on. These roles and practices are *purposively* enacted in their particular contexts, but not in isolation. Our experiences and the contexts in which we carry out our projects of action overlap with the experience of others (as well as our own experience) and other contexts.

To the extent that circumstances from outside our immediate context are relevant, they can be usefully incorporated to the project at hand. This is typically what happens. Our projects of action can be carried out in a very much taken-for-granted manner where we are very familiar with what is at stake and what is required, or when we opt not to give them the attention they merit. Otherwise, our projects of action, which can all be viewed to some extent as "learning experiences," call for varying degrees of systematic planning. Systematic planning in this view requires personal judgment. Within formal educational or public service agency settings, to cite examples of direct interest to the role of educators, projects of action encompassing curriculum development, program planning and evaluation, and policy formation would typically involve us in a very systematic approach (even where we have access to relevant sources from immediate and related contexts) and the exercise of judgment. This gives us an entirely different view of the situation to that prescribed by a behavioristic orientation which steers us towards the taken-for granted deployment of prescriptive blueprints to define the situation at hand.

A theory of action perspective on learning draws our attention to the relevance of past experience as well as to that of purposive action and of immediate context in the construction of meaning. These are very much interconnected constituents of human experience which Schutz refers to as an individual's *stock of knowledge* (past experience), *intentionality* (purposive action), and the *everyday lifeworld* (the context in which every individual carries out her or his projects of action). The stock of knowledge an individual brings to a learning experience is of considerable relevance. It takes its shape not only from the accumulation of past experiences, but also from when and how these experiences were acquired. The stock of knowledge, then, accounts for how an individual constitutes projects of action and deals with problems in her or his everyday lifeworld as well as being the source of past know-how relevant to these immediate situations as they arise. Thus, past experience has an important influence on how we experience present and future events.

The concept of the stock of knowledge offers useful insights for how we as individuals experience our everyday world. By the same token, the stock of knowledge of a social group, which is not merely the sum of the past experience of its individual members, provides the source for investigations into normative behavior, aspirations, learning styles, and proficiencies at the group level.

Clearly, it is contingent on educators to be alert to how the stock of knowledge at both the individual (including themselves) and group levels influence how we constitute and how we go about fulfilling our everyday projects of action. In this way we can gain relevant insight into the *cognitive style* (the way of knowing and acting in the everyday lifeworld) of an individual, ourself, or a particular group. Schutz describes the process in terms of investigating human action according to the structures of *topical (thematic) relevance, motivational relevance,* and *interpretative relevance.* Through these structures of relevance, which are to be conceived of as overlapping and continuous (not discrete) structures, our attention is drawn to how our immediate (or paramount) projects of action are formed and to how they relate to other relevant themes, the motivations that make these projects immediately relevant to us, and the resources brought to bear in understanding and bringing our projects to completion.

How far each of these dimensions is investigated is determined in context by the requirements of the situation at hand. For example, in the case of *motivational relevance,* a straightforward simple reason might suffice for a relevant understanding of the immediate project under consideration. (A student might explain that she studies in order to get a good grade). However, in some instances deeper reflection on underlying motives which influence our projects of action may be required. In any event, how far the level of investigation is pushed with regard to the structures of relevance which account for how our everyday projects are enacted is a matter of judgment. This judgment too, which is learned and to some extent can be taught, is derived from our stock of knowledge and can be accounted for in terms of the structures of relevance.

An individual's everyday projects of action are not carried out in isolation from the activities of others. We are affected, and have to take into account, the experience of other people whose experience overlaps with our own. Though each individual's experience has a meaning structure all of its own, it emerges within an *intersubjective* world in which the individual lives as a human being with other human beings bound to each other through shared dispositions and understandings. Thus, we experience our fellow human beings, in a wide variety of social relationships, as other subjects in the world with their own personal (psychological) environment and agendas.

It is through what Alfred Schutz, drawing in particular upon the research of philosopher Edmund Husserl, refers to as *intersubjectivity* that we are able to arrive at a common understanding (though not necessarily agreement) with others of events and of everyday experience in general. The view of intersubjective understanding as an innate human capacity corresponds to the insights of Jurgen Habermas into communicative action which were addressed in Chapter 4. Thus, the quality of intersubjective understanding improves with the development of communicative competence. Together, these interrelated concepts are critical in making the case for the merits of dialogue, which is so central to the pedagogy of Paulo Freire which is dealt with in the next chapter.

In scarcely any situation we encounter are we completely without some relevant point of reference. The events and objects of our everyday world are not experienced in their uniqueness. They are not given to us in isolation. When confronted with a new problem an individual is almost always able to identify from his or her stock of knowledge something that is familiar—a group in dialogue is better placed in this regard—as a basis from which to proceed. (That is, unless this capacity has been blocked through the negative effects of prior "learning" or as a result of irremediable mental deficiency). Hence, the folly of that pedagogical view, now widely rejected in theory but still discernible in practice, of the human mind as a blank slate on which new knowledge is to be inscribed. Given that learners always bring with them a stock of knowledge and the capacity to make a purposeful contribution to the learning situation, the role of the teacher envisaged by Marin Heidegger (1968) quoted here is more in line with the aspirations of lifelong learning than a pedagogical practice conditioned by the prescriptive methods of behaviorism:

> Teaching is more difficult than learning because what teaching calls for is this: to let learn. The real teacher, in fact lets nothing else be learned than learning. His conduct, therefore, often produces the impression that we learn nothing from him, if by 'learning' we now suddenly understand merely the procurement of useful knowledge. The teacher is ahead of his apprentices in this alone, that he has still far more to learn than they—he has to learn to let them learn. (p. 15)

The commitment called for here is not easy to enact. It requires careful and systematic preparation as well as continuing evaluation.

Although it is well for educators to appreciate the significance of past experience and of learning how to learn, there is an important sense in which we need to *learn how to unlearn*. The concern here is with the fact that an individual's, or a group's, stock of knowledge is formed by negative as well as positive experiences. Our way of knowing and being in the world (cognitive style) is constrained by ingrained habits that limit the human potential to live a life of sensitive awareness and fulfillment. So it is not just a case of building on past experience.

A pedagogy committed to a notion of lifelong learning should also enable each of us to observe within ourselves the effects of these negative experiences which are associated with fear (the need for security), greed, ambition, competitiveness, and violence in its many manifestations. (And by violence here is meant verbal abuse, willful and careless neglect, and the everyday discourtesies we inflict on each other as well as those injurious acts which we immediately recognize as violence). Most of us are able to identify the interrelated tendencies mentioned here at work in society as whole. An approach to learning which encourages us to observe these tendencies at work in ourselves, without any compulsion to pass judgment, is needed if we are to abandon those dysfunctional habits, opinions, and ideas which detract from the quality of our lives.

The self-reflective dimension to lifelong learning envisaged here will be difficult to attain, especially at a time when the discourse on the global imperatives for competitiveness is so prominent within our educational institutions. There seems to be little pause for thought in this current obsession with competition regarding its connections to greed and violence. Yet can there now be any realistic expectation of ever overcoming those interrelated tendencies towards greed, fear, ambition, and violence that stand in the way of a just and rational society unless we are prepared at the same time to observe their manifestations in ourselves? When educators discuss the incidence of violence in today's society (a popular topic in classrooms today), do they also encourage students to observe within themselves the way they perpetrate violence in many forms during their everyday lives? More to the point, are we as educators observing the violence in our own lives? Perhaps this gives us the cue as to where the process of unlearning in the sense described here should begin—with the self-education of educators.

It is not easy to bring about circumstances where careful self-observation that is neither judgmental nor narcissistic becomes an ongoing part of the learning process. A helpful approach would be to give renewed emphasis to the aesthetic and spiritual dimensions of everyday experience which enrich our sense of perception. This approach entails teaching practices, curriculum, and self-directed initiatives concerned with the recovery and development of our capacities to observe *carefully* (as in "full of care" as well as in detail) the beauty and mystery of our immediate environment and the universe as a whole. In carefully observing the things of beauty in our immediate experience (a tree, a bird, a poem, a loved one), we come to understand our relationship to them.

Through aesthetic and spiritual experience we relinquish, at least for a while, those dysfunctional habits, opinions, bits of knowledge, and ideas from the past that are associated with our fears, our greed, and our violence. But we really know this already. Revolutionary social change to overcome problems of inequality and injustice can only come about if they are accompanied, or preceded, by revolutionary change in our understanding of ourselves. Perhaps this is what the slogan "the personal is political" is meant to convey. In any event, we have at this juncture a critical need for a theory and practice of lifelong learning that takes into account the aesthetic, the spiritual, and the political.

Careful observation of one's own experience, which is what is meant by meditation, can be learned. A direct approach to its development is through aesthetic and spiritual appreciation. (This more aesthetic and spiritual approach needs to accompany the kind of pedagogical practices for social change which are described in the next chapter). Hererin lies an immediate challenge for those who are hopeful about the prospects for lifelong learning as an international movement.

The Problem of Accessibility and Making the Connections

Ensuring widespread accessibility to its educational institutions is fundamental to the learning society envisaged by Edgar Faure (1973) and Torsten Husén (1974). In advanced industrial countries the provision of elementary and secondary school education for young people is now virtually taken for granted. In these countries during the past three decades the accessibility of postsecondary education has increased significantly. Yet the provision of elementary education as a right of all citizens has yet to be achieved for the vast majority of the world's population. In the "developing" countries education at both secondary and postsecondary levels is reserved only for the elite and the very fortunate. For the majority, access to state-funded elementary schooling, to the extent that it exists, is still regarded as a privilege.

At the end of the 20th century, then, access to education among the world's population is still very uneven. The provision of basic literacy programs for all of the people has yet to be achieved even in most African, Asian, and South American countries. They are still a far cry from the notion of a learning society where a discourse on lifelong education and lifelong learning makes sense. However, in India, for example, where upwards of 55 million children are working as cheap labor instead of attending school, access to television is now widespread even in communities where few people own a television. Before the century's end, educated Indians will have access to the Internet. And Pepsi Cola will be getting its message over to the young of all classes and religious groups. Yet the majority of India's people will still be illiterate at the turn of the century. The message for educators worldwide in this regard is to keep alive the push for broadcasting educational programs for the masses through the media to support community-based and conventional institutional initiatives. It is now clear that corporate interests will guarantee the worldwide deployment of the latest developments in communications technology. Herein, then, lies a critical pedagogical challenge to ensure that the entire content of the media message does not correspond to that of Pepsi, Coke, IBM, and GM.

Even in the most highly developed of western countries, access to education varies significantly. Elementary and secondary schools for the children of the lower classes are not nearly as well resourced as those attended by middle and upper class children who are more likely to go on to university education and get the better jobs. It is as simple as that. As we have demonstrated in previous chapters schooling is still very much a factor in reproducing class status, in social and economic terms, a fact which runs counter to claims that class analysis no longer has any relevance when it comes to looking at the structure of advanced capitalist societies.

Class structure is still nicely represented in the extent and quality of the educational provision. The current ideological argument for wholesale privatization within the sector of public education has adversely affected, though not eradicated, progressive initiatives to allocate more substantial compensatory resources for the schooling of children from lower class backgrounds and to make universities significantly more accessible to them. And as noted above, in the United States, the mean-spirited ideology of *The Bell Curve* is intended to show that such initiatives are a waste of time, effort, and money because the majority of people born into the lower classes do not have the innate capacities to benefit from what it will take to achieve universal access to good quality educational programs.

The critical pedagogical challenge around making universities more accessible to social groups who are underrepresented calls for initiatives from within the institutions themselves. This approach, combined with support from pressure groups outside the institutions is workable. More extreme approaches represented in the kind of radical strategies that advocate, for example, the immediate allocation of a fixed number of university placements a year from such areas as Chicago's South State Street to Princeton or from Manchester's Moss Side Manchester to Cambridge University would not work. Such initiatives would only serve to confirm the pseudoscientifically based (mis)predictions of *Bell Curve* ideology. Without intensive preparation, people from under-class areas do not have the cultural capital (see Chapters 4 and 5) required to perform well at university. For sure, even in a class structured society the requirements for success at university, compensating for a lack of cultural capital, can be, and is being, taught and learned on an individual basis in under-class contexts. However, the instances remain few and far between.

The question for our times concerning accessibility of postsecondary education is whether universities should or will continue to be regarded as the be all and end all. On this matter, The Faure Report (1973) noted that "in general, the concept of lifelong learning rules out any form of final, premature selection" (p. 203) and then made the following recommendation:

> As educational systems become more diversified and as possibilities for entry, exit and re-entry increase, obtaining university degrees and diplomas should become less and less closely linked to completing a predetermined course of study. (Faure et al., 1973, p. 203–4)

Since Faure we have witnessed a proliferation of institutions offering alternative approaches to adult and continuing education as well as the increasing emergence of nontraditional programs in conventional postsecondary institutions (including universities.)

Within conventional institutional settings, nontraditional initiatives take the form of alternative delivery systems—in particular, as distance education—the granting of credit for previous experience, and flexibility in entrance requirements. The structures to which these initiatives give rise tend to be less centralized and more loosely defined, especially where they are not concerned with the whole apparatus of certification and credentialing. This is certainly the case with learning exchanges and the kind of organized but noncredentialized educational programming which, as a now distant legacy of the radicalized free university classes of the 1960's, is represented in William Draves's book on *The Free University: A Model for Lifelong Learning* (1980). Although the radical social change agenda of such initiatives has been largely abandoned in favor of an entrepreneurial approach, in their flexibility they remain more progressive than current practices governing selection, program planning, and curriculum design in schools, colleges, and universities.

The nontraditional approach to lifelong learning views access to conventional education at all levels as an important option to be exercised in accordance with the needs of learner. Many of the nontraditional institutions offer credentials (certificates, diplomas, and degrees) and seek conventional recognition in the form of accreditation. At present this tendency is more apparent in the United States than elsewhere, but it represents a trend that is likely to spread during the next decade as publicly funded universities continue to face budget restraints and diminishing status.

The mission statement of a typical nontraditional university which relies entirely on a distance education approach reads as follows:

> The mission of Greenwich University is to offer unique opportunities world-wide, for adults to enter flexible, self-paced programs of higher education which are challenging and achievable, and which provide access to qualified faculty in a joint commitment to individualized distance learning. (Greenwich University Catalogue, 1996, p. 3)

Greenwich University does not have a campus. Its administrative offices are based at Hilo, Hawaii. The institution uses its adjunct faculty to supervise students' work. These adjunct faculty members, committed to nontraditional approaches through distance education, tend to take on only the occasional student whose research interests coincide closely with their own. For the most part these adjunct professors are on the faculty of conventional universities.

The credibility of nontraditional distance education colleges varies considerably, and there is no doubt that many of them are unfairly stigmatized with the "degree mill" label accorded to the dubious entrepreneurial activities of some correspondence schools. This view when applied to nontraditional distance education colleges in general is unfortunate because they are, in many respects, at the cutting edge of developments in flexible admission policies, validation of learners' past experience, and enabling learners to shape their projects in accordance with their own immediate aspirations.

Nontraditional education thus runs counter to the elitism and exclusivity often associated with many conventional universities. In these times of institutional restructuring in publicly funded agencies of all kinds, our universities in particular, but also other public service organizations, have much to learn from the aims and practices of nontraditional approaches to education.

Improved access to educational institutions and the growth in nontraditional approaches is in keeping with an emerging discourse on the need for community involvement and interagency cooperation in creating a learning society. This emphasis on community and agency involvement in partnership arrangements with the educational establishment undoubtedly has a lot to do with the search for extra resources in these times of continuing budget cutbacks. Yet the renewal of a concern for connecting community development initiatives with education, and the sense of collective identity entailed, marks a departure from the political ideology of the Thatcher era which disparaged notions of community and society as significant contexts for human action. From that ideological perspective there is no society in this collective sense (according to Mrs. Thatcher who had a marked influence on many of Reagan's policy advisers); rather it viewed the political economy as being made up of individuals who go out each day to compete with each other in the marketplace and rely on home and family for support and sustenance.

This ideological view which simultaneously enthroned and burdened a notion of the nuclear family as the main source of individualistic endeavor in a highly competitive world has widened somewhat in the 1990's. This wider purview, even from the neoconservative right, is acknowledging that communities, apart from the nuclear family, do exist and do have a role in the provision of collective support which is not entirely driven by the profit motive. Along with the prevailing emphasis on the connection between education and employment, then, there is now a movement to strengthen linkages between education and community.

At the institutional level, the community school concept holds out a great deal of promise in terms of lifelong education and the development of a learning society. Community schools are intended to be accessible to all age groups and, because all schools are potentially community schools, they represent a considerable resource base for their immediate neighborhoods. In these times, especially, it does not make economic sense to use publicly funded schools only during the hours when the conventional program for children and young people from kindergarten to graduation is under way.

So far designated community schools tend to be located in lower and underclass areas which are noted for a high incidence of welfare recipients, single parent families, crime, and generalized poverty. The notion is that young people are more "at risk" in such neighborhoods and that the greater participation of adults in the life of the schools accompanied by more involvement on the part of the schools in adult education would alleviate the situation. In middle and upper-class communities there is already a somewhat greater tendency for parents to be involved with school activities and for comparatively easy access to organized adult education. At this juncture, then, it is largely in lower class and underclass areas where publicly funded designated community schools are viewed as strategic locations from which to address the needs of children at risk, to involve parents in the educational process, and to deliver educational and other services to the surrounding community. The everyday problems confronting young people, especially, in these economically marginalized and socially fractured settings cut across the boundaries of schools, social service agencies, and various government departments. In this regard, schools have a stake in the creation of a supportive and relatively stable out of school environments.

Community schools are not a new idea. They are rooted in a tradition that incorporates community education as central to community development. The role of the community school in this view is to build working relationships with community members and organizations in addition to teaching the conventional academic subjects to school age children. As such, they serve as a model for educational innovation and lifelong education. And they also provide for publicly funded education a hopeful rationale based on cooperative initiatives to counter the current move toward privatized charter schools with their emphasis on individualistic entrepreneurship and the cult of competition.

For the community school to fulfill its potential within a learning society, a wider role for the teacher in today's society, a new conception of classroom practices, and a more creative approach to curriculum development in line with community needs are required. In addition to a familiarity with the usual classroom management techniques (a central preoccupation in most teacher education programs), teachers should become conversant with strategies for developing a relevant learning program in conjunction with other teachers and community representatives on school councils. At the same time teachers should understand the need to forge partnerships with parents, community members, and various human service organizations as part of a collaborative process to define educational and community issues, and to establish the most effective way to share resources. As key participants teachers will need to become more committed to, and proficient in, the practice of community development as an educational and motivational process.

These changes can hardly be brought about without radically new approaches to teacher preparation and substantial support for the continuing education of practicing teachers. Colleges of education, which face much criticism these days from both the university community and off-campus sources, are thus presented with a critical challenge to reconceptualize their programs within the nexus of schools and community and under the rubric of lifelong education. What is envisaged here is a more highly qualified teaching force willing to reaffirm the high status that the role of teacher merits and to take on leadership within school communities. While tendencies toward blaming teachers and schools for much of the current social malaise are unfair, it is reasonable at this time, given support from their communities, to expect more elevated levels of performance from teachers and the colleges of education which prepare them.

To a limited extent (but already sufficient to confirm their feasibility), the suggestions made in the preceding paragraphs with regard to the nexus between school and community are already evident in some school programs and the practices of some teachers. Where school programs are not yet tuned into the community school concept, teachers can still expand their own role beyond the classroom into the community. This can, of course, entail bringing members of the community into the classroom setting. Teachers need help. They are overly busy. (Illich is right about today's schools being overburdened with adminis-trivia.) But the flow of energy between classroom and community can be two-way as those educators who incorporate community involvement into their pedagogy have discovered. It calls for commitment, creativity, and careful organization.

The practice of community education with the schools as catalysts can be learned and should be embraced at this time by teachers, their professional associations, and colleges of education. For contrary to Illich's urgings for a deschooled society, we can rediscover within community schools the immediate prospects for building communities of hope. Community schools are about enabling communities to take education into their own hands.

The Politics of Lifelong Education

The guiding principle, invoking here Thomas Hodgskin founder of the mechanics institutes, that the education of a free people should be in their own hands (Halévy, 1956, p. 86), is a reminder that the discourse on lifelong education entails a continuing struggle between autonomy and creativity, on the one hand, and control and prescription, on the other. To the extent that the latter circumstance prevails, the interests of some favored groups in society are being served at the expense of others. Clearly, the state still has a role to play, however reluctant it may be to accept the responsibility, in intervening to rectify the deepening inequalities in the distribution of resources between communities. In this regard, the critical task at this time for educators as engaged intellectuals is twofold: to keep reminding the state of its responsibility for bringing about a more equitable distribution of resources, and to ensure that the movement of lifelong education is toward autonomy and creativity rather than in the direction of control and prescription.

The struggle within the context of lifelong education between autonomy and control is well exemplified in the case of mandatory continuing education (MCE) In a thought-provoking essay entitled "Is Lifelong Education a Guarantee of Permanent Inadequacy?" John Ohliger (1974) drew critical attention to the link between mandatory continuing education and lifelong education. Ohliger is undoubtedly the most prominent critic of MCE and is widely regarded as a source of inspiration, especially in North America, to those who oppose the tendency on moral and political grounds. Nevertheless, the trend toward MCE has gained momentum during the past two decades.

In the professions and occupations that aspire to professional status the justification for MCE is made on the grounds that it serves to protect public interests by guaranteeing practitioner competence. Thus, practitioners in occupations where MCE has been adopted are typically required every year to take a prescribed number of hours of continuing education approved by the occupation's licensing body. The units of MCE completed are regarded as sufficient evidence that the practitioner is keeping up to date and qualified to retain his or her license to practice. Within particular professions MCE is usually applied on a regional basis rather than as a universal mandate. Yet the incidence of MCE is on the increase in medicine, most of the other health service occupations, law, and teaching.

Opponents of MCE argue that it transgresses the principle of voluntary learning that is central to adult and continuing education. Clearly opposition to MCE does not constitute opposition to continuing education for occupational competence. Rather, it raises questions about the reasons for an absence of the kind of commitment which would make people want to learn more about their work without any form of coercion. At the same time, however, there is no doubt that MCE can serve to legitimize the special status of the occupation in the eyes of the public, strengthening to some extent its claims for monopolistic practice. This legitimation of exclusive practice is most apparent in the case of well-established professions such as medicine, law, and accountancy. Further, while there is no evidence that MCE actually serves as a guarantee of competent performance, an indication that the specified number of MCE units have been completed can be used to counter claims of malpractice due to incompetence.

Though some professionals, for the reasons given above, may not be dissatisfied with the imposition of MCE (many are), their willingness sets an unfortunate precedent for less favored members of society. If professionals are willing to accept MCE, it becomes more difficult, for example, to make the case against the imposition of education and training on the unemployed and people dependent on welfare where receipt of their monthly allowance is made contingent upon attendance in school. Here again, it is the compulsion to attend what might otherwise be worthwhile educational programs for adults that opponents of MCE view as morally reprehensible.

In any event by asking whether lifelong education is really about lifelong schooling from cradle to grave, John Ohliger (1974) and other critics of MCE have brought both a moral and a political dimension to the discourse on lifelong learning that was becoming trivialized. From a critical, rather than a merely taken-for-granted, perspective this discourse gains relevance to the extent that it acknowledges the prevailing inequalities in the distribution of knowledge, the relationship of knowledge acquisition to power, and the innate capacities of ordinary men and women to determine their own education and that of their children as social inequities are addressed. Otherwise, as far as democratic education toward a more rational global society is concerned, lifelong education signifies lifelong enculturation to a world increasingly determined, give or take reformist modifications which serve to render minor variations on the vested interests of the status quo, within a nexus of unequal power relations. In such a world talk about the learning society and education for participatory democracy becomes for the majority an exercise in spinning wheels.

Yet an approach to lifelong education which has as its aim the realization of a rational (that is, a more just), genuinely participatory democracy, is conceivable. The beginnings can emerge from the relationship between school and society, from more widespread access to both conventional and nontraditional forms of delivering educational programs, and with the adoption of a more relevant understanding of psychological and social learning processes to replace the entire apparatus of pseudoscientific and coercive pedagogical techniques currently in vogue.

Chapter 7

PARTICIPATORY STRATEGIES

> There is a growing awareness that isolated, competing individuals can rarely confront repressive institutions alone. (Noam Chomsky, *Radical Priorities*)

This chapter is about education for participatory democracy, particularly as it is exemplified in popular education, the pedagogy of Paulo Freire, and participatory research (action research in the context of education and development.) These three interrelated projects are dealt with in the following three sections. Finally, suggestions are made as to how these approaches to education for participatory democracy might be modified and, to an extent, relocated more relevantly within contemporary institutional settings.

Popular Education

Emerging from nonformal educational initiatives developed specifically to serve the interests of the urban and rural poor in Third World countries, popular education has attracted much attention during the past two decades within educational (especially adult education), community development (especially social activist), and academic contexts of the developed world. The basic educational aim of popular education is to help poor people realize their potential for working together toward a more just and equitable society. For the most part, though not entirely, popular education has been associated with the teaching of literacy to adults.

This significant connection to literacy training was well established throughout Central and South America when popular movements for political social change began during the 1950's to incorporate adult education as a means towards achieving their ends. In this view, a primary reason why the illiterate and poor majority lacked the will to act collectively on their own behalf was because they were unable to understand how prevailing social structures were ranged against them. At the same time, conventional forms of education provided in schools, colleges, and universities for those able to attend were regarded as oppressive. They were seen as locations where the norms and structures sustaining an unjust society were legitimized and reproduced. On the other hand, the role of nonformal adult education from the perspective of popular political and social movements, even at the level of basic adult literacy, was to pose critical questions about the prevailing social arrangements and to propose that ordinary men and women had the potential to change them in their collective (class) interests.

Elsewhere, we can discern the origins of popular education in workers' education in Britain. The eminent British historian E. P. Thompson in his study on *The Making of the English Working Class* (1984) traces the historical development within working class culture of popular educational initiatives which, though uneven in their effects, have served over time to check the power of the ruling class. The Danish folk schools and Swedish study circles study represent the kind of state-supported version of popular education that social democratic governments were eager to support before the present era of economic restraints. However, more typical of popular education as it is experienced worldwide are the many nongovernmental organizations that have sprung up from time to time in various parts of the world (most notably in developing countries) to help ordinary men and women fulfill their economic, social, and political needs through group learning.

Gandhi's book on *Rebuilding Our Villages* (1969) remains an important touchstone for popular education initiatives in Asia and in the West, especially where they seek to encompass a spiritual dimension along with a concern for economic, political, and social issues. The editor has this to say in his preface to the book:

> The great merit of Gandhi's views in regard to village reconstruction, therefore, lies just in the fact that while planning for our villages he was not concerned merely with raising their economic standard of living but also with laying the basis for peace, justice and freedom for all. (p. iv)

And Gandhi refers to the nature of the political task in the following terms:

Participatory Strategies

> Here the worker will study the political grievances of the villagers and teach them the dignity of freedom, self-reliance, and self-help in everything. This makes in my opinion complete adult education. But this does not complete the task of the village worker. He must take care and charge of the little ones and begin their instruction and carry on a night school for adults. This literary training is but part of a whole education course and only the means to the larger end. (p. 95)

This "larger end" has to do with organizing for collective action. The political task in India, as elsewhere, is ongoing and yet unfulfilled.

In North America, Highlander Folk School, an informal adult education center for social activists based in Tennessee, has gained international prominence. For advocates of popular education in developed countries the story of Highlander, *Unearthing Seeds of Fire* (Adams & Horton, 1975), has become a major source of inspiration. A fairly recent and instructive study on popular education in Quebec (Chené & Chervin, 1991) describes an advanced North American political economy where well-established state-assisted institutionalized forms of popular education exist alongside marginalized, but more autonomous, community-based projects which the authors refer to as "independent popular education." Yet it is not misleading to claim that the contemporary discourse on popular education traces its origins, and looks for its legitimacy, to politicized nonformal adult education initiatives in the developing countries of South and Central America, Africa, and Asia.

Popular education, then, for the most part occurs outside of the formal education system. For reasons already identified (those that have to do with traditional education's role in the reproduction of existing social arrangements which sustain the status quo), there is a widespread view among social and political activists that popular education's emancipatory potential will be hijacked if it does not take place apart from the formal system. Once it becomes absorbed by the state, it is no longer popular education. Thus, for Vio Grossi (1981, "Popular Education: Concept and Implications," *Convergence,* XIV, 2, p. 73), former regional secretary for the Council of Adult Education of Latin America, "the intent of popular education is to detach itself from the educational efforts that are directed to maintaining a social system that has been accused of being unjust and oppressive." Popular education presents an alternative to the existing paradigm of formal education that has yet to be adequately tested in our schools, colleges, and universities.

In the view represented by Vio Grossi, popular education gains political relevance by challenging from outside of the system the taken-for-granted assumptions and practices of formal and informal education that takes place in schools, colleges, and universities. The notion is that this oppositional stance to traditional education will prevent the co-optation, or domestication, of popular education's commitment to disclose, and ultimately transform, the systemic practices that are inevitably connected to the incidence of widespread poverty and the ongoing expropriation of tribal lands, of racism, sexism, religious bigotry, and environmental degradation. Thus, popular education as a counter-hegemonic practice seeks to maintain a cutting edge to its critical observations of legitimated violence (endorsed or tolerated by the state.)

This politicized approach to popular education is depicted in a paper on "Grassroots Movements, Development Discourse and Popular Education" by Pramod Prajuli (1986), an adult educator with experience of popular education among community-based groups in Nepal. Prajuli opens his essay with this quote from Bertolt Brecht:

> Our concept of what is popular refers to a people who not only play a part in historical development but actively usurp it, force its place, determine its direction. We have people in mind who make history, change the world and themselves. We have in mind a fighting people and therefore an aggressive concept of what is popular. (Prajuli, p. 29)

Applied to popular education Brecht's "aggressive concept of what is popular" constitutes a counter-discourse to conventional approaches to development. These conventional approaches for all of—or because of—the subsidies they provide (with strings attached), and the modernization projects they entail, are held responsible for maintaining the neocolonial status of developing regions in their relationship with advanced political economies, and for widening the gulf between the poor and the rich everywhere.

For Prajuli popular education as counter-discourse calls for the practice of a "bottom up" approach in contrast to the "trickle down" approach which has provided the rationale for modernizing schemes according to conventional development theory. Dependency on foreign aid is to be countered by education for self-reliance. The major focus is to be switched to the concerns of local and civil society rather than those of the state and international agencies. Thus, from this notion of popular education's proper role, the aims and strategies for development should be defined by grass-roots participatory decision making, not by directions from above. According to Prajuli the participants in popular education as counter-discourse "have opted for the transformation of an oppressive social structure instead of merely changing values and attitudes of individuals" (p. 33) and, in line with Brecht's "aggressive concept of the popular," their "battle is political and ideological" (p. 34)

Not all—more likely, not many—of those practitioners who think of their work as popular education can afford to take the firmly stated position marked out by popular education as counter-discourse. Their options for autonomous action and, hence, anti-hegemonic strategies are limited by the fact that so many popular education initiatives are more or less dependent on state funding. And where funding depends on the support of private foundations or individuals, prospects for oppositional strategies are more or less bounded by the political and ideological interests of contributing stakeholders. Rarely are those who influence the dispersal of funds from such sources likely to be in favor of anything like the kind of political and social transformation prefigured by an "aggressive concept of what is popular" and a pedagogy for "the wretched of the earth" (here invoking Frantz Fanon, 1988) in which "the battle is political and ideological."

The reality is that a considerable amount of popular education based in nongovernment organizations (NGO's) which has to rely on funding from the state or outside sources has to deal with the contradictions between the emancipatory aims espoused in popular education discourse and the directions taken by state sanctioned educational policies. These contradictions, and the kind of compromises they typically entail for NGO's in their relationship to the state, prevail in contemporary democratic political economies as well under the clearly more repressive regimes. Funding agencies for NGO's in either context tends to exert social control pressures on the direction to be taken by adult literacy and other community-based education programs. This social control tendency, accompanied by frequent changes in funding criteria, is apparent in the typical arrangements where NGO's operating in more repressive regimes receive their funding from outside sources. Funding stakeholders from outside might find repressive regimes distasteful, but this does not mean they support a counter-hegemonic pedagogical discourse that envisages the overthrow of such regimes which are often supported within the larger design of the United States foreign policy. From this larger context, the World Bank and the International Monetary Fund have been influential in the diversion of funds away from popular education initiatives through their demands for restructuring within the less stable political economies regardless of whether or not they are governed by repressive regimes.

In both nondemocratic, or destabilized, regimes (where the personal risks for popular educators can be significant) as well as under relatively democratic conditions, some NGO's conceptualize popular education (most commonly in the form of adult literacy) as a means to exert pressure "from below" to (re) shape government policy in the interests of the less powerful. Many NGO's, however, work uncritically in line with official policies favoring existing relationships of power. Though the intensity of the political struggle and levels of success experienced by those NGO's which question state policies are variable, the case for characterizing their commitment as popular education is reasonable even where they fall short of Brecht's measure of what constitutes popular practice. The internationally funded literacy programs of the African National Congress during its struggles against the South African regime are examples of NGO educational initiatives in opposition to coercive state power. However, it is just a reasonable to dismiss any claims made by NGO's which support the status quo to identify their adult literacy programs with popular education. This assessment applies all the more as far as popular education in nondemocratic regimes is concerned. Adolfo Esquivel, the Argentinian Nobel Prize-winning poet, making a public speech in his country during the time of the military dictatorship clarifies the issue in the following terms:

> Liberation is directly related to education. . . . under an oligarchical system, with dominant classes, with no alternatives, popular education becomes an alternative. (Oliver, 1987, p. 42)

At the same time, it would be misleading to view popular education for the most part as a revolutionary strategy for the violent overthrow of the state. Well-organized guerrilla movements against oppressive regimes have often incorporated literacy education for the people into their campaigns (notable examples being in South Africa and Latin America during recent times and in China during the 1930's and 1940's). Further, popular education itself has often provided the spark for spontaneous resistance to repressive measures, leading to the formation of class conscious social movements. Even so, popular education tends to be more concerned with unearthing a quiet revolution from below through civic education about the way institutions and government work and political education on ways to influence them. The notion is that by liberating poor people from their "culture of silence," popular education develops a critical consciousness among the masses that will ultimately lead to an unraveling of the prevailing oppressive structures in society since they will no longer be taken for granted as part of the natural order of things. In this view, critical consciousness provides the impetus, or agency, toward social transformation.

Popular education, then, is a pedagogical process for enhancing the critical consciousness of the poor, the marginalized, and the lower classes everywhere who are preoccupied with the day-to-day struggles of survival and, understandably, seek relief, when they can, in recreational activities and in the closeness of their immediate relationships. Among themselves, they may find an outlet in complaining about their everyday living conditions and the unfairness of it all. Yet, from the critical understanding that informs popular education, there is a sense in which they themselves have come to believe that they are fated—even deserve—to live in poverty and can do little about it. The aim of popular education is to remove this fatalistic self-conception by enabling ordinary men and women to recognize the nature and extent of existing social arrangements which order the way they live. Thus popular education is intended to provide the pedagogical context from which a collective expression of a critical consciousness can emerge.

For oppressed people (and from the critical perspective of popular education, involuntary poverty is indicative of systemic violence against the poor), critical consciousness comes with the process of beginning to understand the real meaning of their existence. They begin to "read their world" and, for the first time, to apprehend how their status is accorded them by the prevailing unequal distribution of power. Popular education makes the connection between the unequal distribution of power and knowledge. In this regard, the critical pedagogical task is to legitimize the common sense knowledge already in the hands of the people, to demystify the knowledge that is in the hands of experts (along the lines of Illich's critique), and to facilitate new relevant learning experiences which are tied to collective and individual projects.

One pedagogical strategy for getting marginalized and oppressed groups to appreciate the authenticity of their already acquired stock of knowledge is through collective storytelling of past and present experiences. In this way people retrieve their sense of history and its continuity through their everyday lives. For those experiencing the process, this retrieval of history from below as the history of ordinary men and women narrated by ordinary men and women can be a significant source of empowerment. They begin to see themselves as primary agents in the making of their own history.

Accompanying this emphasis on the retrieval of peoples' history is a renewed focus on the learning of indigenous languages in cultures where they have been relegated, or deliberately suppressed, in favor of the dominant culture's language (typically, the language of the colonizer). Competence in the mother tongue, especially where it has been degraded or in danger of extinction, is also viewed as empowering in terms of the minority group's relationship to the dominant culture. This concern of popular education with mother tongue literacy refers us to what Ivan Illich calls "vernacular values" (Chapter 1) which can be (re)discovered in folk wisdom, literature, theater, poetry, and stories. And this (re)discovery is of critical importance. For as Judith Marshall (1991) in her essay on "The Elusive Art of NGO Literacy" has pointed out:

> Language is never merely a technical question. Language, power and voice are intimately related and tap into the deepest feelings of social identity. To speak or be denied a language has everything to do with one's sense of adequacy and power and space of operation in a given society. (p. 100)

For popular educators, the strategic and moral significance of these subjective reorientations around the recovery of peoples' history and of the mother tongue language are apparent. However, it should be understood that popular education also facilitates a process whereby people bring an objective stance to their critical analysis on the ways a Eurocentric worldview determines dominant forms of economic development, social policies, bureaucratic structures, and what constitutes acceptable behaviors. Within the context of popular education initiatives, community groups with a very low level of literacy are able to engage in a level of critical analysis to match that of university seminars once they grasp the need to investigate the conditions shaping everyday life from an objective as well as a subjective stance. What this means is that they are able to learn how, within the dominant culture, the social structures sustaining existing relationships of power are masked through control of the means of production, of the educational system, of the media, and of mass culture. Otherwise, without an objective stance that accompanies critical analysis, awareness of oppression stops short at sullen and dysfunctional feelings of resentment. Mired in resentment that is informed only by subjective understandings, oppressed people subscribe to what amounts to a conspiracy theory to account for the way things are arraigned against them and in the interests of a unified power elite. With critical analysis, on the other hand, they begin to see that the system is not monolithic, but rife with contradictions and contesting interests. A critical awareness of these contradictions and contestations within the superstructure of society reveals conditions in which there are possibilities for political intervention from below and, ultimately, for social transformation.

The national educational initiative undertaken in Tanzania shortly after it gained independence from Britain is instructive for us in this context because it linked popular education, the pedagogy of Paulo Freire, participatory research in education, and the commitment of the state. In Tanzania we have the typical example of a former colonial dependency desperately low on resources and struggling against the odds to develop an economic base and a democratic form of government with a measure of independence from the growing tide of exploitative neocolonialist hegemony in Africa. Under the leadership of President Nyerere, a consistent advocate from the outset for the education of adults as well as their children, popular education approaches were incorporated into state-supported adult literacy programs, economic development, health education, and community-based projects as part of building the new nation. These initiatives were intended to expand the number of organizations and people committed to new social relationships which prefigured the emergence of genuine participatory democracy. Given needed and reasonably expected economic, political, and moral support from its former colonial exploiters, Tanzania would undoubtedly be a sterling example of how education for the people can be a major force for building a democratic relatively prosperous society despite the destabilizing circumstances experienced by the region as a whole. Even so, the Tanzanian experiment demonstrates that popular education with state support can be linked to development while advancing aspirations toward genuine participatory democracy.

In the developed nations popular education approaches have been prominent in the women's movement, and in the struggles of aboriginal and other ethnic minority groups to claim their just rights. Popular education strategies are also evident in the political activities of labor and farm organizations, and in the formation of environmental, cooperative, and other public interest groups protesting against what they experience as the harmful effects of the prevailing relationships of power in today's society. Though the energies of these popular initiatives have been subdued by the neoconservative backlash which emerged with considerable force in the early 1980's and has continued into the 1990's, the critical current of progressive anti-hegemonic movements retains momentum at the century's end. Popular education still has a role to play in refocusing this momentum.

Paulo Freire: Raising Consciousness, Dialogue, Praxis

The pedagogy of Paulo Freire is widely recognized as the touchstone for popular education. When Adolfo Esquivel made his declaration in defiance of Argentina's ruling military junta linking popular education directly to liberation he was invoking a Freirean notion of critical pedagogy as the practice of freedom. In his best known work, *Pedagogy of the Oppressed* (1981), Freire presents his view of "education as the practice of freedom." (p. 69). In this view liberty is a practice which understands that this is not guaranteed by our present institutions and laws. For Freire "a truly liberating education" opposes that form of education which serves to integrate the young into the norms of the dominant ideology. He advocates a learning process in which men and women deal critically with reality and develop the capacity to participate meaningfully in the transformation of their world. Otherwise, for Freire "education as the exercise of domination stimulates the credulity of students, with the ideological intent (often not perceived by educators) of indoctrinating them to adapt to the world of oppression." (p. 65).

Paulo Freire was born in Recife, northeastern Brazil, in 1921. Though his parents were middle-class, the family situation was adversely affected by the economic crisis of 1929. His father lost his job during the depression, and Freire experienced directly some of the conditions of poverty that were the lot of most children in Recife at that time. Northeastern Brazil is one of Brazil's poorest regions, suffering from the usual problems of underdevelopment such as high rates of unemployment, subsistence level wages, pathetic housing conditions and health services, and widespread illiteracy. No doubt Freire's formative years in Recife had a significant bearing on his lifetime commitment to the poor which led to the development of his "pedagogy of the oppressed."

Although Freire was a practicing Christian and member of the Catholic Church, his work was very much influenced by Marx's analysis of class and ideology And unlike so many socialists of the academy who draw selectively on Marxism as a means for their analyses of objective conditions, Freire still saw relevance in the strategic aspects of its revolutionary project. Thus, Freire was able to recognize some merit in Lenin's thoughts on organization and in Che Guevara's guerrilla tactics (which included strong feelings of love for, and real communion with, the oppressed people he served). This political outlook, which finds expression in *Pedagogy of the Oppressed* but tends to be down-played in much of the Freirean discourse that takes place in the United States, is a development of his involvement with the Catholic Action Movement while an undergraduate student. The Catholic Action Movement was formed to focus attention on the social conditions that were responsible for ongoing hunger and entrenched poverty in regions like northeast Brazil. Freire remained aligned with liberation theology that traces its beginnings to the Catholic Action Movement and which, in the face of official disapproval from the Vatican, receives much of its impetus from the political work of priests who organize against repressive regimes. Liberation theology, very much in evidence among social action groups in Latin America, acknowledges that the Catholic Church has historically played a significant role in supporting colonization and the oppression of aboriginal people.

Freire's pedagogy, then, is informed by an understanding of how centuries of oppression under colonial powers (in Brazil, it was the Portuguese) have been succeeded by a neocolonialism supported by international corporations and the state and favoring the interests of elite groups. Under neocolonialism a privileged minority control most of the land, industrial production, the culture and, hence, the political structure. Meanwhile, the majority experience in relative silence the widespread poverty that comes with the unequal distribution of wealth, political power, and knowledge. In the years since *Pedagogy of the Oppressed* was published the gap between the rich and poor has widened in South and Central America and throughout the world. The Pope publicly deplores this state of affairs and questions the system which sustains them. Could Freire be wrong?

Freire was trained in law at the University of Recife, but soon gave up aspirations to be a lawyer. His early career as an educator, which included experience as a secondary school teacher and work with the rural and industrial poor around Recife, began during the 1940's. He came to understand the significance of adult literacy and popular education and, after a few years studying and teaching the history and philosophy of education at the University of Recife, accepted the directorship of an adult education program sponsored by a newly elected progressive city administration. While in this post Freire completed work on his doctoral dissertation setting out his ideas on the philosophy of adult education. Subsequently, he was appointed professor of the History and Philosophy of Education at the University of Recife.

Freire's reputation for developing successful adult education programs, along with his academic credentials, led to his appointment in 1963 as the head of the National Literacy Program of the Brazilian

Ministry of Education and Culture. This post led to his imprisonment (for over 70 days) and exile in 1964 after the military junta took over in Brazil. Freire then spent a number of years on a UNESCO appointment in Chile working in the area of agrarian reform and adult education. He also helped with national literacy efforts in other South and Central American countries. A period spent teaching in the United States as a consultant at Harvard University was followed by his appointment as special consultant to the Office of Education of the World Council of Churches in Geneva. He continued to influence national literacy initiatives in such countries as Mexico, Nicaragua, and Tanzania. *Pedagogy of the Oppressed* was written while he was working with the World Council. Adult educators and community development workers throughout the world were becoming aware of the significance of Freire's work. In 1988 Freire became secretary of education for Latin America's largest city, Sao Paulo. Had Luis Inacio da Silva, Freire's political ally and a workers' leader, managed to win the 1989 elections—the first popular elections to be held in Brazil in almost 30 years—Freire would undoubtedly have become the nation's minister of education. Da Salva was very close to winning.

Presenting this brief, and somewhat incomplete, summary of the relevant events in Freire's career is in line with his philosophy of consciousness (discernible in *Pedadagogy of the Oppressed* as a phenomenology of education) which attributes a major role to the agency of the individual in effecting personal and social transformation. Thus, while the need for collective action is a central tenet of Freire's pedagogy, it is the emphasis he also attaches to the significance individual initiatives for effecting social transformation that distinguishes Freire's theory and practice from that of orthodox Marxism. With regard to the realization of political and social transformation, conventional Marxist analysis tends to privilege the significance of objective historical conditions and collective action over subjective experience and individual initiative. This distinction pervades Marxist analysis even while it is clear about the dialectical relationship between objective conditions and subjective experience and, by the same token, between individual expression and collective action.

Freire's inclination to move his career between the academy and community-based practice with illiterate people is instructive for popular education. The suggestion here is that the separation of conception from action, of the doer from the thinker, is fallacious. Theory and practice are interconnected. Practice without the kind of careful reflection and conceptual thought which universities traditionally have been able to foster becomes mere activism. From a Freirean perspective, critical reflection is to be engendered in our everyday lives beyond the walls of the academy, the universities are also viewed as contexts for developing concrete projects of action of relevance for the community at large.

Many advocates of popular education drawing on Freire's pedagogy of the oppressed for inspiration are concerned to divorce their practice as much as possible from the activities of the formal educational system. In this regard, they tend to be influenced by the visions of a deschooled society. Yet it is evident that Freire himself has carried out much of his work within the institutional framework of state-sponsored education which he has consistently criticized. Is there too a stark contradiction here between what Freire espoused and what (and where) he practiced? Or do our formal educational systems constitute a relevant context for popular education? This question will be addressed again later in the chapter.

For many adult educators Freire's pedagogy is about consciousness raising. The term coined to describe this concept in the English-speaking world is *conscientization* which is intended to be the equivalent of the Portuguese *conscientizaçao* used by Freire in his studies on *The Pedagogy of the Oppressed* and *Education for Critical Consciousness* (1973). Conscientization describes the movement from naive or primary consciousness toward critical consciousness. Freire quotes from George Hegel's major study on the *Phenomenolgy of the Mind*:

> The awakening of critical consciousness leads the way to the expression of social discontents precisely because these discontents are real components of an oppressive situation. (Freire, 1981, p. 20)

Prior to conscientization, "fear of freedom, of which its possessor is not necessarily aware, makes him see ghosts." (Freire, p. 20). This disabling tendency disappears as individuals begin to see themselves as the subjects rather than the objects of their everyday experience. The newly acquired sense of personal autonomy can be engaged in the transformation of social reality.

The transition to critical consciousness entails the development of capacities to "read the world" and to "find the voice" for expressing aspirations, joyfulness, and discontents. Adult literacy for the majority of poor and dispossessed people is concerned with breaking the "culture of silence" which keeps them marginalized without a critical understanding of what oppresses them, and relatively incapacitated. The capacity for self-expression has a great deal to do with empowerment in a society where access to linguistic competence is differentially accessible in accordance with prevailing class, race, and gender divisions. In this regard, it is important for literacy education not to be caught up merely with the reading and writing—the reproduction—of the dominant culture's worldview.

Thus conscientization through adult literacy and various popular education initiatives is brought about in part through decoding (recognizing, describing, and analyzing) the signs, symbols, and texts that represent this worldview as the way things should be because that is simply the way they are. Decoding, if successful, leads to a critical perception of concrete reality which was previously obscured. It is a process of demystification in which ordinary men and women begin to understand their conditions not as fated and unalterable. Although these conditions are limiting, they are also seen as amenable to change. A critical awareness emerges of the obstacles to development—their causes and consequences, of the relationship between economic, political, and social arrangements, and of both the empowering and inhibiting effects of cultural norms. Conscientization implies an emancipatory goal in which the oppressed move on from critical awareness to defining the directions of their own development.

For conscientization to happen educators have to dispense entirely with what Freire refers to as the "banking concept of education." According to this still prevalent approach to disseminating information, the educational process is largely "an act of depositing in which students are depositories and the teacher is the depositor." (Freire, 1981, p. 58). This common practice is patronizing in that, at best, it views "knowledge [as] a gift bestowed by those who consider themselves knowledgeable upon those whom they consider to know nothing." (Freire, 1981, p. 58). From the students' standpoint education is something that is done to them rather than something they do. Miles Horton, the founder of Highlander Folkschool and a good friend of Freire, provided the antidote for those educators whose practice is still conditioned by their preoccupation with the banking approach. For Horton, "the people, no matter how poor or untutored, would know what they wanted to learn provided that [the educator] could only learn to listen to them and translate what he heard into an educational program." (Adams, 1975, p. 24). The beginnings of consciousness raising comes with teachers asking the people what they want, because they will tell us.

Freire's pedagogy exemplifies the dialogical process. It is the practice of dialogue for which the theoretical grounds are to be found in the work of Jurgen Habermas on communicative action (Chapter 4). Like Habermas, Freire places emphasis on the essentially communicative nature of human beings. In this view, without dialogue there can be no meaningful communication, and in the absence of communication there is no authentic education. Dialogue joins people in a purposeful attempt to reach a common understanding about their shared reality with a view to changing it for mutual benefit. It is an essentially cooperative, democratic undertaking. In contrast to conventional teaching strategies which stifle critical reflection and, at the same time, maintain an objectifying distance between the teacher and students, dialogue requires thoughtful participation and commitment, by the educator in the first instance, to the humanization of the teacher/student relationship. The knowledge brought to the relationship by the student merits the same careful consideration as that of the teacher. Though the latter retains vocational responsibility for the overall organization of the learning context (dialogue is more structured than free-wheeling discussion), in dialogue the teacher also learns and the student also teaches. There is an expectation that students will have a say in determining the course of events in the learning context and in shaping the curriculum.

Dialogue in terms of Freirean pedagogy is often facilitated through the formation of culture circles. Within the context of culture circles participants select themes of relevance to them from which to carry out dialogical explorations of their immediate reality. In this way they begin to understand—"to read"—their world in different ways and to create new knowledge together. The cultural themes are drawn from the everyday life experience of members of the culture and may be introduced by the teacher as generative ideas. However, the educator's identification of a cultural theme ahead of time does not preclude its modification or replacement by one thought by participants to be more relevant to their situation. It is through thematic investigations (similar to that described in the section on the structures of relevance in Chapter 6) that dialogic education develops.

Since Freire's pedagogy calls for a problem-posing approach, there is no intention that a generative theme identified beforehand by the educator will necessarily steer the process. The pedagogical orientation toward problem-posing rather than the assertion of recipes and predetermined objectives helps to foster the critical and emancipatory intent of dialogue. Along with the educator, learners become co-investigators—making knowledge together. For the most part, then, didactic lecturing is viewed as antidialogical because of the way it structures the relationship between educator and students and between students and students, steering the dissemination of information authoritatively from the top down. In a classroom setting where dialogue is preferred, the unilateral authority of educator as lecturer is absent, presenting the opportunity, and ultimately the responsibility, for students to participate actively in the creation of their learning environment. From a Freirean perspective dialogue cannot exist where any form of domination asserts itself. By the same token antidialogue is viewed as essential for maintaining a state of domination.

Although, for Freire, engagement in critical thought is essential to dialogue, he also insists that dialogue is an act of love, of faith in the capacity of ordinary men and women to make and remake the world for the better without recourse to the manipulation of others. Thus, it is only possible to dialogue where one is not fearful of being usurped or preoccupied with maintaining one's self-sufficiency. Along with the rational dimension of dialogue as emancipatory pedagogy, Freire also attributes a great deal to its spiritual, moral, and revolutionary aims. In dialogue the participants are engaging in a process that prefigures the cooperative relationships and genuine participatory democratic arrangements of a transformed society.

So dialogue is more than careful discussion, conversation, or debate. The critical reflection dialogue entails is also action. Reflection (understanding of reality) and action (the transformation of reality) come together in dialogue as praxis. Without action, reflection leads to verbalism and without reflection action is reduced to mere activism. By the same token, theory and practice are not separate entities represented in the typical academic discourse about putting theory into practice. Praxis as the union of thought and action eradicates the notion that certain members of society are thinkers while the masses are "doers."

An important insight that emerges from Freire's pedagogy is that education cannot be neutral. It is inevitably politicized. Where educators refrain from critical discourse and claim that their teaching practices are beyond the fray of politics, they are still political agents in that their posture of nonengagement serves to legitimate the existing relationships of power. This realization does not mean that educators who opt for an emancipatory praxis of education should not always exercise prudence (there is, as previously noted, a strong moral dimension to Freire's pedagogy) in bringing their political commitments to bear on the learning process. Propaganda is antithetical to dialogue and any notion of an emancipatory praxis of education. In the course of dialogue as conceived in Freirean terms, it immediately becomes clear that education is not a neutral entity free from the effects of various interest groups and separate from political contestations.

Emancipatory pedagogical praxis is clearly opposed to the deployment of primers and instructional packages that steer the learning process from the start. The mechanical application of such materials into adult literacy education, for example, undermines the processes of critical interpretation and of gaining voice that are integral to dialogue within the culture circles that are characteristic of Freirean pedagogy. This opposition to prescribed texts and curriculum formats does not extend to the inclusion of materials (newspaper articles, extracts from reports, summaries of news reports, passages from books, and so on) that are relevantly selected in the light of emerging themes. It is important that these materials are identified within a problem-posing framework and directly related to the topic at hand. Contrary to the view of many teachers in the formal education system who have become accustomed to using standard primers and curriculum guides, there is an overabundance of information and creatives ideas for those who take the care to look. The Freirean approach to adult literacy education entails the use of pictures depicting typical scenes from the everyday reality of participants. In critical reflection on these graphic representations and drawings depicting their own concrete experience, students begin acquiring the words to describe their reality. A popular enhancement of this pedagogical strategy is for learners to produce their own educational materials, in this way emphasizing from the outset that in emancipatory praxis students are the producers of their education rather than passive consumers of disseminated information.

In his book *Pedagogy in Process: The Letters to Guinea-Bissau* (1978), Freire gives us a conception of his pedagogical praxis for a newly independent African nation. Freire was invited by the new leadership in Guinea-Bissau to help with the establishment of a national literacy program. From these published letters we see that Freire was anxious to ensure that his presence would be welcome. It is clear that he did not intend to be cast in the typical interventionist role of the expert educational consultant from outside. The literacy program was envisaged as a continuation of the literacy efforts that had been carried out for some time before independence in territories liberated from Portuguese colonial administration by the guerrilla forces of the PAIGC (African Party for the Independence of Guinea and Cape Verde Islands). These literacy efforts, influenced by Freire's pedagogy, had been carried out by guerrillas and party members in the field as part of the liberation movement. By the time Freire arrived in Guinea-Bissau, which gained its independence following the 1974 coup in Portugal itself, the literacy project had already become part of a strategy for national reconstruction.

Taken together the published letters outline Freire's concept of emancipatory education, dwelling on the significance of culture circles, facilitators, consciousness raising, dialogue, and praxis. The advice he offers is accompanied by a sense of humility. Yet he was direct in his criticism of the government's decision to retain Portuguese as the official language of the new nation and, hence, of the school system. While Portuguese was his own mother tongue, and one which he taught in schools and to adults, Freire insisted that it was necessary to relegate the former oppressor's language for the new nation to claim its new identity and a new consciousness.

In opting to retain Portuguese the new government had to take into account that there were several African language groups within its jurisdiction representing competing claims for recognition as a national language. Freire argued that retaining the language of the former oppressor meant that the people would not be able to break away from the Eurocentric worldview that it embodied. Freire did not prevail, and there is no doubt that the retention of Portuguese as the official language is tied to the reproduction of former relationships of power which favor urban elites and landowners at the expense of urban workers, the unemployed underclass, and the rural peasantry. The challenge for Freire's emancipatory praxis of education remains in the African nations that have shed the yoke of colonialism as well as in all other regions of the world at this century's end.

Participatory Research

Drawing much of its inspiration from the work of Paulo Freire, participatory research is very much in vogue among university-based adult educators as well as with popular educators. Although its origins and current practice are still largely associated with Third World contexts, participatory research is increasingly invoked in accounts of community-based housing projects in the poorer neighborhoods of developed countries. In contrast to the prevailing paradigm in social science research, the participatory researcher dispenses with the role of the researcher as detached observer of other peoples' activities. Instead, participatory researchers acknowledge that they are part of, and have an influence on, the project at hand. Their role is not to bring to bear their own predetermined definition of the problem to be investigated. Rather the task of participatory researchers is to help facilitate an investigative process in which the problem to be acted upon is clearly defined through the collective decision making of all those who have a relevant stake in the overall project.

Typically the overall project in developed countries has to do with a community development initiative (North America, Europe, Australasia) around such issues as housing projects for the poor, health and sanitation, and social justice initiatives to advance the interests of aboriginal people and other racial minorities, and of women and children. Ideally, participatory researchers are part of the community or, if from the outside, only offer their services at the invitation of the larger community. The notion is that the research findings and the means by which they are disseminated, through conventional reports, verbal presentations, photographs, videotape productions and a variety of artistic representations (including drama productions), are at the disposal of the community. At the same time, it is understood that the purpose of the project, via the identification of a specific problem to be addressed within the community, is to effect some substantial change as well as to create new knowledge for the better. Thus, participatory research is purposeful and political. It is intended to engender action-oriented community-based endeavors in which the participatory researchers are identified with the interests of the people from the outset. The people, then, are the subjects of their own investigations rather than the objects of conventional research observations undertaken by outside experts.

To a large extent participatory research is viewed as an adult education research process. It is motivated by a belief that educational research should be identified and directed by ordinary men and women for their own benefit rather than to serve the professionalized and bureaucratic agendas of research institutions and government departments. Accordingly, the knowledge gained from participatory research is not intended for agencies outside of the community in which it is generated. Consequently, participatory researchers from outside of the community are most likely to assume a role akin to that of process facilitator (*animateur*) rather than that normally associated with the notion of researcher. Above all, participatory researchers from outside have to achieve a trusting relationship with the community where the project is to take place. The people have to believe that the primary commitment of the participatory researcher concerning the project is to the community's interests, not to some outside agency.

Though it has some marked similarities with action anthropology which developed earlier (Tax, 1964, 1969) in a North American context, participatory research stems largely from the work of a group of village development researchers in Tanzania who had become dissatisfied with conventional social science research methods. Contravening the usual claims about the need for objectivity and neutrality in research design, and for researchers to establish distance between themselves and the "objects" of their research, these activist researchers insisted that the villagers themselves should be active in the design of any investigative initiatives to identify their developmental needs. Thus, research aimed at improving the conditions of poorer communities could no longer claim to be value free if it was to meet the interests of poor people, and researchers could not be uncommitted to the furtherance of these interests. Subsequently, articles by adult educator Budd Hall (1975, 1977) who had spent several years working in Tanzania made the case for participatory research to a wider audience of educational researchers and popular educators, and community development activists.

The Participatory Research Network was formed in 1976 as a program of the International Council for Adult Education (ICAE). Twelve years later, a double issue of ICAE's journal, *Convergence* (XXI, 2 &3, 1988) was devoted entirely to papers on participatory research. *Convergence*, along with other educational publications, featured articles on participatory research in the years before and since the appearance of this double issue proclaiming a new approach for adult education research. The basic principles of the approach echo those of Freirean pedagogy and popular education. These are based on a recognition that ordinary men and women have the capacity to name their own reality, and to become co-investigators in seeking solutions to the problems that beset them in their everyday lives. The investigative process is viewed as collective, dialogical, educative, and emancipatory. Expertise, whether from within the community or brought in from outside, does not direct procedures, but is incorporated to the project at hand according to collective decision making. New knowledge, which should be of immediate and direct benefit, is produced and existing official (certificated or otherwise legitimated) knowledge, typically a monopoly of experts and the elites they represent, is assessed in terms of its use value and reframed to serve the interests of the community. Participatory research openly acknowledges its ideological implications which are formed by an alignment to the interests of the lower classes—to "the oppressed" (Freire), to "the wretched of the earth" (Fanon), to "the victims" (Ryan, 1976) of prevailing relationships of power in today's society.

An instructive example of a participatory research approach in North American context that now represents a more widespread view on how community development should be conducted is provided in an article published a decade ago entitled "Collective Wisdom: Participatory Research and Canada's Native People." (Castellano, 1986). The article recalls how social service agencies in Canada had long since identified the kind of serious malfunctioning of family life in Native communities that also characterizes the experience of aboriginal people, under various forms of neocolonialist governance, in other industrialized and developing countries. Observations concerning the pathologies in Native family life had also been confirmed in conventional social science research which connected the growing incidence of child neglect in with the rapid erosion of traditional community sustaining activities. There is an absence of adequate preparation for dealing with the invasive imperatives of modern life in what were once child-caring Native communities. Consequently, these communities are being increasingly overburdened with dysfunctional families.

The alienating conditions in Native communities referred to by Castellano have been aggravated over the years by inept government policies the harmful effects of which have yet to be healed. Chief among these misguided policies was the practice which took the major part of at least one generation of Native children away from their parents and placed them in residential schools outside of their communities. These residential school children have all reached adulthood, and the residential school policy for Native children has long since been abandoned. (In the decade since Castellano's article appeared, evidence of widespread sexual and other forms of abuse inflicted on Native children in these residential schools has been uncovered). Subsequently, the practice of placing Native children (many of whose parents had been enrolled in the residential schools) with non-Native foster parents has proved equally dysfunctional for the Native community and family life, and especially for the psychological development of young Native people who tend to experience more violence in their lives than is the case for non-Native children. In any event, by the 1980's these wrong-headed policies were recognized as such by Native leaders, educators, and many social service professionals.

In this particular Canadian participatory research case study, then, the author (a Mohawk Indian and professor of Native studies) described initiatives among some of Canada's Native people which address problems associated with child welfare and the deterioration of family life. Prior to these initiatives conventional agencies had not allowed the people themselves to take an active part in problem identification and in working together towards their own solutions. In fact the official forms of intervention, relying on outside expertise, was preventing the emergence of community healing processes which are now understood to be so essential and which, to an extent, are now under way. Paternalistic mediation strategies, though still prevalent, are now more open to question and local knowledge, particularly that of "the elders," who still have special and official status in Native communities is given precedence over that of outside expertise.

The developmental process which emerged in those communities where Native people took on direct responsibility to tackle the issue of family and child welfare is depicted as being guided by the participatory research principles, including the strictly service role of the researcher, outlined in preceding paragraphs. State employed social service personnel from outside the communities were required to be accountable according to locally identified needs. Through this process, different forms of community support and child care were identified. Young adults, including single parents, were the focus of health education using suitable adult education approaches (for example, study circles) carried out by people hired from within the community and competent volunteers from the adult population. Recourse to, and a renewed respect for, the knowledge of the elders assumes particular significance in reconnecting the people with their history in which the care and love of children has been central to the culture. Clearly the challenge is ongoing for Native Canadian communities, as it is for aboriginal people elsewhere in the world.

Although there is a sense of hope for the future among many of these communities, the incidence of child neglect and of violence in the lives of so many young Native people is a matter of grave concern. The situation is compounded by a very high rate of unemployment, welfare dependency, and the imprisonment of young people. At the present time, frustration at the continuation of these circumstances and the prevalence of unequal power relationships between Native communities and the state apparatus is finding expression in the public demands by many of their leaders for aboriginal ("First Nations") sovereignty. At the same time, there are signs among the larger population of serious misunderstandings of the basis for, even a backlash against, Native demands for greater autonomy and just treatment. These developments would now merit careful attention in any participatory research initiatives emerging within Canada's Native communities.

There has been some debate, most notably within the context of academic adult education, about whether participatory research actually constitutes research. Academic critics of participatory research argue from the logical positivist standpoint that seeks to emulate what they see to be the scientific way—that of the natural sciences. In their view of what is proper research in education, the researcher as expert is objectively detached from the experience of the research subjects. The role of the educational researcher is to exercise as much control over research design, investigative procedures, and forms of dissemination as possible so as to ensure objectivity. This systematic approach is to apply even in the case of qualitative research which many educational researchers of the logical positive persuasion have come reluctantly to recognize in recent years as a way to bring more meaningfulness to educational research studies. Thus qualitative researchers have to establish methodological checks to account for their subjective involvement and construct definite categories in which to carry out and report their findings. What this amounts to is that qualitative studies in education that come within a logical positive framework constitute little more than "statistical research without the numbers."

Participatory research clearly does not fit into this logical positivist framework which is antithetical to any declared ideological commitment while blind to its own. Thus, a central principle of participatory research that its investigations must have use value in terms of looking at reality in order to change it is taken to task from a logical positivist standpoint. In keeping with its narrowly reductionist approach, logical positivistism insists that research investigations should be guided by no other aim than to add a definable increment to an already definable store of scientific knowledge. In scientific terms, the results of research are not to be assessed for their use value. (As noted in the critical commentaries on behaviorism in Chapter 6, it is a moot point as to whether logical positivist assumptions that its own methodology correspond to the natural sciences have much validity). The clearly stated aim of participatory research to produce new knowledge in the interests of the poor, and to transform the ways existing knowledge is constituted and made accessible, may be represented as community development, but it is not research (Griffith & Cristarella, 1978).

Even though criticisms of participatory research's claim to research status have some merit, they do not detract from arguments that in any investigations of human action, researchers should avoid imposing their predetermined research categories on groups of other people while reserving for themselves the role of detached scientific observer. And the logical positivist critics of participatory research could be providing a key insight they did not intend. For if the term *research* is not just accepted as artificially and narrowly determined according to logical positivist intent, it makes sense to view community development as a research process which can be assessed as to how well it is carried out.

A more telling critique of participatory research comes from a critical perspective that shares its moral and political commitments. Although participatory research projects are described as starting from the concrete reality of everyday experience, there is a sense in which they are overly idealistic. If logical positivism enthrones objectivity and the need for generalizability, participatory research privileges the subjective and the immediate. In this regard, the discourse on participatory research gives insufficient weight to the effects that wider objective historical conditions have on shaping the everyday lives of people in their communities. Accordingly, there is a tendency for participatory research to exaggerate the potential of community members to bring about immediate and substantial change in their everyday lives. Further, while its most careful advocates are uncomfortably aware of the contradictions entailed, participatory research discourse has not been able to provide adequate clarification of the participatory researcher's role in relationship to the community. This circumstance may be understandable in light of participatory research's inclination to favor spontaneous action from below and its aversion to anything that smacks of vanguard initiatives.

It is reasonable to ask how does the participatory research process get under way—providing the pedagogical context for consciousness raising—in the absence of some form of mediation which introduces know-how not immediately accessible to the community? At some juncture the agency of the researcher is significant. (Otherwise, why the need for signifying participatory research as a specific course of action to be adopted in the first place?) Further, having acknowledged the need to clarify the role of the participatory researcher, a distinction between the role of the outside expert (at some time it might prove useful, for example, to have a lawyer at the community's disposal) and that of the intellectual from within the community should be made.

University-based academics committed to the principles expressed in participatory research discourse, in particular, are faced with a dilemma in deciding on an appropriate role to adopt in what is for them an outside community. How to be invited in the first place rather than inviting oneself? And subsequently, how to play an unobtrusive role, putting aside career interests and being just at the service of a community to which they do not belong and which will somehow ascertain the relevance or otherwise of their experience for a project yet to emerge? Clearly, those of us from the academy who share the same commitments called for in participatory research are not that circumspect about bringing our experience to bear with relevant initiatives in community development efforts where our presence is welcomed. The same is true for those who have actually defined their work as participatory research. The participatory researcher's role either as *animateur*, or as *catalyst*, or as *facilitator* entails agency, mediation, and the possession of know-how not readily available to the community with whom the developmental process is being carried out.

However, as with popular education and Freirean pedagogy, participatory research stands the risk of becoming the means for manipulating people to take on the researcher's agenda which is presented under the guise of affording participation. This kind of manipulation often accompanies the best of intentions and does not necessarily entail a cynically motivated scheme for getting a community to cooperate in the deployment of an already determined plan of action. As far as the involvement of academics is concerned, participatory research has inevitably become commodified—coinage within a written academic discourse which buys promotion and tenure. This tendency toward the commodification of participatory research has come about not from opportunism on the part of academics, but from an overdetermination of the concept as a new method of adult education research, an eventuality for which they do bear some responsibility. Yet, though participatory research is now commodified and overly determined as a method of research, the ethical and political commitments it espouses are still as relevant as ever. Participatory research, promoted largely as a discourse among academic adult educators and activist intellectuals, is community development (the logical positivist critics are right on this) in the interests of, and undertaken with, the poor; that is, as part of the ongoing popular struggle against the unequal distribution of power and resources.

Relocating Participatory Praxis

The tendency with the overall discourse on popular education, Freirean pedagogy, and participatory research has been to favor community-based settings over conventional institutions as strategic locations for emancipatory educational and developmental initiatives. This privileging of community-based settings corresponds with the deschooling ethos examined in Chapter 1. In this regard, the dependency on formal institutions, outside expertise, and agency funding (especially where government agencies are concerned) is viewed as problematic—a circumstance that has to be rationalized. Outside support may be necessary, but it represents a compromise of community-based autonomy. Thus, the discourse on participatory praxis appears to distance itself as much as possible from the economic and political concerns of significant institutions, virtually embracing its status as a marginal activity for emancipatory social change within the larger society.

The position taken here is that our formal institutions present far more significant locations for participatory practices, exemplified in popular education strategies, Freirean pedagogy, and participatory research than has been realized at this time. With the ongoing cutbacks in publicly funded education and other social services more benefits are likely to be gained in terms of supporting social justice issues and endeavors to reduce the effects of the prevailing inequalities of power and knowledge if participatory praxis became more focused within our formal institutions. There are, of course, already instances of popular initiatives within formal institutions that, to some degree, go against the grain even in these times by resisting unjust practices and promoting greater equity. The existence of these initiatives within our schools, colleges, various publicly funded agencies, and our workplaces in general is indicative of the present relevance of institutional settings for the development of participatory praxis. Its relative absence from formal institutions and workplaces coincides with the substantial retrenchment in education and social services and with the top-down restructuring of conventional workplaces that has occurred during the past two decades.

The kind of participatory praxis described in this chapter has maintained its connections with the system even while its discourse privileges community settings outside of formal institutions and invokes a deschooling society ideology. And these connections are not only maintained for the purpose of community development funding and specialized agency support. The proponents of participatory praxis tend to have career affiliations with formal institutions. This is true of Paulo Freire himself and many of the advocates for participatory research. These critical observations are not intended to suggest that within participatory praxis discourse the maintenance of connections between conventional institutions and initiatives in community-based settings is inappropriate. Rather, the contention here is that proponents of participatory praxis, in particular those affiliated with formal institutions, would better serve the interests of ordinary men and women with which they identify if they relocated significant attention to the prospects for emancipatory struggle within our institutions. In this view, the popular movements, especially in Africa, Asia, and Latin America, still remain a central driving force in the struggles toward social justice. Yet, there is a critical task now to take the discourse on popular movements, through participatory praxis, more emphatically into our schools, colleges, and conventional workplaces.

Participatory Strategies

With the critical turn to formal institutions as strategic locations for participatory praxis, the focus of social activists among academics, educators in general, and public service workers is effectively changed. We have to attend, first and foremost, to what is going on within our own institutions in regard to issues around the distribution of power and social justice. In paying attention to normative practices, especially our own, within our workplace settings, we become clearer in the first instance about what we can learn from popular movements and community-based initiatives with a view to the democratic transformation of our institutions. At the same time we come to identify strategies for establishing relevant connections with outside communities, and for making the institutions more accessible to ordinary men, women, and children. When working with communities outside our organizations, we should be clear and confident about the kind of expertise and institutional support we are bringing to the project.

The situation of university-based academic adult educators who advocate the principles of popular education, Freirean pedagogy, and participatory research is a case in point. (Though what follows here applies to the situation of other activist academics and educators). As adult educators they quite rightly feel compelled to be involved in off-campus projects. (How else could they reasonably expect to teach about the practice of adult education?) And as advocates for participatory praxis they also tend to be preoccupied with how they ought to be relating to popular community-based initiatives. This preoccupation is very apparent in the largely academicized discourse on participatory research where the proper role of the researcher receives so much attention. Thus for the academic committed to the principles of participatory praxis there is at presence a crisis of relevance. How to practice what is advocated. How to work with community-based groups on their terms and without imposing academically received thinking on emerging projects. These are, as we have noted, important considerations, but the crisis of relevance among academics inclined toward participatory praxis leads them to seek their legitimation as activists from acceptance by popular movements and community-based activists.

The problem of relevance for the activist academic (a long-standing one for the intellectual involved with popular movements) undoubtedly has to do with a (guilty) sense of the privilege and relative security of being part of a well-resourced institution. The moral dilemma for the individual can be resolved, and has been in many instances, by abandoning the security of institutional affiliation and taking up completely with the popular movement. This is not necessary, or even desirable, from a standpoint that views our institutional settings as strategic locations for participatory praxis. A way into this praxis from an institutional setting is be to bring activists from the popular movements and ordinary men and women from marginalized groups into classrooms and conventional work settings. They too learn from the critical exchanges that ensue. It is no more helpful to idealize the experience of popular movement activists and members of marginalized groups (a marked tendency among many middle-class radical intellectuals) than it is to enthrone the knowledge of academics and other institutionally based experts.

To a significant extent the discourse on popular education, Freirean pedagogy, and participatory research place too much of a burden on the agency of the individual and on the collective agency of the oppressed in their communities to effect social transformation. This tendency is traceable in the philosophical underpinnings of Freire's work from which, as we have indicated in this chapter, popular education and participatory research draw critical insights. Freire's philosophy of learning is informed by a phenomenological orientation (a philosophy of consciousness) which places emphasis on the individual's experiencing of his or her world through purposive action. In contrast to the behaviorist standpoint, our consciousness of the world is formed subjectively through *intentional* awareness. Hence the central importance to phenomenology of the concept of *intentionality*. This concept, most notably elaborated in the philosophical investigations of Edmund Husserl, is traceable to Descartes fundamental insight on human experience—*cogito ergo sum* ("I think; therefore, I am"). Although Freire himself never adequately theorized his view of the learning process in terms of the philosophy of consciousness which underlies it, his considerable emphasis on the capacity of the individual to structure his or her world—on the agency of the individual—is evident in discourses on education which invoke his work.

The overburdening of the potential of the individual, and marginalized groups, is most apparent in the way the terms *consciousness raising* and *empowerment* (both attributable to the influence of Freire's work) have become regular coinage in mainstream educational discourse as well as that of popular education. Within the curriculum of mainstream educational discourse these terms have been effectively psychologized, in a way that is quite antithetical to Freire's project, to denote pedagogical interventions along behavioristic lines for fixing the deficiencies of the individualized learner. In fairness, Freire does make it abundantly clear in his writings that objective historical conditions impose limits on the capacity of both the individual and marginalized collectives to transform reality. And we should understand from our reading of Freire that men and women can, to some extent, work to effect change in the circumstances which nevertheless operate to shape who we are and the way we experience our everyday world.

Thus, there is a dialectical relationship between being acted upon by the world (objective reality) and our acting upon the world (human agency). The latter has been overemphasized at the expense of the former in educational discourse that draws from Freire's work. Part of the reason for this overemphasis on the potential of human agency to understand and change our world is that Freire did not formally address the gap which exists between the philosophy of consciousness that underlies his view of the learning process and a critical analysis of how prevailing relationships of power keep oppressed people in a naive state of consciousness. The enthronement of individual agency in Freire's pedagogy leads us to underestimate the effects of those social norms and institutional arrangements which are systematically reproduced and account for why we take the way things are, or appear to be, so much for granted. It is this critical understanding of how prevailing systemic, largely institutionalized, arrangements shape consciousness and determine our everyday lives which prompts the claim that participatory praxis should focus more on our conventional institutions.

A decade after Marlene Castellano (1986) published her account of the participatory research initiatives in Native Canadian communities, Canada's First Nations' people still experience the lowest incomes, the shortest life expectancy, and the highest rate of incarceration in the country. The evidence is that they are worse off than they were a decade ago. (Sutter, 1996). Contrary to a widespread misconception, reinforced by much publicized accounts of outstanding land-claim settlements and Native self-government agreements, the incomes of registered Natives living on reserves has declined. In view of these circumstances and an understanding that a very high percentage of Canadians believe that Native people have themselves to blame for their problems, popular initiatives emerging within the conventional representative institutions of Native institutions are moving the leadership into making more substantial political demands. Within the provincial federations of Indian Nations and the national Assembly of First Nations, there is now serious debate about sovereignty.

The effects of these recent political initiatives from what are conventional institutions representing Native people are only just beginning to work themselves out. However, it is already clear that the national government will respond by making more substantial political and economic concessions to aboriginal people than hitherto. In the meantime, the heightened political discourse developing within Native representative institutions serves an educative purpose for aboriginal people and the population at large. And, we hope, the kind of community-based efforts described by Marlene Castellano, which to date have been unable to turn around living conditions for Canada's Native people, will gain more impetus and wider support.

In his account of the *lifeworld* and *system world*, Jurgen Habermas (see Chapter 4) provides us with a useful way of looking at the relevant connections between community-based experience and institutional activities. The lifeworld, simply expressed, refers us to the practical projects, feelings, and attitudes that make up our everyday life. It is the source of central values and of the commitments that emerge in community. Thus, the lifeworld constitutes that vital sphere of human experience where continuity of custom and tradition is sustained, where respect and loyalty for community is privileged, and from where a sense of belonging and security is derived. It is these aspects of everyday life, so vital to our well-being that are increasingly taken over by the technical rational imperatives of the *system world* which is guided by the criteria of efficiency. Habermas refers to this tendency as the *colonization of the lifeworld*. Ivan Illich, deriving a metaphor from the custom that emerged in medieval England to allocate tracts of land for the common use of ordinary men and women, defines this same tendency as the *erosion of the commons*. The *commons* stands for those vital aspects of community life that are undermined by the inappropriate deployment of technology and the imposition of bureaucratic regulation.

Like the preeminent liberal sociologist Max Weber (1958), Illich sees the decline of the lifeworld before the drive for efficiency and growing restrictive bureaucratic regulation as an inevitable outcome of modernity. In this view, the strategies and structures of the system world steer and shape the lifeworld. Overall efficiency and technological development occur at the expense of autonomous lifeworld interests. It is not just superstition and blind faith that are undermined. Nothing is sacred, except perhaps the cult of efficiency and, under capitalism today, the ideology of competitiveness. Max Weber's social theory is resigned to the imperatives of the system world which restricts autonomous lifeworld experience, including the expression of human emotional, aesthetic, and spiritual needs, within the confines of what he refers to as the "iron cage." (Oddly, the Chinese Communist Party uses the same metaphor—a bird in a cage—to juxtapose the urge for

Participatory Strategies

free expression with the need for disciplined conduct. No doubt the liberal cage is intended to be somewhat larger.) Illich advocates turning our backs on the conventional institutions where the effects of system world are most deeply embedded. Ultimately, his brilliant polemics against modernity, as we noted in Chapter 1, turn us to a romantic vision of the medieval village.

While his analysis attests to the continuing momentum of system world imperatives over lifeworld interests, Habermas accepts neither the pessimistic rationale for Weber's "iron cage" view of modernity nor the romanticized escapism of Illich's polemics. The system world can be breached by lifeworld interests. Thus, within our conventional institutions (our schools, colleges, and places of employment) which best exemplify the deployment of system world imperatives in the quest for efficiency, greater productivity, and higher profits, there are reasonable prospects for emancipatory discourse. And such a discourse does not take it for granted that the instrumental rationality upholding the institution's aims should be automatically accorded priority. Bureaucratic institutional aims should neither steer the discourse nor necessarily avoid critical review along with other relevant concerns. In this way, the system comes under the purview of lifeworld considerations. Though we are referring here to the kind of initiatives within institutional settings which are typically, though not always, oppositional to official policy and normative regulation, they are sufficient to form the basis of a participatory praxis. This potential, as we have conveyed in Chapter 3, exists even within prisons which epitomize the systematic deployment of efficient control and surveillance over the everyday life activities of human beings.

Clearly, there is not a straightforward correspondence between the system world and conventional institutions on the one hand and traditional community-based settings on the other. Apart from the fact that our notions of conventionally structured institutions and community-based relationships overlap (take our concepts of the family, for example), system world imperatives and lifeworld experience are discernible in both settings. Accordingly, it is important to view participatory praxis as a two-way process furthering the emancipatory interests (on behalf of social justice) in our modern institutions and in our community-based contexts. The latter refers to those enduring, though often beleaguered, community associations, values, and practices that stem from loyalties which the figurehead of neoconservative ideology, Mrs Thatcher, claimed no longer existed except in the form of the nuclear family as handmaiden for the larger political economy. Yet in this two-way process between our key conventional institutions, with all the resources, expertise and legitimation at their disposal and traditional community-based settings, it is time to focus on the former as the critical location for participatory praxis. For educators and social service workers committed to vision of a more just society this means fostering a critical dialogue, incorporating fellow workers, students, and clients, aimed at transforming their own practices and the institutions where they work. The critical discourse envisaged here is one that endeavors to draw in popular education initiatives, the pedagogical approaches exemplified in the work of Paulo Freire, and the views advanced by participatory research on what constitutes knowledge for the people.

Chapter 8

INTERNATIONALIST PEDAGOGY

> Anybody who has experienced the agony of negative equity will know how the heavily indebted countries of the developing world feel. Keeping up with the interest payments is like running through treacle, a soul-destroying and seemingly endless process that redistributes money from the have-nots to the haves. (Larry Elliott)

> As the political leaders of the most powerful industrial countries trumpeted a new crusade against terrorism last week they privately acknowledged a growing threat from extremist dissident groups. (*Guardian Weekly*, July, 1996)

The critical discourse on popular education, Freirean pedagogy, and participatory research described in the preceding chapter is international in scope, and the participatory praxis it prefigures also needs to be understood within the present international context, as an internationalist pedagogy.

A Small World After All

Popular images of the *global village* and *spaceship earth* stemming from the works of such futuristic thinkers as Marshall Mcluhan (1989) and Buckminster Fuller (1969) have been with us for some time. These images convey an understanding that the lives of different peoples of the world and the affairs of nations are becoming increasingly interconnected. Our everyday lives, just like the formulation of government policies are not unaffected by what is going on in other parts of the world. There is a growing sense of humankind's shared destiny on *spaceship earth*. Though far from sufficient, this understanding that we are all in it together gains momentum throughout the world. A concern for cooperative initiatives on a global scale is prevalent within educational and political discourses despite ongoing outbreaks of atavistic tribal hostilities, racial disharmony, and wasteful competition between nations.

The dismantling of the Berlin Wall in 1989 turned what had been a powerful worldwide symbol for the *concrete* separation between nation states into a dynamic vision of a freer flow of people and resources across existing borders. To invoke yet another influential image, the *Iron Curtain* (Winston Churchill's term to describe the stark division between the regions of the Soviet Empire on the one side and the post–World War II western alliance led by the United States on the other) has been raised from the world stage. The Cold War between these two massive power blocs is now seemingly at an end even though Russia, contrary to widespread expectations in the West after the collapse of the USSR, still has to be reckoned with as a major power in the world.

The growing sense of humanity's shared destiny within a global village and the end of Cold War politics, however, appears to have done little to decrease the levels of brutal violence, xenophobia, power struggles among nations, and entrenched inequalities throughout the world. Yet the effects from developments in the format and operative speed of communications technology (conceived in terms of the advance from primitive transportation to jet planes and from the earliest aboriginal means of conveying messages to the Internet) lead to an intelligent awareness that mutual understanding and cooperation is integral to the well-being of the planet. For improvements in communications technology, as well as providing a stimulus for increased productivity and improvements in the distribution of goods and services, also give rise to social problems.

Technological advances can be viewed from a critical perspective as further colonization of the lifeworld by system world imperatives to the extent that they give rise to the disruption of peoples' everyday lives, widespread alienation, and the depletion of natural resources. The critical reference here is to the way technology is deployed in the absence of popular democratic input into the form it should take and the manner of its deployment. In any event, the cutting edge of technological advance—communications—has afforded people wider access to information about world conditions. In terms of global survival, and sooner rather than later, we must concede that the doomsayers do have a point; it is now clear that the problems confronting humanity as a whole are very compelling. It is a small world after all.

It has become virtually commonplace among critical observers of global development to comment, and often on a resigned or cynical note, that international corporate monopolies have most of the advantages to be gained from modern communications media that cut across national boundaries and carry commercial messages to the remotest of communities. No doubt the major corporations, along with the governments of nation states, are way ahead of other interest groups (for example, organized labor and popular movements for social change) in the global context given their ability to transfer funds and make strategic decisions at electronic speed about production (effecting levels of [un]employment and wages), the acquisition and distribution of resources, and marketing.

The clear-cut advantage that corporate business holds over organized nonprofit motivated groups representing the interests of ordinary men and women in a global context is no new phenomenon. What is cause for renewed concern is the extent to which international business corporations are now even more advantageously placed than ever to exploit their advantage. Where national and international policies do not correspond with the global interests of big business, major corporations are increasingly in a position to ignore the authority of national states, the governments of which, in any case, are permeated by power-brokering on behalf of big business. In any event, the influence exerted over the directions of technology development, especially communications technology, and the manner of its deployment has much to do with the global strategic advantages possessed by international business corporate interests.

While there is much substance to the claims that the influence of multinational corporations in global affairs is expanding beyond the restraining capacities of even national governments, it would be overly pessimistic, erroneous in fact, to regard corporate power as monolithic. No doubt international corporations manage to exert enormous influence on national governments, but they are not yet in a position to openly flaunt specified state policy (legislation), especially where governments are in agreement. The association for economic cooperation comprising the United States, Germany, Japan, France, the United Kingdom, Canada, and Italy (the "G7") is very powerful in this regard. In other words, despite the prevalence of successful initiatives to reduce government initiatives that might for almost any reason curb prospects for greater profits and investment, it is too soon to assert that international corporate power has gained complete ascendancy over the authority of the state. To varying degrees, then, the potential still exists for ordinary men and women to influence government policy through collective action that can check, even ultimately supersede, the present momentum of international corporate power.

As for the control by big business over the means and form of global communications (thus, over the medium and the message), this tendency is mitigated by the fact ordinary men, women, and children have access to the media in their roles as employees, consumers, students, and voters. The purposes of business and government would not be served by excluding people entirely from the messages that are conveyed via communications technology. If the much vaunted electronic "information highway" encircling the global village is being built according to the specifications of international business interests, it has been opened up for general use. There is, then, the potential, however small at this juncture, for it to be diverted, reconstructed or deconstructed in ways other than those determined by international corporations.

In the 1950's Dwight Eisenhower, president of the United States and former general, warned us about what he had come to view as the over-arching influence of the "military-industrial complex" on world affairs. His understanding of the symbiotic relationship between the maintenance of military might and industrial productivity could be applied to the situation prevailing across state-capitalist command economies (the USSR, its satellites, the Peoples' Republic of China), the various forms of democracies and dictatorships in the world as well as the United States. Even in the wake of the momentous geopolitical events that signaled an end to Cold War, there can be little doubt that the "military-industrial complex" is still pervasive in shaping global destiny. Yet the military-industrial complex is not securely embedded within the global village. Big business and big armies are made up of people. And people are amenable to learning about alternative future prospects for the way we are on planet earth other than those sanctified by the unrelenting quest for profits and territorial hegemony. This chapter addresses some of the ways educators can help sustain a necessary pedagogical discourse on the destiny of a small planet.

Internationalist Perspectives

Suggesting that educators should view themselves as internationalists is not intended to imply that as individuals or as an organized political force we are in a position to launch radical social transformation on a global scale. Yet teachers of children and adults should, and can, be at the fore of major initiatives fostering individual development and larger social movements which are in quest of the kind of vital changes identified in this chapter. Many educators are already part of such initiatives, of course, and there is a sense in that this kind of commitment entails the adoption of an educator's role even where those involved do not define themselves as educators. An internationalist perspective has moral and political import. It implies an undertaking on the part of educators to embrace their role as members of a world community and to incorporate this understanding into their teaching practices.

In this view, educators are obliged to be informed of world events, whatever our particular "teaching discipline," and to think through the implications of these events for our own immediate communities and everyday working contexts. It is part of our role as educators to resist seeing ourselves, our workplaces, and our communities as insulated from world events. In this regard, it is not enough to rely just on the daily television and radio news sound bites between breakfast or supper and teeth-brushing time. How many educators take the necessary time to read from among the dwindling number of newspapers and news journals which are still mindful about serious reporting and critical commentary? Too few.

Critical dialogue among educators and their students about the coverage of international events by news media can be very instructive. The adoption of an informed critical attitude toward even those publications and broadcasts which have earned a reputation for serious reporting and good journalism means paying attention to format, significant absences, and political ideology as well as content. There is also a critical pedagogical task for educators to take on the high circulation popular press (characterized by the British tabloids and the supermarket weeklies and dailies in North America) for its moral and political irresponsibility, amounting to cynicism, which deliberately panders to prejudice, ignorance, and pornographic inclinations. This task has been neglected for too long because educators understandably wish to avoid being branded as "moralistic" and "politically correct." It takes nerve in today's conventional educational settings to engender a critical discourse which identifies mindless pap as such when it is popular, highly profitable, and passes as news. Yet the fostering of a critical dialogue around the quality of reporting, the political power and moral influence of the media has become even more of an imperative in view of the mounting power of the press barons and technological advances which can place the messages of electronic communications (namely, the Internet) beyond all forms of censorship, including that of parental guidance.

The assumption here is that educators recognize their capacity, and that of their students, to make careful judgments about what constitutes serious reporting and good journalism. Journalists for their part are not loath to pass judgment on the performance of teachers and the quality of education. Schooling, and education in general, is newsworthy. What is needed in this regard is more dialogue between journalists and teachers. Ironically, educators and other intellectuals in authoritarian regimes of the world have less of a problem in identifying, where they are so inclined, the propagandist biases of their countrys' news media. Fortunately, since the end of the Cold War, few of these regimes are still effective at blocking out all news from the outside. Countries like North Korea, for example, being one of the few exceptions at this time, are likely to experience increasing difficulties in preventing noncensored messages from crossing their borders.

The capacity to assess media reports on world events calls for a sense of the impact major historical developments are having on today's global society. Among recent historically significant developments an internationist pedagogy should take into account is the replacement of the former European empires (decolonization) by new forms of geopolitical dependency (neocolonialism), the end of the Cold War and the Gulf War, the industrialization of developing countries and the radical restructuring of the conventional workplace in advanced political economies, the emergence of postwar (World War II) feminism and an increasingly internationally oriented youth culture, and the diminishment of kinship and community ties. All of these more or less interconnected developments have significant implications for pedagogical practice and social learning processes. Educators who are oblivious to these developments and believe they can close their minds and classrooms to the consequences of larger world events are practicing self-deception. The very terms of their employment, the curriculum foisted on them, and the structure of their work environment will alter without them knowing what has hit them. They will never have given themselves a chance to participate critically in the significant decisions affecting their vocational practice.

An internationalist perspective can be readily incorporated into all areas of formal education. These locations encompass, in addition to the classrooms of our schools, colleges, and universities where conventional disciplines are taught, adult literacy classes, continuing professional education, and community-based education initiatives. The pedagogical challenge is to incorporate an internationalist perspective without treating it as a mere add-on to a class but as part of an ongoing dialogical process. Thus any mechanistic tendency to deal with an understanding that an internationalist perspective is required by adding just another unit to the formal curriculum, and dealing with it in isolation from other issues, should be avoided. The reference here is to the kind of positivistic curriculum strategy that treats multicultural education, for example, as simply academic content to be covered for course credit. This approach to curriculum development shortchanges those important moral and political concerns about the issues at stake which can only be adequately addressed through an integrative dialogical approach across many subjects. When it comes to developing an internationalist perspective, the teaching practices and the ongoing commitment of the teacher far outweigh any preconceived curriculum or programmatic texts. In this view educators should conceive of themselves as internationalists putting themselves into practice.

Travel abroad, of course, can enhance international understanding. Yet travel is not in itself a necessity for a person to develop and sustain an internationalist perspective. (The world renowned philosopher, Immanuel Kant, ventured scarcely more than a day's journey away from his hometown of Konigsberg during an entire lifetime.) Some people can travel abroad on a regular basis and yet remain narrowly provincial in their attitudes and profoundly ignorant of world affairs. Travel in this mode may even serve to reinforce entrenched biases, stereotypes, and overall misunderstandings. This is just as likely to be the experience for the frenetic globe-trotting academics and business executives (formal meetings in first class conditions interspersed with tightly scheduled trips to local tourist attractions) as for the pre-packaged sight-seeing of many tourists. In contrast there is the more meaningful experience of those travelers and visitors intent on taking part for a while in the everyday life of people in different lands and cultures. This calls for reasonably lengthy visits, a certain amount of risk-taking and, in the case of westerners traveling in developing countries, a willingness to lower expectations with regard to personal comforts.

With these reservations in mind, there is no doubt that travel can be viewed as a means to enhance international understanding. And from the perspective of an internationalist pedagogy, it would be relevant to place more emphasis at this time on supporting overseas exchange visits for young people, entailing work experience as well as play within another culture. Given the considerable educational benefits of overseas exchange visits for young people, somewhat less emphasis should be placed on the merits of globe-trotting for middle-aged executives, academics, politicians, and comfortably off retirees. The momentum for globe-trotting is already well under way. So is the movement of younger adults—as committed travelers rather than as consumer-oriented tourists—across international boundaries. In any event, the existence these days of a global youth culture, as remarkable in its way as that of the global corporate culture, constitutes a context for an internationalist pedagogy to advance its aims for global communications not entirely steered according to a business corporate ethos or by powerful national state agendas. The experience of a growing number of young travelers moving and living together across national boundaries adds an important dimension to internationalism.

It still makes sense to view organizationally supported travel (study tours, attendance at international conferences, and so on) as potentially beneficial for an educator's development as an internationalist. Yet a critical awareness of how this commitment to an international perspective can be sustained and expanded through access to modern communications technology (electronic mail at this time is becoming available to educators in developing as well economically developed countries) should obviate any compelling sense that keeping in touch with global events requires frequent globe-trotting. Indeed, to enlarge an internationalist perspective in education, it now suffices for us to act locally around issues that have worldwide significance, and to think, and to link, globally.

The Environment

"Think globally, act locally," has become a virtual rallying cry of community-based environmental initiatives in the developed countries of the west during the past two decades. While sensibly recognizing the threat to the very survival of the planet caused by widespread and escalating ecological degradation, the catchphrase holds out a hopeful prospect that an accumulation of voluntary conservationist initiatives at the local level will coalesce to give us a global solution.

Since the early 1970's, then, concern over environmental issues has become very pervasive among the middle and upper classes of western developed nations. Conservationist discourse is very much part of school curriculum. Even elementary school children talk ominously about "the hole in the ozone layer" and of the effects of pollution on the air we breathe, on our rivers and oceans, on our cities and countryside, and on the survival chances of wild animals and plant life. The prevalence of manageable conservationist projects initiated by

Internationalist Pedagogy

schools is testimony to how teachers are attempting to inculcate a sense among children that although the problem of environmental degradation is very serious and part of their everyday lives, they themselves can do something about it. Thus, the pedagogical task is envisaged as the engendering of a relevant critique, taking into account the maturity level of students, which does not impart a disabling sense of despair.

However, this conservationist discourse represents a "green ideology" still largely confined to the middle and upper classes of western developed nations. By and large those who are struggling for basic needs in the so-called economically deprived regions of the world, and the underclass of ethnic minorities and welfare recipients in general, understandably do not register environmental issues as a major priority. Their concerns are much more immediate and the politicians who need their support, or acquiescence, understand these priorities. So with regard to the growing preoccupation with environmental issues, there is some justified resentment in developing countries to the pressure coming from developed nations which can more readily afford conservationist measures. There is, as well, a critical sense that developed countries—as former colonial and now neocolonial powers—bear much of the responsibility for the kind of modernizing tendencies that have led to environmental degradation in the newly developing and still underdeveloped regions of the world.

Even in the wealthier developed nations of the west there is a clear-cut trend, in terms of realpolitik, to place the interests of economic development and profit-making well before those of ecological concerns. Thus, the rhetoric of "sustainable development" (the notion that economic needs can be satisfied at a reasonable level without imposing further ecological damage and a continuing drain on nonrenewable resources) does not yet contain the political force to place the immediacy of the environmental concerns before that of the profit motive. So far, environmentally sensitive decisions that are made in favor of a "sustainable development" approach tend to be localized and cosmetic rather than global in their effects. So, for example, computer scanning can be deployed by the forest industry to ensure that a local community's immediate and narrowly defined view of the trees can be left relatively intact while the surrounding woodlands are devastated. Herein lies a typical corporate commitment to sustainable development: a gesture to "green" aesthetics and sensibilities, the suggestion that some of a rapidly diminishing number of jobs in an increasingly mechanized industry will be available (on a temporary basis) to the community, and a good expectation of quick profits.

There is a saying in the North of England, the earliest among the heavily industrialized regions of the modern era, that "where there's muck, there's brass [money]." The discourse on sustainable development as a global concern can learn from the forthrightness, if not the provincialism of this statement. There needs to be a more widespread understanding of the tie between economic development and environmental degradation which can be relevantly fostered within the context of an internationalist pedagogy. In developed countries, and among the middle and upper classes in general, a critical dialogue needs to be engendered around the additional moral and political responsibilities that attach to power, privilege, and relative wealth with regard to the problem of environmental degradation. The growing interest in environmentally sensitive ecotourism is indicative that the market has cottoned on to the value of the environment itself as a "clean product" (where there's no muck, there's brass), but the contribution of ecotourism to a pedagogical discourse concerned with the survival of the planet is insubstantial.

Perhaps more significant are the educational programs in our schools that encourage young people, in particular, to plant trees, clean up neighborhoods, recycle salvageable waste, and pay more attention to the needs of plant and animal life. Yet meaningful environmental education at this juncture calls for a curriculum, incorporating an internationalist perspective, that pays critical attention to how moral, political, and economic forces shape our ecological destiny. The task for educators in this regard is to draw attention to moral, political, and economic factors affecting the environment in a manner that is appropriate to the maturity level of their students.

Environmental degradation resulting from human action can be viewed as a form of violence against the planet. It is to the even broader issue of violence and its relevance as a central theme for internationalist pedagogy that we now turn.

Unraveling the Motif of Violence

The global village is beset with violence. It is a motif which few can ignore as the end of the most violent century in human history approaches. The evidence is substantial enough: the effects of modernized warfare on a global scale, systematic genocide, and the escalating incidence of torture are the extreme examples of "man's inhumanity to man" in these times. Within our communities and at the individual level we experience a rise in the incidence of violent crimes which are increasingly perpetrated by organized gangs. Even within modern prisons, the epitome of institutionalized control, gangs are formed and are as effective as they are on our streets in fulfilling their credo of violence, inflicting bodily harm on nonmembers. Further, as the century comes to a close we are anticipating that wanton acts of terrorism by disaffected individuals as well as sectarian political groups will escalate. But it is not just violence of human beings against one another which is on the increase. There is an alarming rise in self-inflicted violence, especially among young people, which signifies the extent of our inner turmoil.

These observations about the human tendency toward violence are not news to most of us. Apart from direct experience, the news media ply us with daily information (and they cannot possibly cover it all) on some of the major incidents of conflict throughout the world as well as within our local communities. We also continue to enjoy portrayals of violence in one form or another as entertainment. Whatever else we might say about humanity, there is no doubt that we are a violent species. So with violence so ingrained into human experience and evidently gaining momentum as a means of human expression, what tack are concerned educators to take bearing in mind that the majority of men and women believe themselves to be opposed to violence and that educators are not ethically privileged in this regard?

In view of the immensity of the problems surrounding the incidence of violence in our everyday lives, the challenge for educational discourse is to avoid the path of useless moralizing on the one hand or the sense that there is little to be done except, as law-abiding citizens with a clear-cut stake in the preservation of reliable security measures, to call for more effective control and more clear-cut consequences in the way of punishment. Adding our support to militant demands for increasing the severity of punishment for convicted criminals (which, in any case, has not worked in terms of cutting down on the amount or brutality or criminal activity) serves only to reinforce the overall motif of violence in today's society.

An alternative approach among educators and social service workers at the local levels has been to undertake special initiatives that help those young people "at risk"—that is, those young adults largely from the underclass who are most likely to commit crimes. No doubt such programs, where they exist, can be helpful to some individuals but they scarcely serve to mitigate the overall crisis around the growing violence in modern society and, from a critical perspective, must be viewed as patronizing at best. There is another way for us to begin a serious and hopeful dialogue around the seemingly overwhelming problem of violence in our times. An educational discourse on violence needs to be grounded first of all in an acceptance that as educators we should first look to the violence in ourselves.

Observing the ways in which we ourselves are violent, carefully but without passing judgment, leads us to a better understanding of ourselves and the nature of violence in our communities, institutions, and the world at large. The possibility of an end to violence lies first of all in the recognition that we are violent and that the violence we experience from outside of ourselves mirrors the turmoil within. The generation of this discourse of self-recognition and acceptance of violence within ourselves, which means neither condoning violence nor preaching nonviolence, constitutes a *careful* educative experience which in itself is the antithesis of violence. Clearly, we are not restricting our notion of violence here to the infliction of bodily harm. For we are violent in our tendencies to secure our own position at the expense of others, in our urge to compete, in our feelings of envy and resentment toward others, in our expressions of sarcasm, in our carelessness and failure to attend to the needs of others, and so on. Are not these human tendencies the seeds of those more brutal expressions of violence which have marked the 20th century above all others?

A staunch (self-)determination to become nonviolent—a proclaimed antiviolence stance—is not what is meant here. That way is a form of self-inflicted violence in itself. So is the observation of violence in ourselves which is accompanied by an intent to pass judgment. Rather with careful self-observation comes recognition, understanding, and a transformed way of being in the world. This transformation is educative and pervasive. For if violence is very much part of human experience, so are love, and generosity, and caring relationships. And as careful attention to the ways we experience the world, in particular our relationships with others, leads to generous impulses, so the space for violence dwindles.

This change in the way we view the incidence of violence in our lives, and the obvious options for respectful interactions with one another, does not mean that we should be careless about taking reasonable steps to intervene directly in the prevention of abuse. For example, an adult who witnesses a child being bullied and fails to intervene is being willfully neglectful, which in itself is a form of violence. By the same token, we should not willingly acquiesce when people take advantage of us. Yet at this critical juncture, while leading politicians are making far from reassuring declarations on the world stage about their resolve to fight crime and terrorism, the basic task for educators is to foster a dialogue on violence that begins with a resolve to look closely at the violence within ourselves.

At another level, and taking into account a broader view of the motif of violence which ecompasses more than the direct infliction of bodily harm, a critical task for an internationalist pedagogy in these times is to engender dialogue around connection between the obsession with competition and the incidence of violence. In this critical dialogue educators need to provide a context in which we can observe more closely the interconnections between the push for instilling competitiveness on the one hand and the reinforcement of tendencies toward self-centered individualism, aggression, greed, envy, and resentment on the other. Clearly, we are suggesting a critical alternative here to the discourse which is currently flooding our schools, colleges, and workplaces about the necessity for us to be competitive in order to survive in the global economy. Too little attention is being paid in this discourse to the fact that there are inevitably a lot of losers and to how they react to their position in the competitive stakes. The ideological rhetoric asserting that the gains of the winners—the economic spoils—will "trickle-down" to benefit the losers, though still prevalent, has proved false.

Even for those of us who have participated more or less successfully in competitive sports and continue to enjoy them as a spectacle, it can be instructive to observe how they are increasingly connected to the legitimation of self-absorbed individualism, exploitation, a nationalistic fervor that represents nationalism as a force still to be feared, and various other forms of aggressive behaviors. For clear-cut evidence we have only to check with recent major international sporting events—the Olympic Games and the World Cup Soccer Competition. The same tendencies are also observable in school and college sports programs. Although these observations should not be taken as a call to oppose competitive sports—a futile as well as a threatening and undesirable gesture—the time has come to examine critically the social effects that come from the extent to which competitive sports have been elevated, especially within our schools and colleges. The consequences may well become apparent in the emergence of more convivial forms of healthy and skillful exercise that are not driven by the notion that "when it comes down to it, winning is everything."

The preoccupation with competitiveness is central to the ideology of advanced capitalism which an internationalist pedagogy needs to examine on a continuing basis to uncover how it privileges some social groups and regions of the world at the expense of developing nations and the majority of men, women, and children in our "global village." According to the 1996 United Nations Human Development Report, if present trends continue the widening gap between the developed and the underdeveloped nations will move from inequitable to inhuman (Sutel, 1996.) This conclusion is largely derived from the study's assessment of life expectancy, education, and purchasing power. In the developing world 86 countries are now worse off economically than they were 10 or more years ago. Of the world's richest nations, only three (Canada, Finland, and Iceland) are worse off than they were a decade ago. And all three rank highly in the national league. (According to the study Canada, a member of the privileged G7 group of nations still enjoys the best quality of life.) About a quarter of the world's population have been left behind and are worse off than they were 15 years ago. The poor of the global village get poorer while the policies of organizations like the G7, the International Monetary Fund (IMF) and the World Bank favor the interests of the richer (creditor) nations and international business. From the perspective of an internationalist pedagogy, these tendencies are to be viewed within a nexus of exploitation which is beginning to draw in the terrorist activities of dissident political groups. The alarming message for the citizens of the richer nations at the century's end is that we can no longer be immune from the violent consequences attendant upon the massive inequalities in the distribution of wealth throughout the world.

In these circumstances the critical task of internationalist pedagogy is to educate people about how the leading nations are failing the world's poor. In the absence of a modest program of debt relief, Zambia spent 35 times as much on debt payment between 1990 and 1993 as it did on education (Elliott, 1996). The same source revealed that 12% of the IMF's $40 billion in gold reserves could wipe out the IMF debt of the world's 20 poorest countries. However, the IMF opts to maintain "an armlock on the debtor nations" (Elliott). The task of an internationalist pedagogy in this regard is to show why this armlock on the poorer nations has to be released in the interests of the entire world community. At this critical historical juncture the pressing necessity for a commitment to transfer resources to the poorest countries while lowering restrictions on immigration to the richer countries has to be more widely understood.

Even though their various contributions toward effecting world order with justice, prosperity, and happiness remain in doubt, international organizations are plentiful enough. Accordingly, an internationalist pedagogy does not need to burden itself with a concern for forming new organizations and formalized networks. The challenge of constituting a critical discourse which focuses on the global agendas of existing international organizations is sufficient. And this critical discourse needs to highlight encouraging initiatives as well as highlighting shortcomings. The United Nations, for example, still has a crucial role to play in formulating global agendas and, for all its limitations, does provide a context for illuminating and even providing some check on the expansionist aspirations of the superpowers. Thus, closer observation of the roles of the UN, of its potential as well as the pitfalls it encounters, serves a critical educative purpose in terms of an internationalist pedagogy. On the question of human rights, the UN has already confirmed that it is able to provide significant, even if still insufficient, support for indigenous people around the world in their struggle around land claims and language protection. The UN's involvement with indigenous groups in Guatemala is a notable example of this kind of support.

Contrary to the currently fashionable deconstructionist sensibilities of postmodernist analysis, which has exerted a considerable influence on critical pedagogy as well as social theory and literary criticism, internationalist pedagogy is guided by a critical insight that the potential for a participatory global democracy resides within the rational discourse of international organizations like the UN. In this view, it makes sense to engender a rational discourse that holds out hopeful prospects for a democratically conceived global agenda to address the crucial issues of our times. This is the larger purpose of an internationalist pedagogy.

Epilogue: The Educators Themselves Must Be Educated

The final chapter and the book in its entirety has been largely concerned with the necessity for us to acknowledge this imperative—that we must focus on the education of the educators—if we are to recover and reaffirm the status of educators. This entails an understanding that the role of educator encompasses moral and political dimensions as well as the need to be knowledgeable. In view of widespread cynicism about politicians in general, growing skepticism in many countries about the authority of church leaders, and substantial evidence that mainstream journalists are tending more toward entertainment than informed reporting, these are times for educators to take on more of a leadership role within their communities. This responsibility is there for community educators and public service workers as well as teachers.

With regard to school teaching, the entrance requirements to colleges of education are far too lax at the present time. Fairly rigorous and well publicized selection procedures (which should take into account other qualities in addition to academic achievement) would allow candidates to prepare themselves more thoroughly in advance. Candidates who are not immediately accepted should be notified of what they need to do prior to seeking admittance at a future date. As for teacher education programs, they need to become more intellectually demanding while cutting down drastically on the busy work of methods courses. Field-based internships, where teaching strategies can best be identified and refined, should be more central to a teacher preparation than is typically the case. The college courses provide the context for careful reflection (from sociological, psychological, historical, and other relevant perspectives) on what education students encounter during their field-based experience. Good teaching (should there be any other kind?) is very exacting. And so teacher education programs must become more demanding in terms of theory and practice than they are at present.

If there is a need to ensure that beginning teachers are sufficiently well educated for a vocation seeking to advance its status along the lines we have outlined, it is at least as important that they commit themselves to the development of their own continuing education in cooperation with other educators. In paying attention to their own continuing education, teachers exemplify what is meant by lifelong learning which, as noted in Chapter 6, has become so much a part of today's educational discourse. And in the discourse on the forms continuing education for teachers should take, it is well to bear in mind that being "practical" does not preclude being "intellectual." The two qualities are interconnected (teachers as intellectuals are practical), and this should be apparent in the way continuing education is developed.

The above observations also apply in kind to the preparation and continuing education of all public service workers who can be defined by the very nature of their vocational commitment as educators. This is a vocational commitment sustained by a conviction that, despite the pervasive end-of-century sense of global crisis, there still remain reasonable prospects for ordinary men and women to make this planet a wonderful place to live. Education is the key.

REFERENCES

Adams, Frank (with Myles Horton). (1975). *Unearthing Seeds of Fire: The Idea of Highlander*. Winston-Salem, NC: John F. Blair.
Adorno, Theodor. (1950). *The Authoritarian Personality*. New York: Harper.
Adorno, T., & Horkheimer, M. (1972). *Dialectic of Enlightenment* New York: Herder & Herder.
Apple, Michael. (1986). *Ideology and Curriculum*. New York: Routledge.
Associated Press. (1997). Torture Charge Has New York Back on Ropes. *The Star Phoenix,* August 16, p. B17.
Barron, Daniel. (1992). Information Power: the Restructured School Library for the Nineties. *Phi Delta Kappan*, vol. 73, no. 7, pp. 521–25.
Belanger, Paul. (1991). Adult Education in the Industrialized Countries. *Prospects*, vol. 21, no. 4, pp. 491–500.
Bergson, Henri. (1946). *The Creative Mind*. New York: The Philosophical Library.
Bowles, S., & Gintis. H. (1976). *Schooling in Capitalist America*. London: Routledge.
Bordieu, P., & Passeron, J. (1977). *Reproduction in Education, Society and Culture*. London: Sage.
Bronner, S., & Kellner, D. (Eds.). (1989). *Critical Theory and Society*. New York: Routledge.
Bruder, Isabelle. (1990). Restructuring: The Central Kitsap Example. *Electronic Learning*, vol. 10, no. 2, pp. 16–19.
Buffamanti, D. (1994). How We Will Learn in the Year 2000: Reengineering Schools for the High Performance Economy. *Journal of Industrial Teacher Education*, vol. 31, no. 4, pp. 87–95.
Carr, David. (1991). Living on One's Own Horizon: Cultural Institutions, School Libraries, and Lifelong Learning. *School Library and Media Quarterly*, vol. 9, no. 4, pp. 217–222.
Castellano, Marlene. (1986). Collective Wisdom: Participatory Research and Canada's Native People. *Convergence*, vol. xix, no. 3.
Chené, A., & Chervin, M. (1991). *Popular Education in Quebec.* Washington, DC: American Association for Adult Continuing Education.

Chomsky, Noam. (1965). *Aspects of the Theory of Syntax*. Cambridge, MA: MIT Press.
Chomsky, Noam. (1977). *Language & Responsibility*. New York: Pantheon.
Collins, R. (1979). *The Credential Society*. New York: Academic Press.
Cremin, Lawrence. (1961). *The Transformation of the Schools, Progressivism in American Education—1876-1957*. New York: Knopf.
Crick, Malcolm. (1976). *Explorations in Language & Meaning*. New York: Wiley.
Dahlberg, Lucy. (1990). Teaching for the Information Age. *Journal of Reading*, vol. 34, no. 1, pp. 12-18.
Dewey, John. (1957). *Nature and Human Conduct*. New York: Random House.
Dewey, John. (1960). *The Quest for Certainty*. New York: G. P. Putnams.
Dewey, John. (1977). Education vs. Trade Training: Dr. Dewey's Reply. *Curriculum Inquiry*, vol. 7, p. 37.
Draves, William. (1980). *The Free University: A Model for Lifelong Learning*. Chicago: Association Press.
Editorial (1997). *The New York Times*. August, 20, p. A20.
Elliott, Larry. (1996). Caught on the Horns of a Global Dilemma. *Guardian Weekly*, July 7, p. 13.
Fanon, Frantz. (1988). *The Wretched of the Earth*. New York: Grove Press.
Faure, Edgar, & Associates. (1973). *Learning to Be: The World of Education Today & Tomorrow*. Paris: UNESCO & Toronto: Ontario Institute for Studies in Education.
Foucault, Michel. (1977). *Discipline and Punish: The Birth of the Prison*. New York: Pantheon.
Foucault, Michel. (1980). *Power/Knowledge*. New York: Pantheon.
Freire, Paulo. (1981). *Pedagogy of the Oppressed*. New York: Continuum.
Freire, Paulo. (1973). *Education for Critical Consciousness*. New York: Seabury Press.
Freire, Paulo. (1978). *Pedagogy in Process: The Letters to Guinea-Bissau*. New York: Seabury Press.
Fromm, Eric. (1969). *Escape From Freedom*. New York: Avon.
Fuller, R. Buckminster. (1969). *Operating Manual for Spaceship Earth*. Carbondale, IL: Southern Illinois University Press.
Gelpi, Ettore. (1979). *A Future For Lifelong Education*, Vol. 2. Translated by R. Ruddock & others. Manchester, UK: Manchester Monographs.
Ghandi, M. K. (1969). *Rebuilding Our Villages*. Ahmedbad, India: Navajivan Press.
Goodman, Paul. (1969). *Paul Goodman on Education*. Berkeley, CA: Pacific Tape Library.
Gramsci, Antonio. (1971). *Selections from the Prison Notebooks*. New York: International Publishers.
Greenwich University. (1996). *Catalogue*. Hilo, Hawaii: Greenwich U. Press.
Gregson, Jonathan. (1995). New Relief for those Autumn Headaches. *University 95*. London: The Observer, August 20, p. 3.
Griffith, W., & Cristarella, M. (1978). Participatory Research: A New Method-

References

ology for Adult Educators? Vancouver, Canada: Dept. of Adult Education, University of British Columbia.
Grossi, Vio. (1981). Popular Education: Concept and Implications. *Convergence*, vol. xiv, no. 2, pp. 70–73.
Habermas, Jurgen. (1971). *Toward a Rational Society: Student Protest, Science, and Politics*. Boston: Beacon.
Habermas, Jurgen. (1984). *The Theory of Communicative Action*, Vol. 1. Translated by T. McCarthy. Boston: Beacon.
Habermas, Jurgen. (1987). *The Theory of Communicative Action, Vol. 2*. Translated by T. McCarthy. Boston: Beacon.
Habermas, Jurgen. (1985). Questions and Counter Questions. In R. J. Bernstein (Ed.), *Habermas and Modernity*. Cambridge, MA: MIT Press.
Halévy, Elie. (1956). *Thomas Hodgskin*. London: Ernest Benn.
Hall, Budd. (1975). Participatory Research: An Approach for Change. *Convergence*, no. 8, pp. 24–32.
Hall, Budd. (1977). Creating Knowledge: Breaking the Monopoly. *Working Paper No. 1*. Toronto: International Council for Adult Education.
Hancock, Vicki. (1995). Information Literacy for Lifelong Learning. *B.C. Business Education Association Journal*, vol. 7, no. 1, pp. 27–29.
Heath, Shirley. (1994). The Best of Both Worlds: Connecting Schools and Community Youth Organizations for All-Day, All-Year Learning. *Educational Administration Quarterly*, vol. 30, no. 3, pp. 278–300.
Heidegger, Martin. (1968). *What Is Called Thinking?* New York: Harper & Row.
Herrnstein, Richard, & Murray, Charles. (1994). *The Bell Curve: Intelligence and Class Structure in American Life*. New York: Free Press.
Hiatt, Diana. (1994). No Limit to the Possibilities: An Interview with Ralph Tyler, vol. 75, no. 10, pp. 786–789.
Hobsbawn, Eric. (1995). *Age of Extremes: The Short Twentieth Century*, 1914–1991. London: Abacus.
Holt, John. (1976). *How Children Fail*. New York: Delta.
Holt, John. (1977). *Instead of Education*. New York: Delta.
Husén, Torsten. (1974). *The Learning Society*. London: Methuen.
Illich, Ivan. (1970). *Deschooling Society*. New York: Harper.
Illich, Ivan. (1973). *Tools for Conviviality*. New York: Harper.
Interviewer. (1974). The Father of Behavioral Objectives Criticizes Them: An Interview with Ralph Tyler. *Phi Delta Kappan*, vol. 55, no. 1, pp. 55–57.
Jacoby, Russell, & Glauberman, Naomi (Eds.). (1995). *The Bell Curve Debate: History, Documents, Opinions*. New York: Random House.
Jalaluddin, A. K. (1990). Educational Applications of Computers for Lifelong Education. *Prospects*, vol. 20, no. 2, pp. 197–211.
James, William. (1950). *The Principles of Psychology,* Vol. 1. New York: Dover Publications.
James, William. (1971). *Essays in Radical Empiricism and a Pluralistic Universe*. New York: E. P. Dutton.

Kaufmann, Paula. (1992). Information Incompetence. *Library Journal*, vol. 17, no. 9, pp. 37–39.
King, Edmund. (1992). The Young Adult Frontier and the Perspective of Continuous Change. *Comparative Education*, vol. 28, no. 1, pp. 71–82.
Knowles, Malcolm. (1980). *The Modern Practice of Adult Education: From Pedagogy to Andragogy*. New York: Cambridge Books.
Knowles Malcolm. (1986). *Using Learning Contracts: Practical Approaches to Individualizing and Structuring Learning*. San Francisco: Jossey-Bass.
Knox, Alan. (1979). Enhancing Proficiencies of Continuing Educators. In Knox, A. (Ed.), *New Directions For Continuing Education, No. 1*. San Francisco: Jossey-Bass.
Kozol, Jonothon. (1968). *Death at an Early Age*. New York: Bantam.
Lindeman, Eduard. (1961). *The Meaning of Adult Education*. Montreal: Harvest Row.
Malikova, Z. A. & others. (1990). Pedagogical Science at the New Stage. *Soviet Education*, vol. 32, no. 3, pp. 57–70.
Marcuse, Herbert. (1966). *One Dimensional Man*. Boston: Beacon.
Marcuse, Herbert. (1969). *Essays on Liberation*. Boston: Beacon.
Marcuse, Herbert. (1978). *The Aesthetic Dimension*. Boston: Beacon.
Marshall, Judith. (1991). The Elusive Art of NGO Literacy: Some Issues and Reflections. *Convergence*, vol. xxiv, no. 12, pp. 93–104.
Marx, Karl. (1989). *A Contribution to the Critique of Political Economy*. Maurice Dobb, (Ed.). New York: International.
Marx, Karl. (1990). *The Economic & Philosophic Manuscripts of 1844*. Dirk Struik, (Ed.). New York: International.
Mason, Robb. (1992). Education and Change in Rural Areas in the 1990's: Chicken Little Was Not Wrong. *Education in Rural Australia*, vol. 2, no. 1, pp. 7–17.
McCarthy, T. (1985). Reflections on Rationalization in The Theory of Communicative Action. In R. J. Bernstein (Ed.), *Habermas & Modernity*. Cambridge, MA: MIT Press.
McLean B., & Milovanovic D. (1997). *Thinking Critically About Crime*. Vancouver British Columbia: Collective Press.
McLuhan, Marshall. (1967). *The Medium is the Message*. New York: Bantam.
McLuhan, Marshall. (1989). *The Global Village: Transformations in World Life and Media in the 21st Century*. New York: Oxford Univ. Press.
McTaggart, R., Singh, M. (1986). New Directions in Action Research. *Curriculum Perspectives*, vol. 6, no. 2, pp. 42–)6.
Nadler, Leornard. (1980a). The Field of Human Resource Development. In L. Nadler, (Ed.), *Corporate Human Resource Development: A Management Tool*. Madison, WI: American Society for Training and Development.
Nadler, Leornard. (1980b). What is Human Resource Development? In L. Nadler, (Ed.), *Corporate Human Resource Development*. ASTD.
Niemi, John. (1978–9). The Meaning of Lifelong Learning. *Yearbook of Adult Continuing Education*. Chicago: Marquis Academic Media.

References

Ohliger, John. (1974). Is Lifelong Education a Guarantee of Permanent Inadequacy? *Convergence*, vol. 7, no. 2, pp. 47–58.

Oliver, Leonard. (1987). Popular Education and Adult Civic Education: The Third World is a Different Place. *Convergence*, vol. xx, no. 1, pp. 40–50.

Ontario English Catholic Teachers Association. (1994). New Basics, Lifelong Learning, Student Employment, Technology & the Arts. *Reporter*, vol. 19, no. 3, pp. 6–9.

Oran, Gilda. (1993). Meeting the Challenge. *Preventing School Failure*, vol. 38, no. 1, pp. 5–6.

Ornstein, Allan. (1994). Curriculum Trends Revisited. *Peabody Journal of Education*, vol. 69, no. 4, pp. 4–20.

Ortega y Gasset, Jose. (1964). *What is Philosophy?* New York: W. W. Norton.

Parnell, Dale. (1978). *The Case for Competency-Based Education*. Bloomington, Indiana: Phi Delta Kappan Fastback, No. 118.

Popper, Karl. (1965). The Logic of Scientific Discovery. New York: Harper & Row.

Prajuli, Pramond. (1986). Grassroots Movements, Development Discourse, and Popular Education. *Convergence*, vol. xix, no. 2, pp. 29–39.

Ray, Boris. (1991). Technology and Restructuring Part 1: New Educational Directions. *Computing Teacher*, vol. 18, no. 6, pp. 9–16, 18–20.

Reimer, Everett. (1971). *School is Dead: Alternatives in Education*. New York: Doubleday.

Rensi, Edward. (1993). McDonald's CEO Discusses Education, Students, and Change. *High School Magazine*, vol. 1, no. 2, pp. 25–27.

Rinne, Risto. (1991). Learning to Unlearn: What Can We Expect from Education? *Life and Education in Finland*, no. 4, pp. 8–13.

Rogers, Carl. (1969). *Freedom to Learn*. Columbus, OH: Merrill.

Ryan, Kevin. (1978). An Interview with Lawrence A. Cremin. *Phi Delta Kappan*, October.

Ryan, William. (1976). *Blaming the Victim*. New York: Vintage.

Schutz, Alfred. (1970). *Reflections on the Problems of Relevance*. New Haven & London: Yale University Press.

Scott, Ted. (1991). Issues in Education in Remote Rural Australia. *Education in Rural Australia*, vol. 1, no. 1, pp. 7–11.

Sharratt, Gene, & others. (1992). Vocational Education in Rural America: Agenda for the 1990's. *Rural Educator*, vol. 14, no. 1, pp. 21–26.

Shipley, Carol. (1992). Empowering Children: Play-Based Curriculum for Lifelong Learning. Scarborough, Ontario: Nelson Canada.

Skinner, B. F. (1976). *About Behaviorism*. New York: Vintage Books.

Smith, Robert. (1982). *Learning How to Learn*. New York: Cambridge Books.

Spady, William. (1978). *Report on the United States Office of Education Invitational Workshop on Adult Competency Education*. Washington, DC,: U.S. Government Printing Office.

Staples, Brian. (1994). Life-Centred Schools . . . : Or What Would Our Schools Be Like if We Really Believed in the Concept of Lifelong Learning? *Learning*, vol. 6, no. 4, pp. 7–13.

Sutel, Seth. (1996). Canada Enjoys Best Quality of Life: UN. *The Star Phoenix*. Saskatoon, Canada: The Associated Press, July 16, p. C8.
Sutter, Trevor. (1996). Native Living Standard Worse than Ever. *The Star Phoenix*. Saskatoon, Canada: Associated Press, July 10, p. A8.
Tax, Sol. (1964). *Horizons of Anthropology*. Chicago: Aldine.
Tax, Sol. (1969). The People Versus the System—Dialogue in Urban Conflict. *Proceedings, Community Service Workshop*. Chicago: Acme Press.
Taylor, Frederick. (1967). *Scientific Management*. New York: W. W. Norton.
Terkel, Studs. (1975). *Working*. New York: Avon.
Thompson, E. P. (1984). *The Making of the English Working Class*. New York: Penguin Books.
Toepfer, Conrad. (1994). Vocational/Career/Occupational Education at the Middle Level: What is Appropriate for Young Adolescents? *Middle School Journal*, vol. 25, no. 3, pp. 59–65.
Tonegawa, Keiko. (1991). In Japan: Quest for Individuality and Flexibility. *School Administrator*, vol. 48, no. 6, pp. 27–29.
Turlington, Ralph. (1979). Good News from Florida: Our Minimum Competency Program is Working. *Phi Delta Kappan*, vol. 6, no. 9, May.
Tyler, Ralph. (1950). *Basic Principles of Curriculum and Instruction*. Chicago: University of Chicago Press.
Walker, Martin. (1991). Sentencing System Blights Land of the Free. *Guardian Weekly*, June 30, p. 10.
Watkins, Karen. (1989). Business and Industry. In S. Merriam & P. Cunningham, (Eds.), *Handbook of Adult and Continuing Education*. San Francisco: Jossey-Bass.
Weber, Max. (1958). *The Protestant Ethic and the Spirit of Capitalism*. New York: Scribner.
Whitehead, Alfred, N. (1929). *The Aims of Education and other Essays*. New York: Macmillan.
Wordsworth, William. (1904/1950). *The Poetical Works of William Wordsworth*. New edition by Ernest De Selincourt. London: Oxford University Press, p. 460.

INDEX

Aboriginal peoples, 147, 149, 167–68, 185; and participatory research, 157–60, 167; studies in, 36
Abuse, 159, 182. *See also* Violence
Academics, 49, 72, 75, 166; as globe-trotters, 177–78; and participatory research, 160, 162–163, 165
Access to education, 99, 129–36; admission policies, 133. *See also* Nontraditional education
Accountability, 41, 48, 50, 116
Accreditation, 132
Activism, 141, 150, 163, 165–66
Adams, F., 141, 152
Administrators, 34, 97, 116; competency-based education, 44, 48; and busywork, 85
Adorno, T., 65–67, 73
Adult and continuing education, 46, 110, 113; alternative approaches of, 131–32; and community schools, 134; competency-based education in, 42, 47; and employment, 84; as higher education, 39; and human resource development, 91–93; International Council on Adult Education, 158; and job skills, 53, 83, 86; as participatory praxis, 165; and participatory research, 157, 160, 163; popular education in, 139–42, 147, 149; and self-directed learning, 115; as social reproduction, 64; standardization of, 38, 41; and teachers and parents, ix, 135, 186; rationality in, 65; and voluntary learning, 137. *See also* Continuing professional education; Life-long education; Mandatory continuing education
Adult educators, role of, viii, 20–21; as activist intellectuals, 163; and dependencency on "how-to junk," v; deskilling of, 32; proficiencies for, 113; in universities, 156, 165; and work in prisons, 62
Adult literacy: emancipatory approach of, 144, 149, 151–52, 155, 176; as state supported, 45, 143, 147, *See also* Literacy education
Aesthetic dimension, 67, 74–75, 79, 129; restrictions on, 69, 73, 101, 168
African National Congress, 144
Agency: critical consciousness of, 145, 166; and dialectics, 167; at individual level 125, 150; of learners and teachers, 119, 124, 154; of participatory researcher, 162–63
Alienation, 95, 103, 105, 172
American Enterprise Institute, 122
Animateur, 157, 163
Apple, M., 64, 70
Associated Press, 56
Autonomy: and behaviorism, 116, 118; for community interests, 141, 143, 151, 163, 168; as creative experience, 67, 136; and Native peoples, 160; of teachers and students, 33, 47–48, 50–52, 54, 116; in work setting, 31, 81, 93

Barron, D., 112
Behaviorism: and competency-based education 41–45, 49; critique of, 116–25;

Behaviorism—*(continued)*
defined as ideology, 35–38; and intentionality, 166; as logical positivism, 161
Behavior modification, 60–61
Belanger, P., 113
Benjamin, W., 66, 68
Bergson, H., 46
Bordieu, P., 8
Bowles, S., 88
Brecht, B., 142–44
Bruder, I., 112
Budget cutbacks. *See* Cutbacks
Buffamenti, D., 112
Bush, G., 40, 57
Business and industry: competency-based education in 44, 47; as controlling influence, 20, 24, 59, 173–74; and downsizing against "labor," 93–94; involvement in education and training, 23–24, 40–41, 64–65, 86, 94–95, 99; and in global context, 97, 100, 173, 177–78; and information age, 101–2; postmodern critique of, 76. *See also* Corporate interests
Business-like education, 101–3. *See also* Training
Busyness syndrome, 47, 52–53, 83–85, 103, 186

Carr, D., 112
Castellano, M., 158–59, 167–68
Catholic Action Movement, 149
Censorship, 176
Certification, 106–7, 114, 132
Charter schools, 102, 134
Chené, A., 141
Chervin, M., 141
Child care, 82, 123; and neglect, 159
Chomsky, M., 119–20, 139
Church, Catholic, 7, 28, 30, 149, 185; and Freire, 148; Illich and, 8, 14, 22, 27, 75–76
Churchill, W., 172
Civil society, 74, 142; and civic responsibilities, 86; civil liberties in, 56
Class, 88, 130, 140, 148, 151; consciousness of, 144–45; as divisive, 103, 122; reproduction of, 64, 73 130–31. *See also* Underclass; Working class
Classrooms, 44–45, 74, 107, 135, 166; and influence of behaviorism, 34–35, 37; business shaping of, 40, 83–84, 89: in community schools, 134–35; and international perspectives, 176–77;
Clinton, W., 57
Cognitive style, 126, 128
Cold War, 172, 174, 176
Collective action, 72, 140–41, 145, 150, 174; in community development, 133–34; and interests in, 96,140; and participatory research, 156, 158; through storytelling, 145; and undermined by 4, 49
Colleges of Education, 50, 107–8, 135, 186
Collins, R., 88
Colonization, 149, 155–56; of language, 146; and lifeworld, 168, 172; as neocolonialism, 142, 147, 159, 176, 179
Commons, the, 10–11, 168
Communication(s), 69, 81, 88, 92, 153; in communicative action, 69, 127, 152; and communicative competence, 45, 61, 69–74, 127; effected by competency-based education, 48–49; as news media,173, 175; in prisons, 61; and communicative rationality, 69–70; as technology, 101, 130, 172–74, 178
Community, 20, 32, 63, 71, 168–69; and collective action, 82, 141, 151, 163, 165–66, 178; and community development, 27; 133–35, 139, 150, 156–58, 161–64, 168; participatory research education in, viii, 133, 135, 143, 146–47, 176, 185; hope for, 136, 159; and media support, 130; international influences on, 173, 175–76; and schools, 29, 113, 133–36; system world, 136, 169–70; violence in, 180–82
Competence, 14, 39–42, 87–88, 104–6, 137; and behaviorism, 120; in information technology, 112; and learning processes, 116; in mother tongue, 146, as competency-based education, 41–96, 119
Competitive ethos, 40, 94, 128, 172; as ideology, 133–34, 168; and violence of, 182–83
Computerization: effects of, 11, 38–39, 44, 120
Consciousness raising, 148–56, 162, 166–67. *See also* Critical pedagogy
Conservationism, 178–79

Index

Consumerism, 81, 84, 95, 104
Continuing professional education, 86, 106, 111, 176
Contradiction, 66, 68, 70, 88, 147; in participatory research, 162; and the state, 143
Conviviality, 49, 183. *See also* Illich
Cooperation, 81, 134, 147, 153–54, 172
Corporate interests, 32, 51, 97, 101, 130; and advanced technology, 114; in movement of capital, 94 ; effects on education, 104, 108; in global context, 173–74; need for skilled workers, 95
Correctional ethos, 57–62
Cremin, L., 43–44
Crick, M., 118–19
Criminality, 60, 123, 134, 180–82; crime rates on, 56–57; and criminology discourse, 60
Cristarella, M., 161
Critical pedagogy, outlines of vi–ix, 12, 53–54, 63–68, 148; as common sense knowlege, 145; culture critiqe in, 73–75; against "end of history," 29, 174; and Habermasian analysis, 68–72; in institutional settings, 55, 61–62, 72, 131; internationalist perspectives in, 175; and the media, 46; as participatory democracy, 185; and postmodernism, 76–77; research *on* and *in*, 25–26; of workplace, 32, 79, 100, 103–8
Critical perspectives, vii, 152, 155, 175, 181; as dialogue, 72, 75, 179–80, 182–83; and discourse, v, 27, 165, 171, 184; of educators, 74, 77; in reflection, 63, 144–45, 151, 153–54; and thought, 4, 53, 85, 154
Critical theory, v–vi, 63–64; of Frankfurt School, 65–66; lifeworld and system, 71–72; and rationality, 68, 75–77; as theory and practice, 26, 28
Cult of efficiency, 7, 34–35, 65, 67
Culture, 146, 149, 160; and cultural capital, 88–89, 98, 131; as mass culture, 67, 73, 75, 146; norms and themes in, 152–53; "of fear," 56; "of passivity," 100, and "of silence," 144, 151
Culture Circles, 153, 155–56
Curriculum: aesthetic dimension in, 129; and behaviorism, 34, 36–37, 116–17,
119–21, 124; and career counseling, 89; as competency-based education, 41–42, 44–46, 48–52; conservation discourse in, 178, 180; and critical pedagogy, viii; democratization of, 51–52; design and development of, 25, 38, 124–25, 132, 134; deskilling by, 33; as dialogue,153, 155; in everyday life, 37; and fads, 96; in Freire's work, 166; and guides for teachers, 155; as hidden, 64; international perspective on, 176–77; and life-long learning, 109–11; in nontraditional institutions, 114; as prepackaged, 20–21, 47; in prisons, 58; and rural settings, 112; 114–15; standardization of, 37, 39–41, 53–54; and teacher autonomy, 50–52; technocratic rationality of, 24, 35, 70; in world of work, 23, 81, 86, 91, 97, 100, 104–7
Cutbacks: and critical pedagogy, 109; as downsizing and restructuring, 94–95, 100, 114; in education, 2–3, 20–21, 29–30 41, 132–33, 164; educators against, viii; as legitimized, 88; in other publicly funded services, 2, 23–24, 29, 88

Dahlberg, I., 112
Deconstructionism, 27–28, 75–77, 185. *See also* Postmodernism
Descartes, R., 166
Deschooling, 1, 3 12, 20–21; and community, 163; in contrast to competency-based education, 142; critical pedagogy and, 63; and popular education, 151; as postmodern discourse, 28, 75; shortcormings of, 17–18, 22–24, 164; as utopian, 19, 29–30, 51, 62, 72
Deskilling, 31–54, 84–85, 105; as alienated work, 54, 85, 105; and behaviorism, 34–35, 38; in competency-based education, 41, 44, 47, 49; of teaching role, 32, 38, 50, 52, 84
Developing countries: and competitiveness, 183; conservationist discourse on, 179; education in, 86, 114, 130, 141; and employment, 83, 85; international perspective on, 171, 176, 184; neocolonialist status of, 142, 159; nongovernment organizations in, 140. *See also* Third World

Development: and communications technology, 172; in cooperative relationships, 81; critical views on, 13, 27, 29, 66, 152, 184; in global context, 176; and human potential, 83; in Native communities, 160; participatory praxis in, 158, 163; and popular education, 142, 147
Dewey, J., 31, 46–47, 86–87, 121
Dialectical relationship, 150, 167
Dialogue, 70–71, 113, 127, 148–56; defined, 153; international scope of, 177, in just society, 170; and participatory research, 158; in prisons, 61; and self-directed learning, 116; between teachers and journalists, 176; on violence, 181
Discourse, defined, vi
Distance education, 114, 132. *See also* Nontraditional education
Draves, W., 132

Ecology, 12; degradation of, 178–180; and ecologists, 80–81; as ecotourism, 180. *See also* Environment
Educators' role, vii–viii; 1–5; as facilitator, 115; and internationalist, 174–78; as lecturer, 152–53. *See also* Teaching
Eisenhower, D., 174
Elliot, L., 171, 184
Employment. *See under* Jobs; Unemployment; Work
Empowerment, 145–46, 151–52. *See also* Freirean pedagogy
Engels, F., 12
Enterprise culture, 96–97,102
Environment, 80, 113, 128–29, 142, 147. *See also* Ecology
Esquivel, A., 144, 148
Ethical concerns, 10, 39, 71, 73; in behaviorism, 36; corporate interests and, 69; and "deep" ecology, 81; and human resource development, 92; in just society, 52; and participatory research, 163; *See also* Moral considerations; Values
Expertise: and behaviorism, 36; claims of, 39; in institutions, 170; as intervention, 159–60; and participatory praxis, 163, 165
Experts, 63, 115; and correctional discourse, 60; deconstruction of, 76; dependency on, 3–4, 9–10, 16; and expert knowledge,105, 145, 166; monopoly of, 158; and participatory research, 157; as researchers, 25, 160; and self-directed learning, 116; standardization by, 39–40; and Taylorism, 34. *See also* Professionalization

Family, 19–20, 59, 73, 76; in community, 71, 169; in Native settings, 159–60; and Thatcher ideology, 133, 169
Fanon, F., 143, 158
Fascism, 7, 65–66, 95–96; and applied eugenics, 123
Faure, E., 109–11, 113–14, 129, 131
Ford, H., 34, 40
Foucault, M., 59, 75
Fourier, C., 18
Frankfurt School, 55, 65–70, 75–77
Freire, P.: formative years and career, 148–50; and Freirean pedagogy, 127, 139, 147–56, 158, 163–67, 170–71
Friedman, M., 14, 21
Fromm, E., 66
Fuller, B., 171

Galton, F., 123
Gandhi, M., 62, 140–41
Gelpi, E., 105
Gender, 64, 88, 151
Gingrich, N., 23
Gintis, H., 88
Glauberman, N., 123
Global society, 137; agendas in, 184–86; and the environment, 179–80; and learning technologies, 102; as marketplace, 50, 83, 94, 100–101, 128, 183; as "global village," 171–72, 180, 183–84. *See also* International perspectives
Goddard, H., 123
Goldman, E., 75
Goodman, P., 1, 5, 9, 13, 51,
Gould, S., 123
Gramsci, A., 62, 74
Gregson, J., 97
Griffith, W., 161
Grossi, V., 141
Guardian Weekly, 55, 171
Guevara, E. (Che), 148
Gulf War, 176

Index

Habermas, J.: on lifeworld and system, 71–73, 141, 168–69, 172; and communicative competence, 69–74, 127, 152; critical pedagogy and, 75; and Frankfurt School, 65–68
Halévy, E., 136
Hall, B., 158
Hancock, V., 112
Heath, S., 113
Hegel, G., 151
Hegemony, ix, 72, 147, 174; and counter-hegemony, 24, 74, 104, 142–43, 147
Heidegger, M., 127
Helstein, R., 82
Hernstein, R., 122–23
Hiatt, D., 121
Highlander Folk School, 141, 152
Hobsbawn, E., 2
Hodgskin, T., 136
Holt, J., 1, 5, 13, 20, 38, 51; and case for home schooling, 9, 18–21
Hoover Institute, 122
Horkheimer, M., 55, 65–67, 73
Horton, M., 141, 152
Humanism: on human action, 118–19, 124, 126, 161, 180; against behaviorism, 35, 37–38, 116, 118–19; as experience and development, 28, 80, 82, 103, 124, 181–82; nature and potential in, 80, 128; perspectives on, 45, 83, 86–87; and humanists, 90, 97
Human resource development, 86, 91–92, 106, 111
Husen, T., 113–14, 129
Husserl, H., 127, 166

Illich, I.: as activist priest and radical intellectual, 5, 7–9; and alternative view of deschooled society, 13–22; on the "commons", vernacular values, tools for conviviality, 10–13, 146; formative years of, 5–7; and critique of Illichian view, 17–19, 22–30, 72; on home schooling and experts, 9–10; and reseach, 24–28 ; schooling and enthronement of expertise, 1–5;
Illiteracy, 20, 140, 148, 150
Inacio da Silva, L., 150
Instrumental rationality, 65–66, 68–71, 73, 76–77, 168–69; in behaviorism, 35, 116

Intelligence: and behaviorism, 117; as intelligence quotient (IQ), 121–23
Intentionality, 37–38, 166
Internationalist pedagogy; for the oppressed, 7; outlines of, 171–86
International Monetary Fund (IMF), 143, 184
International perspectives, 142, 149, 172–78, 184–85; on lifelong learning, 113; as social movement, 129
Internet, 11, 130, 172, 176
Internships: for students in workplace 106-7; and teacher training, 186

Jacoby, R., 123
Jalalludin, A., 112
James, W., 46, 119
Jobs, 79, 82–91, 94–100, 103–4; as low-skilled, 47; training for, 106, 130; uncertainty of, 53 ; and university education, 110. *See also* Employment; Unemployment
Just society, v–vi, vii–ix, 28–29; in critical dialogue 170; and critical theory, 77; deschooling discourse and, 5; ethics in, 53; and global restructuring, 100; lifelong learning and, 123; political commitment to, 99; popular education for, 139; postmodernism on, 76; prison as instructive, 62; and schools, 70, 140; violence and, 128

Kant, I., 177
Kaufmann, P., 112
King, E., 112
Knowledge: as "knowledge about" and "knowledge of acquaintance," 119; of academics, 166; emergence of, 111; as deposited, 152; and dialogue, 153; distribution of, 137, 145, 149; as local, 160; making of, 153; monopoly of, 25; in participatory research, 157–58, 160–61, 164, 170; as resource, 102; industries based on, 96
Knowles, M., 115
Knox, A., 113
Kozol, J., 1, 5, 9, 18, 38, 51

Labor, 92–93, 105–6, 173; and conception of work, 82; Marxian view of, 80; organizations of, 147

Language: as cooperative, 81; in communication, 69; and culture, 146; protection of, 185; and the state, 156; vernacular values in, 11
Learning how to learn, 110, 113, 115, 127–28. *See also* Self-directed learning
Learning packages, 36, 38, 120.
Learning society, 110, 113–14, 129–30, 134, 138
Leisure, 81–84, 103
Lenin, V., 148
Liberal education, 91; in adult education, 111
Liberation theology, 22, 27, 149
Licensing, 105, 136
Lifelong education; accessibility of, 129–36; and art, 113; conceptual distinction from lifelong learning, 109–10; as critical pedagogy, ix; learner and learning in, 112, 115–24; politics of, 136–38; a theory of lifelong learning for, 124–29; and skill exchanges, 161; and work, 82
Lifelong learning (*See* Lifelong education): as educational discourse, 186
Lifeworld, 118, 125–26, 168–69; and behaviorism, 120; colonization of, 71–72, 172; distinguished from system world, 71
Limbaugh, R., 23
Lindeman, E., 46, 120
Literacy education, 110, 130, 152; and Gandhi, 141; guerrilla movements in, 144; as popular education, 139–41, 146
Logical positivism: as behaviorism, 36, 118; and participatory research, 160, 163; in (conventional) research, 161–62
Lowenthal, L., 66
Lower classes: *See* Working class
Luxemburg, R., 62

Making music together, 67; in critical pedagogy, 75
Malcolm X., 62
Malikova, Z. 112
Mandatory continuing education, 15–16, 136–37
Mandela, M., 62
Manhattan Institute for Policy Research, 122

Marcuse, H: on negation and prospects for resistance, 66–68, 71, 73
Marginalized groups, 166–67, 172; and critical consciousness, 145
Marketplace: education in, 97, 102–3; and the environment, 180; as ideology 86, 133; and marketing, 173; wage cuts in, 99
Marshall, J., 146
Marx, K., 12, 79–80, 105; and influence on Freire's work, 148, 150
Mason, R., 112
McCarthy, T., 67
McDonald's, 111
McLean, B., 56
Mcluhan, M., 46, 171
McTaggart, R., 63
Meaning in context, 37, 125
Mechanics' Institutes, 136
Media: on crime rates, 57; and critical pedagogy, 29; and educational broadcasting, 130; as mass media, 103; and "medium as message," 46, 116; as news, 175–76, 181; popular education and, 146; as prepackaged, 73; and social learning processeses, 103; influence on young, 5, 95
Medical profession, 25–26, 28; mandatory contiuing education in, 137; and medical model, 60–61
Milovanovic, D., 56
Moral considerations, 68–69, 79, 181, 185; and dialogue, 154; for educational leadership, 49; on the environment, 180; international perspectives and, 175, 177; in participatory research, 161; and popular education, 147; on retraining, 106. *See also* Ethical concerns; Values
Murray, C., 122–23

Nadler, L., 191
Native people. *See* Aboriginal
Natural sciences: influence on behaviorism, 35, 118, 120, 160; and human sciences, 36; as logical positivism, 161; participatory research and, 160
Neoconservatism, 1–2, 21, 29, 41, 51; backlash of, 147; and communities, 133, 169; effects on education, vii, 17,

Index

23, 28, 40; for employers, 106; and social programs, 123; sustaining privilege, 64
New Deal, 88–89
New Right. *See* Neoconservatism
New York Times, 2
Niemi, J., 110
Nietzsche, F., 76–77
Nongovernment agencies, 140, 143–44
Nontraditional education, 114, 131–33, 138
Nyerere, J., 147

Observer, The, 97
Ohliger, J., 136–37
Oliver, L., 144
Oppression, 145–46, 148, 151–52, 158, 166–67
Oran, G., 112
Ornstein, A., 111
Ortega y Gasset, J., 118
Outcomes-based education, 117, 119, 121; and learning, 50, 96
Owen, R., 18

Panopticon, 59
Parents: expectations for children's education, 87, 134–35
Parnell, D., 43
Participatory democracy, 45, 63–65, 67, 69, 73; and international pedagogy, 185; and popular education, 139, 142, 147; worker oriented, 104
Participatory research, 139–40, 156–67, 170–71; in formal institutions, 164; and praxis, 163–71
Passeron, J., 8
Pavlov, I., 117
Pedagogy of hope, 30, 62
Peoples' history, 146, 160
Pepsi Cola, 130
Phi Delta Kappan, 43, 109, 121
Philosophy of consciousness: in Freire's work, 150, 166–67
Pope, the, 149
Popper, K., 119–20
Popular education, 139–47, 170–71; and Freirean pedagogy, 148–49, 151–52, 158, 166; as participatory praxis and research, 156, 163–66; concept of the "popular," 142; in popular movements, 173
Postmodernism, 75–77; and critical pedagogy, 185; criticism of, viii, 27–30.
Poverty, 123, 139–40, 145, 148–52; and participatory research, 156, 161, 163; widening gap between rich and poor, 142
Power relations, 64, 72–73, 76, 138; and busywork, 85; competency-based education and, 46; in communicative competence, 70; and dominant culture, 146, and environment, 180; in global village, 172; legitimation of, 154; of Native people with the state, 160; and the oppressed 167; in particpatory practice and research, 158, 163–65; and popular education, 145, 147; reproduction of, 156; and structure of work, 105
Prajuli, P., 142
Prisons, 25, 55–63; education in, 58, 61–62; and gangs, 181; oppositional initiatives in, 169; as paradigm case, 59; purpose of, 56–57
Privatization, 29, 102; of education, 21, 102–3, 107, 130
Professionalism: as distinguished from professionalization, 105–6
Professionalization, 25–26, 59–60, 106; dependency on, 10; as monopoly, 12, 14; and status, 50, 106; *See also* Expertise; Experts
Proudhon, P., 18

Qualitative research, 161
Quest for certainty, 46–47; and teachers, 51

Racism, 64–65, 95, 122–23, 142; socialization to, 88
Ray, B., 112
Reagan, R., 13, 40, 97, 124, 133; and Reaganism, 23
Realpolitik, 29, 179
Reductionism, 36, 45, 118, 120–21, 161
Reimer, E., 1, 5, 9, 13, 38, 51
Relevance: and competent performance, 46; concept of, 124–26, 153
Rensi, E., 111
Research, 6, 15, 24–28, 99, 158; influence

Research—(*continued*)
of behaviorism on, 37, 118; and role of researcher, 156-58, 160-61, 163, 165
Resistance, 67-68, 71-75, 144; to business influence, 86-87; and busywork, 85; in schools, 17, 24; by teachers, 33, 35, 50-52
Restructuring, 23-24, 33, 114, 164; of workplace, 176; of universities, 133; by World Bank/IMF, 143. *See also* Cutbacks
Rinne, R., 113,
Rogers, C., 37, 45, 116, 124
Ryan, K., 43
Ryan, W., 158

Saint-Simon, C., 18
Schooling: role in social reproduction and socialization, 64-65, 88, 130. *See also Illich*
Schools, 3-5; reinvesting in, 28-30. *See also* Illich
Schutz, A., 124-27
Scott, T., 112
Self-directed learning, 115-17, 120-21; as self-education, 128-29
Sharratt, G., 112
Singh, M., 63
Skinner, B., 35, 37-38, 117-118; and IQ testing, 121-22
Smith, R., 113
Social control, 17, 88; in competency-based education, 46, 143; and prisons, 55, 58, 62
Social Darwinism, 123
Social justice, 6, 29-30; in economic context, 24; in educational institutions, 64, 73, 122; international persectives on, 184; in the marketplace. 102-3; participatory praxis for, 157, 164-65, 169; and popular education, 140-41; in prison education, 61
Social movement, 140, 144, 175
Social norms, 68, 96, 140, 167
Social policy, 89, 146; programs of, 121-23
Social reality, 55, 151; relationships and, 80, 89, 127, 147; reproduction of, 64-65
Social science research, 156-57, 159
Spaceship earth, 171-72
Spady, W., 44

Spellman, F. (Cardinal), 7-8
Spirituality, 113; dialogue on, 154; as learning process, 129; need for, 168; and popular education, 140
Stalin, J., 65
Standardization, 38-41; of curriculum, 33, 44-46, 48-50, 53, 54; of primers for teachers, 155; and testing, 36; in workplace, 47, 94, 96
Standards, 79, 121
Staples, B., 112
Stock of knowlege, 125-28; and collective storytelling, 145
Study circles, 140, 160
Study tours, 178
Surplus labor force, 33, 48
Surveillance and control, 48, 61; exemplified in prisons, 58-59, 62, 169
Sustainable development, 13, 179-80
Sutel, S., 184
Sutter, T., 167

Tax, S., 157
Taylor, F., 34-35, 44
Teaching, viii, 4-6, 20, 35, 38-39; and academic subjects, 86; agency in, 119, 124-25; as autonomous, 20, 33, 47, 50-52; and "teacher bashing," 17, 51; behaviorism and, 35-38, 116-17, 120; and busywork, 84; careful observation in, 129; competency-based education and, 41, 44-50; in community, 134-35; as complex, 121; as consciousness raising, 152; on conservation, 179; coping in, vi; as custodial, 16; dependency in, v; deskilled, 21, 32-33, 38-39, 50-51; dialogue and 35; as expertize, 5, 14, 76, 115, 152; in Freire's early career, 149; Heidegger on, 127; internationalist perspective and, 175, 177; and leadership, 185; and journalists, 176; learning packages in, 47; lifelong learning and, 109; mandatory continuing education in, 137; and politics, 153-54 ; preparation for, 35, 107, 115-17, 135, 185-86; in prison settings, vii, 58, 68; and professional status, 106, 135; as resistance, vii, 17, 33, 35, 51-54, 73; and self-directed learning, 115; effects of standardization on, 39-40; strategies

Index

to revalue, 54; and teachers' work, 32, 41, 84; in technical education, 108; technology and, 112; and world of work, 79, 87, 90, 104, 107
Technical education, 86, 90–91, 96, 108 110
Technical rationality: *See* Instrumental rationality
Terkel, S., 79, 81–83
Thatcher, M., 13, 23, 40, 97, 124, 133
Third World, 139, 156. *See also* Developing countries
Thompson, E., 140
Toepfer, C., 111
Tonegawa, K., 112
Trade unions, 97, 105–7; for teachers, 49–50; and trade unionists, 107; worker education and, 111
Training, 53, 85, 87–94, 137; in prisons, 60; for women, 100
Tyler, R., 121

Underclass, 2, 23, 134, 179; and cultural capital, 88, 131; and IQ discourse, 122–23; relationships of power and, 156; youth of, 98, 181. *See also* Welfare
Unemployment, 2–3 12–13, 52; in global context, 173; and Native people, 160; social programs for, 123; of teachers, 33; and training 137; under-development and, 148. *See also* Jobs; Work
United Nations, 183–84; UNESCO in, 105, 150
Universities, 27–28, 90, 140, 142, 150–51; accesibility of, 130; business influence on, 39, 41, 97 101–4; Colleges of Education in, 135; and competency-based education, 45, 49; employment for graduates, 99; fiscal restraints, 108; different to further education, 111; and international perspectives, 176; and lifelong learning, 110, 112–14; nontraditional education in, 131–33; and participatory research, 162; popular education and, 141, 146; and courses in prisons, 61. *See also* Academics

Values, 82, 168; of business, 101; of bourgoise, 64; and compassion, 68; in community, 71, 169; of labor, 80; and technical rationality, 66. *See also* Ethical concerns; Moral considerations
Violence, 20, 128–29, 180–85; on environment, 180; in global context, 172; and Native children, 159; the state and, 142; as systemic, 145; and young adults, 95. *See also* Abuse

Walker, M., 56
Watkins, 91, 93
Weber, M., 57, 66, 168–69
Weitling, M., 18
Welfare, 93, 115, 159–60; and welfare state, 24, 29. *See also Underclass*
Whitehead, A., 91
Wordsworth, W., 55, 57, 60
Work, 31–32, 34, 79–82, 169; and businesslike education, 101–3; and busyness, 84–85; critical pedagogy of, 103–7; under current conditions, 47–49, 52–54, 93–101, 156, 183; distinction between work and employment, 82–84; links to education, training and employment, 40, 64–65, 85–93, 111–12, 133, 137, 174–77; and participatory praxis, 164–65; worker education, 111, 114–15, 140–41
Workers. *See under* Labor; Work
Working class, 19, 72, 106, 158. *See also* Class; Work
World Bank, 13, 143, 184
World Council of Churches, 150

Young adults, 93–100, 103, 111–12, 129; and the environment, 180; international perspectives and, 176–78; and participatory research, 160; at risk, 134; and violence, 181